LAND O...

Currently the global strategist of one of the world's largest banks, Sanjeev Sanyal divides his time between India and Singapore. A Rhodes Scholar and an Eisenhower Fellow, he was named Young Global Leader for 2010 by the World Economic Forum. He has written extensively on economics, environmental conservation and urban issues, and his first book, *The Indian Renaissance: India's Rise After a Thousand Years of Decline*, was published by Penguin in 2008.

PRAISE FOR THE BOOK

'A selective, charming, and unusual history of the subcontinent with a delightful surprise in every chapter.' —Gurcharan Das

'A fast-paced account of a few high points of Indian history—but a history deeply entangled in India's geography. With Sanjeev Sanyal's eye for detail as well as the overall picture, the land comes alive: the rivers, mountains, forests, villages and mines, all play their part in the unfolding of events that will determine India's destiny, from the Indus civilization to the Partition.' —Michel Danino

'This is a refreshingly different book. It is neither history, nor geography. It is more like a collection of nuggets that straddle both . . . Genetics and tectonics to modern India, the nuggets make for wonderful reading.' — Bibek Debroy

'Sanyal writes of a country's future even as he looks back at her history . . . the writing is infused with wit and intelligence.'—*The Hindu*

'An imaginative book that connects geology to history and culture . . .' —*Tehelka*

[Sanyal] is a powerful storyteller who traverses the corridors of history, mythology and epic seamlessly.' —*Financial Express*

'Wonderfully establishes the sense of continuity that has existed in our civilizational customs . . .' —*Pioneer*

SANJEEV SANYAL

Land

of

the

Seven

Rivers

A BRIEF HISTORY OF
INDIA'S GEOGRAPHY

PENGUIN BOOKS

An imprint of Penguin Random House

PENGUIN BOOKS

USA | Canada | UK | Ireland | Australia
New Zealand | India | South Africa | China

Penguin Books is part of the Penguin Random House group of companies
whose addresses can be found at global.penguinrandomhouse.com

Published by Penguin Random House India Pvt. Ltd
7th Floor, Infinity Tower C, DLF Cyber City,
Gurgaon 122 002, Haryana, India

Penguin
Random House
India

First published in Viking by Penguin Books India 2012
Published in Penguin Books 2013

39 38 37 36 35 34 33 32 31

ISBN 9780143420934

Typeset in Dante MT by SŪRYA, New Delhi
Printed at Thomson Press India Ltd, New Delhi

www.penguin.co.in

MIX
Paper
FSC FSC® C010615

To Varun and Dhruv,
that they may know where they came from . . .

Contents

Author's Note　　　　　　　　　　ix

Introduction　　　　　　　　　　　1

1. Of Genetics and Tectonics　　　　11

2. People of the Lost River　　　　　36

3. The Age of Lions　　　　　　　　70

4. The Age of Merchants　　　　　　106

5. From Sindbad to Zheng He　　　　138

6. The Mapping of India　　　　　　176

7. Trigonometry and Steam　　　　　211

8. The Contours of Modern India　　259

Notes　　　　　　　　　　　　　306

Index　　　　　　　　　　　　　323

Author's Note

This book is about the history of India's geography although I do not have any formal training as either a historian or as a geographer. Yet, as I wrote this book, it felt like I have been preparing for it for all my adult life. Ideas, facts and conversations that I seem to have hidden away somewhere in my head all came tumbling out as I wrote out the chapters one by one. My profession as an economist, my love of old maps and wildlife, my studies of urban habitats and my many travels through India and South-East Asia began to slowly fit together into a mosaic.

Still, it was no easy journey. I read through ancient religious texts, the writings of medieval travellers and scores of academic papers on seemingly unrelated and arcane topics. Often it took several readings before I could make sense of them, but I struggled on because, as my family and friends will attest, the topic had become an obsession. It drove me eventually to take time off from my professional career to travel around India for two and half years to collect material. Indeed, I discovered that many of the texts make sense only if one has actually visited the places to which they refer. I would probably have kept going if my editors at Penguin had not simply taken the draft away from me.

Given the eclectic nature of this book, it could not have been written without the advice and support of many people. Let me begin by thanking Ravi Singh and Michel Danino, who were ready with advice and encouragement at every stage of the book. This book benefitted greatly from their extensive collections of papers and books. I am grateful to Divyabhanusinh Chavda, Vidula Jayaswal, R.S. Bisht, Pratik Bhatnagar, Mahesh Rangarajan, Partha Majumdar, Manoshi Lahiri, Susheel Menon, Ramachandra Guha, Jose Dominic, Abdul Hakim, Lalji Singh and Jacob Thomas for their many suggestions. Let me also thank the Lal Bahadur Shastri National Academy of Administration (Mussourie), the Survey of India (Dehradun), the World-Wide Fund for Nature, the Archaeological Survey of India, Madhya Pradesh Tourism, The Sushant School of Art and Architecture, Vivekananda Kendra and the Institute of South East Asian Studies, Singapore.

I enjoyed the hospitality of many kind hosts on my travels. Let me take this opportunity to thank Suresh Neotia, Upendra Gupta, Sajjan and Sangita Jindal, Dushyant Singh, Abhijit Pandit, Sheila Nair, Maharaj Gaj Singh, Ranjit Barthakur, Shree Raman, Vineet Saran and Praveen Rengaraj. My dear friends Jayant Sinha, Peter Ruprecht, Ashish Goyal, Siddharth Yog and Arvind Sethi read drafts at different stages and gave me useful insights on style and readability.

Of course, the book would not have been possible without the diligence and enthusiasm of my editors Udayan Mitra and Ameya Nagarajan. It was a pleasure working with them. I am also grateful for the support of my extended family, particularly my father, with whom I continue to debate the meaning of the *Rig Veda*. Lastly, I wish to thank my wife Smita who put her life on hold for almost three years, accompanied me on my travels and patiently heard me read out the very first draft of each chapter.

Introduction

As we make our way through the second decade of the twenty-first century, India is undergoing an extraordinary transformation. This is visible everywhere one looks. After centuries of relative decline, the Indian economy is reasserting itself. The result is an urban construction boom that defies imagination. Almost overnight, whole new cities are being built. Nowhere is this more true than in Gurgaon where I lived as I wrote this book. Where there had been wheat and mustard fields till the mid-nineties, there are now malls, office towers, apartment blocks and highways. Even as I write these words, I watch yet another condominium block rise up.

Boomtowns like Gurgaon, however, are merely one facet of the changes being experienced by India. Mobile telephones and satellite television, combined with rising literacy and affluence, have changed the dynamics and aspirations of rural and small-town India. The children of farmers are moving to the cities in the millions. By all accounts, India is likely to become an urban-majority country within a generation and its cities need to prepare for the influx of hundreds of millions of people. Existing cities will expand, new cities will rise and villages will be transformed. The old ways are clearly declining.

The economic rise of India is to be welcomed in a country that has long been plagued by poverty but change is not without its price. Natural habitats are being drastically altered and often ravaged by activities like mining, sometimes legal but often illegal. I am told that there are now barely 1706 tigers left in the wild[1]. Dams and canals are altering the fortunes of sacred rivers even as factories and cities empty their untreated waste into them. As urbanization and modernization churn the population, communities are being torn apart and with them we are losing old customs, traditions and oral histories. Many reminders of the country's history are being paved over by new highways and buildings.

I am very conscious that we live in a time of rapid change. However, it is important to remember that India is an ancient land. In the long course of its history, it has witnessed many twists and turns. Cities have risen and then disappeared. There have been 'golden' periods of economic and cultural achievement as well as periods of defeat and humiliation. Over the centuries, many groups have come to India as traders, invaders and refugees, even as Indians have settled in foreign lands. The country has endured dramatic changes in climate and natural habitat. In short, India has been through all this many times before.

The scars and remnants of this long history are scattered all over the landscape. If one cares to look, they will stare back even from the most unlikely of places. New Delhi, the national capital, is a good example. It is merely the latest in a series of cities to have been built on the site. Amidst the frenetic pace of modern life, the older Delhis live on in grand ruins, place-names, urban villages, traditions, and sacred sites. Even older are the ridges of the Aravalli Range, arguably the oldest geological feature on Earth.

Much has been written about Indian history but almost all of it is concerned with sequences of political events—the rise and fall of empires and dynasties, battles, official proclamations and so on. These are undoubtedly important but I have little to add to what has already been said about the emperor Akbar's *mansabdari* system or the Morley-Minto reforms of 1909. However, history is not just politics—it is the result of the complex interactions between a large number of factors. Geography is one of the most important of these factors. Moreover, this relationship works both ways—just as geography affects history, history too affects geography.

This book is an attempt to write a brief and eclectic history of India's geography. It is about the changes in India's natural and human landscape, about ancient trade routes and cultural linkages, the rise and fall of cities, about dead rivers and the legends that keep them alive. Great monarchs and dynasties are still important to such a history but they are remembered for the way in which they shaped geography.

Thus, the book focuses on a somewhat different set of questions: Is there any truth in ancient legends about the Great Flood? Why do Indians call their country Bharat? What do the epics tell us about how Indians perceived the geography of their country in the Iron Age? Why did the Buddha give his first sermon at Sarnath, just outside Varanasi? What was it like to sail on an Indian Ocean merchant ship in the fifth century AD or to live the life of an idle playboy in Gupta-era Pataliputra? How did the Mughals hunt lions? How did the Europeans map India? How did the British build the railways across the subcontinent? The process of change still goes on and, in the last chapter, we will look at the huge shifts being caused now by the process of urbanization and rapid economic growth.

While the primary focus of this book is on the history of India's geography, the converse, too, is a secondary theme that runs through the book. In other words, the book is also about the geography of India's history and civilization. One cannot understand the flow of Indian history without appreciating the drying up of the Saraswati river, the monsoon winds that carried merchant fleets across the Indian Ocean, the Deccan Traps that made Shivaji's guerilla tactics possible, the Brahmaputra river that allowed the tiny Ahom kingdom to defeat the mighty Mughals and the marshlands that dictated where the British built their settlements. Furthermore, the book will also consciously bring out the technologies—from kiln-fired bricks and ship building to map-making and railways—that have influenced the way we think of India.

The very idea of India, its physical geography and its civilization, has evolved over the centuries. Yet, despite all these changes, it is astonishing how India's civilizational traits have survived over millennia. The ox-carts of the Harappan civilization can still be seen in many parts of rural India, essentially unchanged but for the rubber tyres. The Gayatri Mantra, a hymn composed over four millennia ago, is chanted daily by millions of Hindus.[2] This is not just about longevity but about a civilizational ability to take along an incredible mix of ideas, cultures and lifestyles that, despite their apparent differences, are still a part of the overall patchwork. There are still remote tribes that retain a hunter–gatherer lifestyle that has changed little since the first humans entered the subcontinent. This is not just about a lack of 'development'. The Sentinelese tribe of the Andaman Islands deliberately retains its Stone Age culture and ferociously resists outside contact despite repeated efforts by the government. Who are we to 'civilize' them?

One of the persistent misconceptions about Indian history is that Indians have somehow never conceived of themselves as a nation and, consequently, never cared about their history. This idea was often repeated by colonial-era officialdom for obvious political ends. As Sir John Strachey put it in the late nineteenth century, 'The first and most essential thing to learn about India—that there is not, and never was an India.' Half a century later, Winston Churchill would echo the same point when he said that 'India is a geographical term. It is no more a united nation than the equator'. A corollary to this point of view was the argument that since Indians were never conscious of their nationhood, they did not care for their history (or their freedom).

Curiously, this colonial-era idea has somehow remained alive—it is still not uncommon to hear people, even scholars, say that Indians are an ahistorical people. As we shall see, this is totally incorrect. There is more than enough evidence to show that Indians have long been conscious of their history and civilization. Indeed, from very ancient times, Indians have gone out of their way to record their times as well as to create linkages to those who came before them. This sense of civilizational continuity is so strong that foreign rulers, including the British, have repeatedly acknowledged Indian civilization even as they have tried to give themselves legitimacy.

Indeed, the British systematically drew on the political symbolism of India's past. In front of the Rashtrapati Bhavan (Presidential Palace) in New Delhi is a tall column called the Jaipur Column. It is a sandstone shaft topped by the 'Star of India'. There is an inscription on its base, conceived by Lord Irwin and Sir Edwin Lutyens, that reads as follows: 'In thought faith,/ In word wisdom,/ In deed courage,/ In life service,/ So may India be great.' The column was a gift from the princely state of Jaipur and was erected by the British when they built a new imperial capital in the early decades of the twentieth century.

At that time, the British may not have known that India would become independent a few short years after they had completed the project. However, it is as if they were very conscious that they were inheritors of a very ancient imperial dream. They would have been aware that in the context of India's long history, the period of British rule would one day become just a speck. Therefore, by erecting the column, they were determined to leave a stamp of their times. In doing so, they were following a practice that went back at least to the third century BC.

Delhi has several other imperial columns. One stands in the fourteenth-century ruins of Feroze Shah Kotla. The column stands erect amidst the crumbling walls of the old palace complex, oblivious to the cheering crowds of the nearby cricket ground and the swirling traffic of ITO. The polished sandstone shines as if it was put there recently. Yet, this column carries an edict by Emperor Ashoka from the third century BC. It is one of two Ashokan columns that Sultan Feroz Shah Tughlaq got transported with great care to his new city (the 'New' Delhi of its time). This one is said to have been brought from Topara near Ambala, Haryana and erected here in 1356 AD. The other pillar—brought from Meerut—stands near Bara Hindu Rao Hospital on the North Ridge, not far from Delhi University, at the northernmost point of the Aravalli range.

The Sultan appears to have realized that the two columns were very old and represented a great imperial power. The one in Feroze Shah Kotla is said to have been carefully wrapped in cotton and silk and transported on a forty-two-wheel cart pulled by two hundred men, and finally brought by boat to its current location. The Sultan was very keen to know what the inscriptions said. He asked the local Brahmins to translate them but the Brahmi script had been long forgotten and they were unable to help.[3] It would be another five centuries before the script was deciphered.

Yet another of Delhi's imperial columns is commonly called the Iron Pillar and stands in the Qutub Minar complex in South Delhi. It is made of almost pure iron and yet has not rusted despite being exposed to the elements for fifteen centuries. The inscription is dedicated to the Hindu god Vishnu and tells of the exploits and conquests of a king called Chandra (often interpreted to mean Emperor Chandragupta Vikramaditya of the fifth century AD). The column was probably brought to Delhi either in the late eleventh or early twelfth century and placed in the middle of a temple complex. The temples were destroyed and replaced by mosques in the late twelfth century when the city passed into the hands of Turkish conquerors. However, the pillar was allowed to stand. Why? Perhaps the new rulers wanted to link themselves to the past. Perhaps they wanted to overshadow it with their own column, the stone tower of Qutub Minar built to commemorate the victory of Islam.

Over the centuries, the Delhi of the Qutub Minar would be replaced by newer Delhis, each built by an emperor who proclaimed a new era. The city we see today was decreed in 1911 by George V, Emperor of India. The official proclamation was read out at Coronation Park to the far north of the city. It is the same spot where Queen Victoria had been proclaimed the Empress of India. Here, too, a column stands to commemorate the event.

Again and again, we see how a primordial imperial dream symbolized by the columns has survived over millennia. Whether Muslim or Hindu, Indian or British, successive rulers appropriated this idea and its symbols to strengthen their rule. It survives in modern India in the form of the Mauryan lions in the national emblem and the chakra (or wheel) in the national flag—symbol of the 'Chakravartin' or Universal Monarch. The founding fathers of the Indian Republic, too, were conscious that they were inheritors of a very old civilization.

The imperial dream is but one of many extraordinary continuities in India's ancient civilization. Some of them are overt but many more lie hidden. Take for instance, the ratio 5:4 which implies that the length is a quarter longer than the breadth (1.25 times). This ratio was commonly used in the town planning of Harappan cities in the third millennium BC. The city of Dholavira in Gujarat, for example, is 771 metres by 617 metres. Over a thousand years later, the same ratio appears in Hindu texts like the *Shatapatha Brahmana* and

Shulbha Sutra that use the ratio in their precise instructions on how to build fire-altars for Vedic ceremonies.[4]

Another millennium later we find the same ratio mentioned in the vastu shastra texts (these texts are still used in the same way the Chinese use feng shui). In the sixth century AD, the great scholar Varahamihira states that a king's palace should be built such that the length is greater than the breadth by a quarter. The Iron Pillar of Delhi mentioned earlier is also designed in the same ratio: the overall length of the pillar is 7.67 metres while the section above the ground is 6.12 metres, a ratio of 5:4.

It is obvious that this ratio was considered special for a very long time. So when the seventeenth-century Mughal emperor Aurangzeb wanted to praise his vassal Maharaja Jai Singh, he called him 'Sawai' (meaning that he was worth a quarter more than any other man). This title was used by Jai Singh's descendants till the kingdom of Jaipur was absorbed into the Indian Republic. Even today, a tourist visiting Jaipur will see a small flag fluttering above the old royal flag—it's the extra quarter—a reminder of the old town planners of Dholavira. It is appropriate, therefore, that Jai Singh is remembered mostly for the town planning of the city of Jaipur.

Not all the continuities of Indian history are linear. Some of them are circular. The Jews came to India as traders and refugees in the first century AD and settled along the south-western coast. Almost two thousand years later, their descendants would return to the modern state of Israel. Similarly, Arabs traders came to India in the Middle Ages to seek their fortune. From the 1970s, their descendants, the Moplahs of Kerala, would return in large numbers to the oil.

rich Arab states to work for their distant cousins. Most interesting of all was the fate of the Timurid dynasty, better known as the Mughals. In the fourteenth century, Taimur the Lame would capture Delhi and massacre its inhabitants in the tens of thousands. His direct descendant, the last Mughal emperor Bahadur Shah Zafar, would watch helplessly as the British sacked Delhi in 1858 and put his sons to death.

Of course, the history of India's physical geography is older than that of its civilization or even that of the human race. The subcontinent has been a distinct geological entity for millions of years. Therefore, to understand India we must go back to the very beginning.

1

Of Genetics and Tectonics

The Indian subcontinent was not always located where it is today but was once attached to Africa and Madagascar. This is a relatively recent discovery. Till the early twentieth century, it was assumed that most geological features were due to vertical rather than horizontal movements in the earth's crust. Thus, the positions of the continents were considered to be essentially fixed. This was first challenged by the hypothesis of continental drift, proposed by Alfred Wegener in 1912 and expanded in his book *The Origin of Continents and Oceans* published in 1915. He suggested that the present continents once formed a single land mass that drifted apart like icebergs. The hypothesis explained an observation that had puzzled map-makers like Ortelius since the sixteenth century—the fact that land masses, especially those on the opposite sides of the Atlantic, seemed to fit together neatly like a jigsaw puzzle.

Wegener's arguments would have to wait for half a century before adequate scientific evidence could be found to support it. In the late fifties and sixties a great deal of new geological data proved that the earth's crust was a patchwork of plates that were moving relative to each other. This led to the modern theory of plate tectonics. It is still a very new field and our understanding is still evolving. Nonetheless, the broad contours of the story are now clear.

It appears that most of the earth's land mass was joined together a billion years ago in a supercontinent called Rodinia. It was probably located south of the equator but there is still a great deal of debate about its exact shape and size, and where India's land mass fit into it.[1] This supercontinent broke up around 750 million years ago and the various continents began to drift apart. Very little is known about this period (loosely dubbed the Pre-Cambrian period). Existing life forms were no more than single-cell organisms like bacteria. However, there is one remaining relic from the Pre-Cambrian period that is still very visible—the Aravalli range. It is arguably the oldest surviving geological feature anywhere in the world.

The Aravallis were once tall mountains, possibly as high as the Himalayas. Over hundreds of millions of years they have been eroded down to low hills and ridges. Yet, these diminutive hills have been witness to many important events of Indian history. The northernmost point of the Aravallis is the North Ridge near Delhi University. Today, college sweethearts cuddle among the ancient rocks, oblivious to both passers-by and history, but the North Ridge was the stage for an important turning point in Indian history. It was here that a small British garrison held out in 1857 against a much larger force of Indian rebels and pounded the walls of Shahjehanabad (what is now called Old Delhi). The British eventually received reinforcements and stormed the city. Mughal emperor Bahadur Shah Zafar was exiled to Burma and his sons were executed. Thus ended the great Mughal dynasty.[2]

From Delhi, the Aravallis extend into Haryana. As I write, I can see the low rocky ridges holding out against an onslaught of Gurgaon's modern buildings. Sadly these ancient hills are now being destroyed by indiscriminate mining. One of the worst examples of this can be seen on a side branch of the range near Jodhpur, Rajasthan. Ask to be driven to Balsamand Lake, an eleventh-century lake on the outskirts of the city. The lake is often dry these days due to the wholesale destruction of its water-catchment area.[3] Along its banks is an area of several square kilometres where the terrain has been gouged out by stone quarrying (some legal, some illegal). The air is filled with the sound of drills and dynamite, the dust and smoke of trucks laden with stone. Not a single tree stands against the glare of the relentless desert sun. It is a vision of hell.

Farther south, near the Gujarat–Rajasthan border, the Aravallis briefly lay claim to being mountains rather than mere hills. The Guru Shikhar peak at Mount Abu rises to 1722 metres above sea level. This is a sacred place of temples and legends. The Rajput warrior clans claim that their ancestors arose from a great sacrificial fire on this mountain. Not far from Abu is the beautiful lake-city of Udaipur. This was once the capital of the kingdom of Mewar, which bravely fought medieval invaders against impossible odds. The hills and valleys still ring with ballads of how Rana Pratap and his army of Bhil tribesmen refused to surrender to the Mughals. Long before all these events, however, the Aravallis witnessed a major shift in the evolution of life on this planet.

Fossil records suggest that around 530 million years ago, there was a sudden appearance of a large number of complex organisms. This is called the Cambrian Explosion although it still took millions of years. Over the next 70-80 million years, we see an astonishing array of life forms evolve. Meanwhile, the continental land masses began to reassemble and, around 270 million years ago, they fused into a new supercontinent called Pangea.[4] It is now thought that this cyclical assembling and breaking up of supercontinents has always been a part of the geological history of the earth.

A map of Pangea would show the Indian craton wedged between Africa, Madagascar, Antarctica and Australia. It was on Pangea that the dinosaurs appeared 230 million years ago. However, the earth remained restless and Pangea began to break up around 175 million years ago during the Jurassic era. It first split into a northern continent called Laurasia (consisting of North America, Europe and Asia) and a southern continent called Gondwana (Africa, South America, Antarctica, Australia and India). Note that the name Gondwana is itself derived from the Gond tribe of central India.

We now see a sequence of rifts that separate India from its neighbours. First, India and Madagascar separated from Africa around 158 million years ago and then, 130 million years ago, they separated from Antarctica. Around 90 million years ago India separated from Madagascar and drifted steadily northwards.[5]

A large number of dinosaur remains have been found in Raioli village of Balasinor taluka, Gujarat. The site was identified in 1981 and appears to have been a popular hatchery as thousands of fossilized dinosaur eggs have been found there. Fossilized bones have also been found including those of a previously unknown predator that was 25–30 feet long and two-thirds the size of the Tyrannosaurus Rex. The animal has since been named Rajasaurus Narmadsensis (means Lizard King of the Narmada). The site is now protected and is being converted into a Dinosaur Park.[6]

As the Indian craton drifted northwards towards Asia, it passed over the Reunion 'hotspot', which caused an outburst of volcanic activity. Most of these eruptions happened in the Western Ghats near Mumbai and created the Deccan Traps. This is not the type of volcanic eruption that one associates with the perfectly conical Mount Fuji in Japan. Rather, it was more like a layer-by-layer oozing that created the stepped, flat-topped outcrops that geologists call Traps. The term is apt for, in the late seventeenth century, Shivaji and his band of Maratha guerillas would use this unique terrain to trap and wear down the armies of the Mughal emperor Aurangzeb. The volcanic episode did not last very long—perhaps just thirty thousand years—but it was a dramatic phenomenon and there are some scholars who feel that it may have contributed to the extinction of dinosaurs. Looking out from Lord Point at the hill station of Matheran, one can clearly see the geological impact of all the volcanic activity.

Meanwhile, India kept up its relentless northward journey and, 55–60 million years ago, it collided with the Eurasian plate. This collision pushed up the Himalayas and the Tibetan plateau. What are now tall mountains were once under the sea, which is why marine fossils are quite common high up in the mountains. The process is not over—the Indian plate is still pushing into Asia. As a result the Himalayas are still rising by around 5 mm every year (although erosion reduces the actual increase in height). The actual line of collision between the Indian and Eurasian plates is called the Indus-Yarlung-Tsangpo Suture zone. The holy Mansarovar lake sits in a trough along this zone. Overlooking the lake is Mount Kailash,

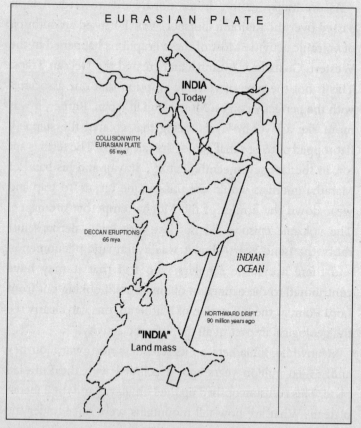

The northward drift of the Indian land mass

home of Lord Shiva according to the Hindu tradition. Not surprisingly, intense tectonic pressures make the Himalayas seismically unstable and prone to frequent and powerful earthquakes. Given the lack of vegetation, Ladakh is a good place to visually appreciate the impact of all these geological processes.

The broad contours of the above narrative of India's geological history are generally accepted. However, there remain many unresolved issues and several findings that do not neatly fit into the story. One puzzle relates to the discovery of a large number of insects preserved in amber found in Vastan, 30 km north of Surat, a geological zone called Cambay Shale. It is a big finding that includes 700 species, representing 55 families. These insects are not unique to India, but very similar to those found in other continents and as far away as Spain. The problem is that the currently accepted view about the northward drift of the Indian craton would mean that the subcontinent would have been an isolated island for tens of millions of years at the time when these insects emerged. So, how did these insects get to India? It is possible that there were islands that allowed them to hop across to the subcontinent. Perhaps, the date of the Indo–Asian collision was earlier than generally accepted. Frankly, we really do not know.[7]

Nonetheless, India's relentless push into Asia continues, making the subcontinent tectonically very active. As we shall see in the next chapter, it is very likely that a tectonic event diverted the course of a major river and, with it, the course of Indian civilization. The danger still lurks. The 2005 earthquake in North Pakistan and Pakistan-occupied Kashmir registered a magnitude of 7.6 on the Richter scale and claimed eighty thousand lives. However, much more powerful earthquakes have been recorded along the mountain range. The Assam earthquake of 1950 registered a magnitude of 8.6; it is one of the most powerful earthquakes ever recorded. Fortunately, the epicentre was in an area that was then relatively sparsely populated and so it killed only 1500 people. A similar earthquake in a densely populated area today would kill hundreds of thousands if not millions. Given tectonic pressures, it is only a matter of time before this happens. This is why the Himalayan range is one of the most dangerous places to build large dams.

With the Indian plate wedged into Asia along the Himalayas, the stage was set for the formation of the youngest of India's geological features—the Gangetic plains. They started out as a marshy depression running between the Himalayas and an older mountain range called the Vindhyas. Silt brought down by the Ganga and its tributaries slowly began to fill up this hollow to create a fertile alluvial plain. Note that this process is so recent that early humans would have witnessed it. We know that the Ganga repeatedly changed its course and shifted southward leaving behind oxbow lakes that can still be seen.

The Ganga's southward drift was arrested only when it nudged into the Vindhyas near Chunar (close to Varanasi). It is the only place in the plains where a hill commands such a view over the river, making Chunar fort a coveted strategic location. It was once said that he who controlled Chunar fort also controlled the destiny of India. A walk through the fort is a walk through Indian history. The walls resonate with tales of the legendary King Vikramaditya, the Mughals, Sher Shah Suri and Governor-General Warren Hastings. There are remains here from each era including an eighteenth-century sundial. Do not miss the neglected British graves below the walls. Their headstones make for interesting reading. Just south-west of the fort are the quarries that, in the third century BC, supplied the stone used by the Mauyans to carve the lions of Sarnath, now the national symbol. We will return to them in Chapter 3.

POPULATING INDIA

When India collided with Asia, it rejoined the broader ecological milieu of the rest of the world. Many people assume that the similarities between present-day Indian and African mammals (elephants, rhinos, lions, etc) are due to the fact that India was once attached to Africa. As we have seen, this cannot be the case because India separated from Africa during the age of the dinosaur.[8] The entry of large mammals into India was due to its geographical re-attachment to Eurasia and the shifting climatic zones that allowed or forced these animals to migrate into India. Take for instance a genetic study of the frozen remains of a Siberian mammoth that died 33,000 years ago. The scientists of the Max Planck Institute in Leipzig found that the Asian elephant is more closely related to the mammoth than to the African elephant. It appears that the genetic lines of the Asian and the African elephant separated six million years ago whereas the Asian elephants and the mammoths diverged only 440,000 years ago.[9]

Moreover, many Indian animals came into the subcontinent from the east. The tiger is one such example. There is some disagreement about the exact origins of the big cat. Some scholars claim a Siberian origin while others prefer to locate it in South China. Two-million-year-old remains of the tiger's ancestors have been found in Siberia, China, Sumatra and Java. However, the animal is a relative newcomer to India. The genetic data as well as fossil finds suggest that the Bengal tiger came to inhabit India fairly recently, perhaps no more than 12,000 years ago.

Meanwhile, where were the humans? There is now general consensus that, anatomically, modern humans evolved in Africa around 200,000 years ago. This fits both genetic data as well as archaeological remains. Genetic studies show that the San tribe of the Kalahari (also called the 'Bushmen') are probably the oldest surviving population of humans. Members of this tribe show the greatest genetic variation of any racial group and are therefore likely to be direct descendants of the earliest modern human population.[10]

Modern humans, of course, were not the first hominids to have walked the earth. More than a million years ago, pre-modern humans like Homo erectus used stone tools and had wandered as far as China and Java. At the time that modern humans were evolving in Africa, their close cousins, the Neanderthals, were already well established in Europe and West Asia. In other words, we are the last survivors of a large family tree and, in the early stages, it would not have been obvious that we would emerge as the most successful species. Indeed, there is evidence that our first attempt to leave Africa was a failure. Archaeological remains in the Skhul and Qafzeh caves in Israel show that modern humans may have made their way to the Levant about 120,000 years ago. Their passage may have been helped by the fact that the planet was enjoying a relatively wet and warm inter-glacial period that allowed them to wander up north. However, this climatic period did not last and a new Ice Age started. The early settlers either died out or were forced to retreat. Neanderthals, better adapted to the cold, probably reoccupied the area.

For the next 50,000 years, our ancestors remained in Africa. Around 65–70,000 years ago, a very small number, perhaps a single band, crossed over from Africa into the southern Arabian peninsula.[11] It is amazing that despite all their superficial differences, all non-Africans are descendants of this tiny group of wanderers.[12] This means that non-Africans have very little genetic variation. This has important implications for our susceptibility to global pandemics.

Climate and environment had a very significant impact on the expansion of modern humans.[13] Our planet goes through natural cycles of cooling and heating. When early humans made their way out of Africa, the earth was much cooler and much of the world's water was locked in giant ice-sheets. As a result, sea-levels were as much as 100 metres lower than today and coastlines and climate zones would have been very different. Thus, the early band of humans migrating from Africa to southern Arabia would have had to make a relatively short crossing across the Red Sea. Furthermore, they would have found an Arabian coastline that was much wetter and more hospitable.

It appears that modern humans next made their way along the coast to what is now the Persian Gulf. The average depth of the Persian Gulf is merely 36 metres.[14] With sea-levels 100 metres below current levels, this area would have been a well-watered plain—a veritable Garden of Eden. The groups of early humans would have found this a very attractive location and probably enjoyed a significant population increase. Expansion into Central Asia and Europe would have been difficult at this stage because of the Ice Age. However, they would have spread out along the Makran coast into the Indian subcontinent. Note again, that the Indian coastline would have been different from what we see today and, in many places, the shore would have been 25–100 km out from current contours.

At some stage, branches of the Persian Gulf people pushed their way farther into the Indian subcontinent. The landscape being traversed by these early migrations *had* supported other hominid populations.[15] In Europe, we know that the Neanderthals steadily withdrew westwards till one of the last bands died out in a cave in Gibraltar. However, it is unclear what happened to the pre-modern hominids of Asia. The eruption of the Toba volcano in Sumatra 74,000 years ago may have played some role in their extinction as excavations in Jwalapuram show that peninsular India was covered in volcanic ash from the eruptions. Experts still disagree on the impact but it is possible that the eruption may have decimated the population of pre-modern hominids that lived in the subcontinent at that time. This would have cleared the way for new immigrants, who appear to have spread quickly through the subcontinent and then through to South East Asia. Some scholars believe that the indigenous tribes of the Andaman and Nicobar Islands may be remnants of the earliest migrations into the region.

One branch eventually reached Australia around 40,000 years ago and became the ancestors of the aboriginals. Genetic studies confirm that the Australian aboriginals do have a genetic link with aboriginal tribes in South East Asia. However, for a long time researchers could find no direct genetic link between present-day Indians and native Australians. Some scholars even argued that this group may have avoided India altogether and used a route through Central Asia.[16] A study published in 2009 by the Anthropological Survey of India finally found genetic traces to link some Indian tribes with native Australians.[17] Note that these are very tiny traces—966 persons from twenty-six tribes were tested but only seven individuals showed possible genetic links. Still, we have a possible solution to the puzzle. The researchers also suggested that the Indian and Australian groups had separated about 50–60,000 years ago.

Meanwhile, a sizeable population remained in the vicinity of the Persian Gulf and the subcontinent for several thousand years. Scientists think that many important genetic lineages emerged from this area at this time. During the relatively warmer inter-glacial periods, sub-branches would have spread farther out into Europe, Central Asia and so on. However, note that temperatures would have still been far lower than present-day levels and that there would have been several climatic cycles. This means that we are not dealing with a landscape that is static. Research into the Persian Gulf people is still relatively new and hindered by the fact that the area is now mostly underwater. Nonetheless, scholars like Jeffrey Rose are painstakingly reconstructing the history of what they call the 'Gulf Oasis'.

This is a stylized and simplified account of what happened over tens of thousands of years. We are dealing with very tiny

Stone Age bands of fifty to hundred individuals over vast expanses of time and space. Their movements would not have been systematic or linear. There would have been random wanderings, retracements and dead ends. Just as there were groups coming into the subcontinent, there were groups going out. Indeed, geneticists feel that India may have been the source of a number of important genetic lineages that are now found worldwide. Natural calamities, hunger, tribal wars and, most importantly, disease would have decided who survived and who did not. It is important to remember that a tiny difference in the constellation of circumstances in the Stone Age could show up as a dramatic difference in the genetic make-up of today's population.

There are plenty of remains of these early humans in Stone Age sites scattered across India. Bhimbetka in central India is one of the most extensive sites in the world although it was only discovered in the 1950s. It is now a UNESCO World Heritage site. The hilly terrain is littered with hundreds of caves and rock shelters that appear to have been inhabited almost continuously for over 30,000 years.

The country's climate and wildlife would have gone through a lot of change over this long period. For instance, the finding of beads and ornaments made from ostrich-egg shells show that the bird was once common in India. It is possible that the Stone Age fashion industry pushed it into extinction by targeting the eggs. Bhimbetka has rock paintings of animals and hunters from the Stone Age as well as of warriors on horseback from a later time (perhaps the Bronze Age). The paintings provide intriguing glimpses of the ancient origins of Indian civilization. As the BBC's Michael Wood puts it,

'Looking at the dancing deity at Bhimbetka with his bangles and trident, one can't help but recall the image of the dancing Shiva'.[18]

The last full-blown Ice Age started around 24,000 years ago, reached its peak around 18,000–20,000 years ago and then warmed up. From 14,000 years ago, the ice sheets were melting rapidly, the sea-levels were rising around the world and weather patterns were changing. The Persian Gulf began to fill up 12,500 years ago.[19] Around 7500–8000 years ago, the Gulf Oasis was completely flooded. One wonders if this event is remembered as the Great Flood in Sumerian and Biblical accounts.

The Persian Gulf people would have been pushed out in waves by rising seas and desertification. Recent archaeology does suggest a spike in new habitations on higher ground appearing around 7500 years ago.[20] We also see growing evidence of maritime activity. A small clay replica of a reed boat and depiction of a sea-going boat with masts from this period have been found in Kuwait. In other words, by this time we are dealing with a Neolithic population capable of farming, domesticating animals and building boats. Some groups would have made their way into Central Asia, taking advantage of warmer temperatures. Others would have made their way into Europe where earlier migrations had already pushed out the Neanderthals. By this time, groups from South East Asia had already established themselves in China and the warmer climate would have allowed them to expand. Modern Chinese are now thought mainly to be descendants of the South East Asians group with inputs from people coming via Central Asia.

Meanwhile, what was happening along the Indian coastline? We know that the Indian coastline also moved several kilometres inland to roughly approximate what we would now recognize. Does this account for the fact that the Indians too have their own account of the Great Flood? According to this ancient legend, Manu, the king of the Dravidas, was warned by the god Vishnu about the flood. So he built a large ship and filled it with seeds and animals. Vishnu, in the form of a fish, then towed it to safety. Manu and the survivors are then said to have rebuilt civilization. The parallels with the story of Noah are obvious.

While the sea moved inland all along the coast, computer simulations suggest that there were two places where very large land masses were inundated. One was where we now have the Gulf of Khambat (Cambay), just south of the Saurashtra peninsula of Gujarat. The other land mass extended south from the Tamil coast and would have included Sri Lanka. Were there large human populations living in these areas at the time of the floods? It is very difficult to tell since the sites are under water.

In 2001, however, marine archaeologists identified two underwater locations in the Gulf of Khambat that seem to be remains of large settlements that would have been flooded 7500 years ago.[21] There is still a great deal of controversy over the exact nature of these discoveries but, if true, these findings would be truly remarkable. Since I have not personally examined the evidence, I reserve my judgement for the moment. Still, it would be reasonable to say that the changes in weather patterns and the sharp rise in sea-levels must have caused significant displacements in Neolithic populations during this period.

It is often argued that migrant Neolithic groups from the Persian Gulf area took the knowledge of farming to other regions. There is indeed evidence that some of the first crops to be farmed systematically in the subcontinent, around 7000 BC in Mehrgarh, Baluchistan, were West Asian species such as wheat and barley. Thus, it used to be thought that Indians learned to farm from West Asian migrants and only later managed to domesticate local plants such as eggplant (brinjal), sugarcane and sesame.[22] More recently, however, researchers have uncovered evidence that Indians may have independently developed farming, including the cultivation of rice. If there were large urban settlements off the Gujarat coast, they too surely knew how to farm. Was farming developed by the people who lived in the submerged cities and was the technology then carried by refugees to the interiors? Or, were there parallel innovations in different places? We are still learning a lot of things about this period, and it remains a developing story.

Whatever the truth about the submerged cities and the invention of farming, we know for sure that India supported a fairly large human population by the end of the Neolithic age. Who were these people? How are they related to present-day Indians?[23]

WHO ARE THE INDIANS?

Till the early twentieth century, it was believed that India was inhabited by aboriginal stone-age tribes till around 1500 BC when Indo-Europeans called 'Aryans' invaded the subcontinent from Central Asia with horses and iron weapons. Indian civilization was seen as a direct result of this invasion. Although the date was entirely arbitrary and not backed by any textual or archaeological evidence, this theory appeared to fit the pattern of later Central Asian invasions as well as explain certain linguistic similarities between Indian and European languages. Most importantly, it was politically convenient at that time as it painted the British as merely latter-day Aryans with a mission to civilize the natives.

This theory, however, had to be drastically revised when remains of the sophisticated Harappan civilization were discovered. They proved that Indian civilization clearly predated 1500 BC. Oddly, the 'Aryan invasion theory' was not thrown away. It was now argued that a people called the Dravidians (supposed ancestors of modern-day Tamils) created the Indus cities and that these cities were destroyed by the invading Aryans. This theory too ran into trouble. There is virtually no archaeological or literary evidence of such a large-scale invasion. As we shall see, the Harappan cities did not suddenly collapse but suffered a slow decline as a key river dried up and environmental conditions deteriorated.

Just by looking around, it will be obvious to anyone that India is home to a bewildering array of castes, tribes and language groups. Some of these groups came to India in historical times—Jews, Parsis, Ahoms, Turks to name a few. However, there are also many populations that have lived in the country for a very long time. Further complicating the picture is the fact that there has been a great deal of internal migration over thousands of years. So, where a group is found today may be very different from where it originated. Over the centuries most groups have mingled and yet a few have retained their unique identity to this day. In isolated pockets such as in the Andaman and Nicobar islands and in the North-Eastern states there are still tribes that have remained separate from the mainstream since prehistoric times.

Given this multiplicity, it is very difficult to generalize about the ethnic origins of all Indians. Nonetheless, twenty-first-century genetic studies provide some clues about how the Indian population came to resemble today's complex milieu. This too is an evolving area of study, but we are getting some sense of the broad contours.

The first thing that should be clear from the outset is that there are no 'pure' races. With the possible exception of some tiny isolated groups, the vast majority of Indian tribes, castes and communities are a mixture of many genetic streams. This merely confirms what we can all see—that Indians come in all shapes, sizes and shades—and these can vary quite a lot even within the same family. Nevertheless, some patterns of genetic distribution are discernible.

The first clue came with a 2006 study that India's population mix has been broadly stable for a very long time and that there has been no major injection of Central Asian genes for over 10,000 years[24]. This means that even if there had been a large-scale influx of so-called Indo-Europeans, it would have taken place more than 10,000 years ago, long before iron weapons and the domestication of the horse. Similarly, the study suggests that the population of Dravidian speakers has lived for a long time in southern India and the so-called Dravidian genetic pool may even have originated there.

More recent studies have added colour to these discoveries. A study led by David Reich of Harvard Medical School, published in *Nature* in 2009, suggests that the bulk of the Indian population can be explained by the mixture of two ancestral groups—the Ancestral South Indian (ASI) and the Ancestral North Indian (ANI).[25] The ASIs are the older group and are not related to Europeans, East Asians or any group outside the subcontinent. The ANIs are a somewhat more recent group and are related to Europeans.

Not surprisingly, Ancestral North Indian genes have a larger share in North India and account for over 70 per cent of the genes of Kashmiri Pandits and Sindhis. However, it is interesting that ANI genes have a large 40–50 per cent share even in South India and among tribal groups of central India. Indeed, there is no 'pure' population of Ancestral South Indian. The only populations without a large ANI input live in remote places like the Andaman Islands. Incidentally, there are also no pure ANIs.

There may be a temptation to equate the ANI–ASI data to the old Aryan–Dravidian racial theory. One should be careful doing this for a number of reasons. First, the ANI and the ASI are not 'pure' races in the nineteenth-century sense. Rather, they are merely different genetic cocktails that each contain many strands. Second, the terms Aryan and Dravidian are not just about genetic ancestry but carry strong cultural connotations. While the ANI genes are more widespread amongst speakers of Indo–European languages and the ASI genes in Dravidian-language speakers, there is a tendency to extrapolate this to cultural innovations of much later times. For instance, the people called Aryans are usually linked to the Vedic tradition while the Dravidians to the Sangam literary tradition. This is not meaningful to the ANI–ASI framework because we are dealing with genetic mingling that started well over 10,000 years ago, a lot earlier than the Vedic tradition, Sangam literature or the Harappan civilization.[26] We are dealing with small bands of hunter–gatherers and early farming communities rather than the thundering war-chariots, iron weapons and fortified cities that are said to have been part of an Aryan–Dravidian rivalry.

In other words, after thousands of years of mixing, Indians are most closely related to each other and it is pointless splitting hair over who is more Aryan and who is more Dravidian. The story of Manu, the Indian Noah, sums up the genetic findings surprisingly well. He was said to have been the king of the Dravidians prior to the flood but is repeatedly mentioned in the Vedic tradition as an ancestor!

A word of caution: India is a large and diverse country and there are many communities that will not fit a simple ANI–ASI framework. In the country's north-east and along the Himalayas, for instance, we find large genetic inputs from Tibeto–Burmans. In historical times alone we know of genetic inflows of Arab, Ahom, Turk, Jewish, Iranian and European extract. The deliberate North–South axis of the ANI–ASI approach should not be expected to explain all genetic variation across the country. It is merely the starting point of a very interesting line of study that could not only explain our pre-history but also provide key tools for next-generation medicine. One point, however, is clear—that Indians are a mongrel lot who come in all shapes, sizes and complexions. Genetics has merely confirmed what we can all see.

Of course, the genetic links of North Indians to some Europeans and Iranians corroborates linguistic linkages that were discerned in the nineteenth century. Most of the evidence is centred around a gene mutation called R1a1 (and more specifically a sub-group R1a1a).[27] This gene is common in North India and among East Europeans such as the Czechs, Poles and Lithuanians. There are smaller concentrations in South Siberia, Tajikistan, north-eastern Iran and in Kurdistan (that is, the mountainous areas of northern Iraq and adjoining areas). Interestingly, however, the gene is rare among Western Europeans, western Iranians and through many parts of Central Asia. In other words, we are dealing with R1a1a population concentrations that are separated by vast distances from each other. How did they get there?

A study by Peter Underhill et al published in 2010 in the *European Journal of Human Genetics* found that the oldest strain of the R1a1a branch was concentrated in the Gujarat-Sindh-Western Rajasthan area, suggesting that this was close to the origin of this genetic group. European carriers of R1a1a also carried a further mutation, M458, that is not found at all in their Asian cousins.[28] Since the M458 mutation is estimated to be at least 8000 years old, the two populations appear to have separated before or during the Great Flood. Thus, the genetic linkages between North Indians and East Europeans are best explained by the sharing of a distant common ancestor, perhaps from before the end of the last Ice Age. We do not really know why the Asian and European branches separated, although it is tempting to assume that it had something to do with climatic changes.

Note that the most common lineage in Western Europe is R1b. This is related to R1a1 and possibly also originated in the Persian Gulf area but the two lineages separated a long time ago—probably during or before the last Ice Age. Compared to R1a1, India has relatively low concentrations of R1b. My interpretation is that we are dealing with two major genetic dispersals occurring from the Persian Gulf-Makran-Gujarat region at different points in the climatic cycle—one occurred at the onset or during the last Ice Age with R1b carriers heading mostly west, and another occurred around the time of the Flood involving R1a1 carriers.

The genetic and cultural links between North Indians and eastern Iranians are due to the second dispersal but possibly with additional inputs from a later migration of some lineages north-westward from India.[28] As we shall see in the next chapter, there is reason to believe that some Indian tribes moved westward to Iran and beyond during the Bronze Age. In addition, cultural linkages could have been kept alive by trade. The spread of Indian culture to South East Asia in ancient times and, more recently, the accelerated popularity of the English language in the post-colonial period show that one does not need either conquest or large-scale migration to drive linguistic and cultural exchange. The reality of complex back-and-forth linkages make it very difficult to decode history using the linguistic layers. This may explain why traditional timelines based on linguistics were far shorter than those being suggested now by genetics and archaeology.

CASTES OR TRIBES?

There is one further insight that genetics hints at—the dynamics of India's caste system. India is not unique in having developed a caste system. Through history we have seen different versions of the caste system in Japan, Iran, and even in Classical Europe. What is remarkable about Indian castes is their persistence over thousands of years despite changes in technology, political conditions, and even religion. The system has even survived centuries of strong criticism and opposition from within the Hindu tradition.

It was once thought that the caste system had something to do with the Aryan influx and the imposition of a rigid racial hierarchy. However, as geneticist Sanghamitra Sahoo and her team have shown: 'The Y-chromosomal data consistently suggest a largely South Asian origin for Indian caste communities'.[30] Genetic studies suggest that Indian castes are profoundly influenced by 'founder events'. Roughly speaking, this means that castes are created by an 'event' when a group separates out and turns itself into an endogamous 'tribe'. Over time this process leads to a heterogeneous milieu of groups and sub-groups, sometimes combining and sometimes splitting off. The result is that, despite centuries of mixing, we do not have a unified population but a complex network of clans. This is a good description of the messy 'Jati'-based social system that exists to this day

Genetics also tells us that there is no real difference between groups that we differentiate today as 'castes' and 'tribes'. As India's leading geneticist, Dr. Lalji Singh puts it, 'It is impossible to distinguish castes and tribes from the data. This supports the view that castes grew directly out of tribe-like organizations during the formation of Indian society. The one exception to the finding, that all Indian groups are mixed, is the indigenous people of the Andaman islands . . .'[31]

In order to appreciate the messiness of the Jati system of castes, note the distribution of the R1a1 genetic haplogroup, the genes many Indians share with Eastern Europeans.[32] Their distribution in India across region and caste is telling. It is present in high concentration among high-caste Brahmins of Bengal and Konkan as well as in Punjabi Khatris, but it also shows up in tribes such as the Chenchus of Andhra Pradesh. In other words, a Chenchu tribesman is closely related to an upper-caste Bengali 'bhadralok' and a blond Lithuanian. You never know where you will bump into relatives. A paper published in the *Journal of Human Genetics* in January 2009, argues that the R1a1 lineage probably originated in India. The study argues for 'the autochthonous origin of R1a1 lineage in India and a tribal link to Indian Brahmins'.[33] Thus, we may well be dealing with a particularly successful Neolithic clan that branched out in different directions and whose descendants experienced very different fates.

There is a difference between the genetic reality and the rigid and strictly hierarchical 'Varna' system of castes described in the Manusmriti (Laws of Manu). The Manusmriti is often used by scholars as the framework to understand the phenomenon of castes. It now appears that the formal 'Varna' based caste system described in the text is a scholarly abstraction that may never have existed in reality.[34] Instead, what we have here is a very flexible and organic milieu consisting of Jatis that can adapt easily to changing times by allowing for evolving social equations. For instance, the system can spontaneously create new castes whenever new groups need to be accommodated. Similarly, groups can be promoted or demoted in status according to prevailing social conditions. This fits what we know from historical experience—including the formation of the warrior Rajput caste in the medieval period. In the past, these groups vied with each other to move up the pecking order. Today we have the opposite situation where they vie to be classified as 'backward' in order to benefit from affirmative action. The logic of collective action is the same.

2

People of the Lost River

As we move from prehistory to history, we are immediately confronted by a problem of plenty. The early history of India has two parallel sources, but there is a great deal of disagreement about how they fit together. On one hand there is the archaeological evidence of the sophisticated cities of the Harappan Civilization (also called Indus Valley or Indus–Saraswati civilization). On the other hand, there is the literature of the Vedic tradition. Their geographies and timelines roughly overlap but archaeologists and historians have long had difficulty reconciling them. Indeed, this has remained a hot topic of discussion among scholars and often deteriorates into a political debate. I do not claim to have resolved the debate. Therefore, I will tell the two stories separately. I will then focus on the one thing that the two sources agree on: the drying of a great river that the

Rig Veda calls the Saraswati. No matter which way one looks at it, the drying of this river was an important geographical event that defined early India.

THE HARAPPAN CIVILIZATION

Till the early twentieth century, as already discussed in the previous chapter, it was believed that Indian civilization began with the 'Aryan Invasions' that were supposed to have taken place around 1500 BC. These European-like Aryans were supposed to have come from Central Asia and to have conquered the subcontinent and then 'civilized' the native population. It should not be lost on the reader that this theory evolved in an intellectual milieu in which Rudyard Kipling was composing poems such as *The White Man's Burden*. The theory was based on the discovery of some linguistic affinities between European languages and Sanskrit. The date of 1500 BC was mostly arbitrary. It ignored the fact that both ancient texts and folk traditions have always maintained a much older timeline, but these were considered mythical and dismissed. To be fair, there were no known archaeological equivalents of Egyptian pyramids or Sumerian cities to prove an older history.

However, new discoveries would radically challenge this view in the early decades of the twentieth century. When the Lahore–Multan railway line was being built in the late nineteenth century, wagon-loads of bricks were removed from old mounds to be used as ballast. The bricks were of exceptionally good quality and most people assumed they were of relatively recent origin. In the winter of 1911–12,

D.R. Bhandarkar of the Archaeological Survey of India decided to visit one of the sites in Sindh called Mohenjodaro (which literally means Mound of the Dead). He came away unimpressed. In his view, the bricks were of a 'modern type' and the locals had told him that they were from a town that had been abandoned just two hundred years earlier. He could not have been more wrong. Fortunately, in the 1920s, Rakhal Das Banerji and Sir John Marshall of the Archaeological Survey decided to revisit the site. Another team led by Daya Ram Sahni began to excavate another site called Harappa in Punjab (both these sites are now in Pakistan). They soon realized that mounds of bricks scattered along the Indus Valley were the remnants of a much older civilization, a contemporary of the Sumerians, the Minoans and the ancient Egyptians. It was named the Indus Valley or Harappan civilization.

Soon, more and more sites began to be discovered. The reason that the Harappan sites were ignored for so long is that they lack grand structures like the Pyramids of Giza that stare out at a visitor. There are large buildings that have been given names like 'granary', 'assembly hall', 'citadel' and 'college' but these designations are essentially arbitrary. We do not know what these buildings were really used for and, in most cases, we have little more than foundations and lower walls. There is nothing that is obviously a great palace or a temple. One of the few major buildings that we can definitely identify is the 'Great Bath' in Mohenjodaro but even in this case we do not know if the structure was used for religious rituals (as in later Hindu temples), a bathing pool for the royal family or some completely different purpose.

Yet, the Harappan sites are remarkable for their attention

to urban design and active municipal management. At its height, the Harappan civilization was very consciously urban. A large city like Mohenjodaro (now in Pakistan) may have had a population of around 40–50,000 people. Furthermore, we see meticulous town-planning in every detail—standardized bricks, street grids, covered sewerage systems and so on. Similarly, a great deal of effort was put into managing water. The solutions varied from city to city. Mohenjodaro alone may have had 600-700 wells. At Dholavira in Gujarat, water was diverted from two neighbouring streams into a series of dams and preserved in a complex system of reservoirs.[1] Many houses, even modest ones, have their own bathrooms and toilets connected to a drainage network that emptied into soak-jars and cess pits. The toilet commodes were made up of big pots sunk into the floor. Most interestingly, as historian Upinder Singh points out, the toilets came equipped with a 'lota' for washing up.[2] This must count as one of the most important and enduring of Harappan contributions to Indian civilization. Unfortunately, the toilet design did not survive quite as well as the lota.

DEALING WITH SLUMS AND TECTONICS

Dholavira is a good example of a large Harappan urban centre. It is on an island in the strange salt-marsh landscape of the Rann of Kutchh. At the centre of the settlement is a 'citadel' which consists of a rectangular 'castle' and a 'bailey'. It is thought that the citadel contained the homes of the elite as well as public buildings. The castle, which is the oldest part of the city, was heavily fortified with thick walls and was probably meant to withstand military attack. Early scholars had a belief that the Harappan civilization was uniquely peaceful and that there are no signs of military activity. I disagree. As the citadel at Dholavira suggests, defence was a key consideration. The times and technologies may have been different, but human nature was the same. Indeed, examinations of Harappan skeletons has often found wounds that are likely to have been inflicted in battle.

In front of the citadel there is a large open ground that could have been used for many purposes—military display, sport, royal ceremonies or perhaps the annual parading of the gods. Archaeologists have found tiered seating for spectators along the length of the ground. Beyond the ceremonial grounds was the planned area where the common citizens lived. This division into a Citadel and Lower Town is quite common in larger Harappan settlements. Interestingly, as the city grew, it continued to attract migrants who could not be fitted into the planned city. This led to the growth of informal settlements just to the east of the original Lower Town. As we shall see, the problem with slums is a recurring theme in India's urban history and we find them in Mughal Delhi, colonial Bombay and in virtually every modern Indian city. The difference is that the political leadership of Dholavira responded by expanding the urban limits and incorporating the slums into the city. According to Dr R. S. Bisht, who led the excavation of the site, we can still discern how the civic authorities redeveloped the slums and imposed Harappan municipal order on them. Thus, Dholavira ended up with three sections—the Citadel, a Middle Town (i.e. the old Lower Town) and a new Lower Town (the new extension).

The city also had to respond to the vagaries of nature. Dr Bisht mentions earthquakes that repeatedly affected Dholavira, including a particularly severe one around 2600 BC.[3] We were violently reminded of the tectonic instability of the region when an earthquake measuring 7.8 on the Richter scale killed 20,000 people in the state of Gujarat on 26 January 2001. The epicentre was not far from Dholavira.

Thus, the picture is not the popular one of a rigidly pre-planned city but of an evolving urban settlement that was responding in various ways to natural and human challenges. When one visits an archaeological site, one tends to admire the ancient masonry in isolation. In reality, Dholavira was a living city that would have been crowded with soldiers, traders, artisans, and bullock-carts. Imagine the heat and dust, the sound of children playing, and street-vendors haggling with their customers. Moreover, like successful cities of today, there would been a large population of 'outsiders' including migrants, foreign merchants, refugees and so on. This would have been true not just of Dholavira but all major urban clusters. A recent study of the composition of teeth from a burial site in Harappa found that many of the city's inhabitants had come to the city from outside.[4]

Given the geographical spread of the civilization, it is not surprising that there are regional variations. Nonetheless, there is an extraordinary level of standardization including weights and measures, the characteristic terracotta seals and so on. This has led many commentators to argue that there was a centralized empire that imposed order over the whole system. Unfortunately, we know nothing about the political structure and, as already mentioned, we have yet to find any building

that can be definitely identified as an imperial palace or a
political centre. In fact, we know almost nothing for sure
about historic events, political leaders, religion and language.
The Harappans did have a script but it has not yet been
deciphered.

THE MERCHANTS OF MELUHHA

Despite our near-total ignorance about the political history of
the civilization, we now know a great deal about its geography.
Over the last century, thousands of sites have been found and
several new sites are being discovered every year. It appears
that the subcontinent was very populous even at this early
stage. The core of the Harappan civilization extended over a
large area, from Gujarat in the south, across Sindh and
Rajasthan and extending into Punjab and Haryana. Numerous
sites have been found outside the core area, including some as
far east as Uttar Pradesh and as far west as Sutkagen-dor on
the Makran coast of Baluchistan, not far from Iran. There is
even a site in Central Asia called Shortughai along the Amu
Darya, close to the Afghan-Tajik border. Thus, the
geographical spread, the number of sites and implied
population of the Harappan civilization dwarfs that of
contemporary Egypt, China or Mesopotamia. What the
Harappans lack in grand buildings, they make up for in the
sheer scale of their civilizational reach and in the extraordinary
municipal sophistication of their cities.

We also know that the people of the civilization were
actively engaged in domestic and international trade. For land
transport, the Harappans used bullock-carts that are almost

exactly the same as those that can still be seen in rural India. Cart ruts from Harappa show that even the axle-gauge was almost exactly the same as that of carts used in today's Sindh. The streets of Mohenjodaro, Harappa and Dholavira would have been full of these bullock-carts ferrying goods and merchants. Thousands of years later, French traveller Tavernier would speak of how seventeenth-century Indian highways were clogged by bullock-cart caravans that could have as many as 10,000–12,000 oxen. He goes on to describe how, when two such caravans met on a narrow road, there would be a traffic jam and it could take two or three days for them to pass. One can imagine Harappan highways would have been quite similar.[5] Perhaps it was one of the great continuities of Indian history.

The numerous rivers of the region would have been useful waterways for ferrying goods and people. A dry dock has been discovered at Lothal in Gujarat where vessels would have docked. It is a short drive from modern Ahmedabad and is worth a day-trip. Little more than foundations and drains have survived of the urban settlement and the visitor may need help from the friendly staff of the archaeology museum (across the car park) to make sense of it. However, the dock—the world's earliest known—is an impressive structure. It was connected by a canal to the estuary of the Sabarmati river and a lock-gate system was used to regulate water flow during tides. Next to the dock are the remains of warehouses. Standing on the brick blocks of the warehouses, I imagined the humourless customs officials who would have peered suspiciously at the merchandise being unloaded from the boats.

There is strong evidence that the Harappans traded actively with the Persian Gulf. The merchant ships likely hugged the Makran coast, perhaps with a pit stop at Sutkagen-dor and then sailed on to the ports of the Persian Gulf. Mesopotamian tablets mention a land called Meluhha that exported bead jewellery, copper, wood, peacocks, monkeys and ivory.[6] These sound like goods that Indians would have exported. It is also likely that they exported cotton textiles since the Harappans were the world pioneers in the spinning and weaving of cotton.[7] To this day, the Indian subcontinent remains a major exporter of cotton textiles and garments.

Strangely, we have no idea what the Harappans imported. Hardly any object of Mesopotamian origin has been found at Harappan sites. Perhaps they imported consumables like dates and wine but we really do not know. The same can be said about trade with Iran and Central Asia. As already mentioned, archaeologists have found a Harappan outpost in Shortughai on the Afghan–Tajik border. What were they doing there? One intriguing possibility is that they were there to buy horses. The inability to breed good-quality horses would plague India right into the nineteenth century and force Indian rulers to import large numbers from Central Asia and Arabia. Marco Polo would comment on this in the thirteenth century. We will return to this issue later.

WHAT HAPPENED TO INDIA'S FIRST CITIES?

We now know that this civilization did not suddenly appear or disappear. Excavations in Mehrgarh, near Quetta in Balochistan, show the gradual evolution from Neolithic village to an increasingly more sophisticated culture from around 7000 BC. The earliest recognizably Harappan sites date to 3500 BC. This early phase lasts till around 2600 BC. We then enter the Mature phase from 2600 BC to 2000 BC. This is when the great cities were at their height. Note that this is a Bronze Age culture and there is no systematic use of iron. Then, from around 2000 BC we have a steady disintegration that lasts till 1400 BC—what is usually called Late Harappan.

This is a simplified timeline. In reality, cities rose and fell and were sometimes rebuilt on older sites. Some areas flourished when others were in decline. Nonetheless, there are clear signs that the overall civilization was in severe stress after 2000 BC. We see steady deterioration in municipal governance till one by one the great cities are abandoned. What went wrong?

It was once believed that Aryan invasions from Central Asia had caused the collapse of the Indus Valley Civilization. However, there is no sign that Harappan cities were laid waste by invaders. The evidence strongly points to the wrath of nature. A number of studies show that the area which is today the Thar desert was once far wetter and that the climate gradually became drier. However, the exact trajectory of this change is somewhat disputed. It is possible that the process of drying was already under way when the Mature Harappan period began. However, around 2200 BC, we find that the monsoons had become distinctly weaker and there were prolonged droughts. In fact, this is a widespread phenomenon that also affected Egypt and Turkey.[8] By itself, this would have caused an agricultural crisis for a heavily populated region. However, the Harappans were hit by an even bigger problem—the drying up of the river system on which the civilization was based.

A simple map of Harappan sites would be enough to illustrate that the largest concentration of settlements is not centred around the Indus but around the dry riverbed of the Ghaggar. It is now little more than a dry riverbed that contains water only after heavy rains (it saw an exceptional flow after the heavy monsoons of 2010). However, surveys and satellite photographs confirm that it was once a great river that rose in the Himalayas, entered the plains in Haryana, flowed through the Thar–Cholistan desert of Rajasthan and eastern Sindh (running roughly parallel to the Indus) and then reached the sea in the Rann of Kutchh in Gujarat. Indeed, the strange marshy landscape of the Rann of Kutchh is partly due to the fact that it was once the estuary of a great river. Although much of this course is now dry desert and often hidden under sand, satellite photographs show that there is still a substantial amount of underground water along the old channels. This has been confirmed by drilling wells that have given fresh water at shallow depths even in the middle of the Thar desert!

The Ghaggar emerges from hills just east of Chandigarh but is joined by a number of other seasonal rivers in the plains of northern Haryana. There is evidence that the Ghaggar and/or some of these rivers were perennial in ancient times. Moreover, satellite images show that both the Sutlej and the Yamuna once flowed into the Ghaggar, which would have made the Ghaggar a mighty river. However, at some point the Ghaggar appears to have lost its main sources of glacial melt from the Himalayas even as the Sutlej and the Yamuna, its largest tributaries, abandoned it for the Indus and the

Ganga respectively. Tectonic shifts appear to have played a role in this. As a result, we find that the river no longer flowed to the sea. The Ghaggar may have struggled on with the help of rain-fed seasonal tributaries but even these failed as the climate changed. The sequence of events may have taken decades or centuries to play out and different parts of the

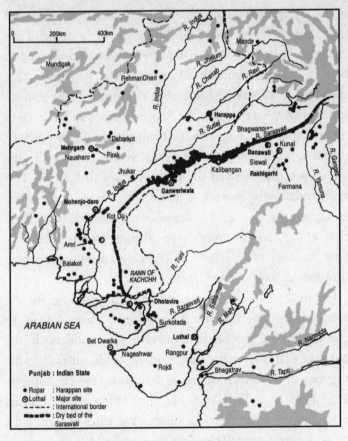

Dry Bed of the Saraswati River
(source: *The Lost River: On the Trail of the Sarasvati* by Michel Danino)

Harappan world would have experienced different sub-cycles. Cities on the banks of the Indus, for instance, may have suffered floods as Sutlej waters suddenly entered their ecosystem. The Pakistan floods of 2010 provide a glimpse of what this may have felt like—especially if such an event had caused the Indus itself to shift course.

What does the drying of the Ghaggar tell us about the fate of the Harappans? It appears that the climate was wetter and the Ghaggar was in full flow during the early phase of the civilization. Perhaps the earthquakes of 2600 BC, attested to both at Kalibangan and Dholavira, were related to the tectonic shifts that affected either the Yamuna or the Sutlej. Interestingly, we find that the mature Harappan phase takes off only after the Ghaggar was already drying. One wonders if the drying weather and the dying river created a climatic sweet-spot that allowed the urban centres to flourish. This may explain why there is a dense concentration of mature Harappan sites in the Thar desert, around the time we think that the Ghaggar may have already started to dry. Unfortunately, around 2000 BC, conditions again took a sharp turn for the worse.

Eventually, the lack of water began to weigh against the Harappans. Their carefully managed cities began to disintegrate and they began to migrate. This would not be the last time that cities in the subcontinent would suffer from the vagaries of too much or too little water. One can imagine long lines of bullock-carts, heavily laden with personal belongings, leaving their old villages and cities in search of a more secure future. The scene was replayed in 2010 when Pakistan was devastated by floods. In the north, the Harappans moved north-east to the Yamuna and Ganga. In Gujarat, the cities in Kutchh were abandoned in favour of new settlements in the Narmada and Tapti valleys to the south.[9] The late Harappan sites show a degree of cultural continuity but there is a clear shift towards smaller settlements. The old urban sophistication has clearly broken down. Thus ended India's first experience of urbanization.

WHERE DID THE HARAPPANS GO?

The archaeological evidence suggests that they slowly drifted east and south, and that their culture and genes lived on in India. However, archeologists and historians disagree bitterly on this. Romila Thapar, an eminent historian, is of the opinion that the 'material culture shows no continuities'.[10] In contrast, B.B. Lal, a former Director General of the Archaeological Survey and one of India's most celebrated archaeologists, argues that 'many of the present day cultural traits are rooted in the Harappan Civilization'.[11]

We have already discussed the similarity between modern-day bullock carts and those used by the Harappans. However, B.B. Lal puts forward a formidable body of evidence that the Harappan legacy is not just visible in later Indian civilization but is present in everyday life to this day. Take for example, the 'namaste'—the common Indian way to show respect to both people and to the gods. There are several clay figurines from Harappan sites that show a person with palms held together in a namaste. There are even terracotta dolls of women with red vermilion on their foreheads. Is this the origin of the 'sindur' used by married Hindu women? All of these are intriguing thoughts but we cannot be absolutely sure that these had the same meaning for the Harappans.

In his recent book, Michel Danino has collected even more examples of continuity. We have already discussed the persistence of the ratio 5:4 in the previous chapter. We see the use of such ratios in many facets of Harappan life. They also had a standardized system of weights and measures, many of which are echoed two thousand years later in the *Arthashastra*, a manual on governance and political economy written in the third century BC. Danino calculates that the standard length used by the planners at Dholavira was 1.9 metres which is the same as the unit called *dhanush* (i.e. bow) used in the *Arthashastra*. He then shows that this unit was divided into 108 sub-units of 1.76 cm each. This fits with the 108 *angulas* (i.e. finger-widths) that made up a *dhanush*.[12] In fact, the old systems appear to have survived in a few places into the twentieth century. Till India switched a few decades ago to the metric system, the traditional weights and measures used in some parts of the subcontinent bore a striking resemblance to those used by the Harappan people. According to John Mitchiner, the difference was less than 1.8 per cent—not bad for a time lapse of over four thousand years!

Most interesting of all, chess pieces that look remarkably like modern equivalents have been found at Harappan sites. It has long been known that chess originated in India but it is extraordinary that the game, or something similar, was being played more than four thousand years ago. Even the famous town planning of the Harappans may have survived in later times. The streets of Kalibagan, a large site in Indian Punjab, are laid out with widths in a progression of 1.9 m, 3.8 m, 5.7 m and 7.6 m—the same as those prescribed in the *Arthashastra*. In short, the Harappans did not just disappear; they live on amongst us. They merged with the wider population and seeded what we now know as the Indian civilization. However, Indian civilization has parallel roots, in particular the Vedic tradition and its continuous history to this day. It is to this that we now turn.

THE RIG VEDA

The Vedas are the oldest scriptures of the Hindu tradition and consist of four books—Rig, Sama, Yajur and Atharva. They consist mostly of prayers, hymns and instructions on how to conduct rituals and fire sacrifices. They were composed and compiled over several centuries by poet-philosophers (or rishis). The Rig Veda is the oldest of the four and organized in ten sections. It is the oldest extant book in the world and remains in active use. Indeed, it is considered by most Hindus to be the most sacred of texts and one of its hymns, the Gayatri Mantra, is chanted daily by millions. It has been variously translated by scholars over the centuries. Here is my interpretation: 'As you light up the Heavens and the Earth, O Radiant Sun, So light up my Mind'.

The Rig Veda is composed in a very archaic form of Sanskrit and is undoubtedly very old. However, there is a great deal of disagreement about exactly how old. The dates range from 4000 BC to 1000 BC.[13] Dating it is no easy task since it was probably compiled over decades or even centuries and remained a purely orally transmitted tradition till the third century AD. Nonetheless, it is clear that the Rig Veda belongs to the Bronze Age as it does not mention iron.[14] The earliest possible mention of iron comes in the Atharva Veda which was compiled many centuries later and talks of a 'krishna ayas' or dark bronze. Since we know that iron was in use in India by 1700 BC,[15] this would roughly date the Atharva Veda. Allowing for a few centuries between the composition of the first and last Veda, it would not be unreasonable to say the Rig Veda was compiled no later than 2000 BC.

Since the nineteenth century, the Rig Veda has been used to reconstruct early Indian history. At the outset, let me point out that this is fraught with difficulty. The book is mainly concerned with religion and philosophy, and is not meant as an encyclopaedia of social and political conditions. It is a bit like guessing the history of the Roman Empire by reading the New Testament. Nonetheless, it does provide an interesting glimpse of a Bronze Age society, its social customs, its material and philosophical concerns, its gods and its tribal feuds. With one exception, however—it is difficult to discern actual historical events from the hymns.

The geography of the book, by contrast, is very clear. To the east, the book talks of the Ganga river and, to the west, of the Kabul river. It also shows awareness of the Himalayan mountains in the north and the seas to the south (i.e. the Arabian Sea). This is a very well defined geographical area and, interestingly, roughly coincides with the Harappan world.

Most interesting of all, the Rig Veda speaks repeatedly of a great river called the Saraswati. It is described as the greatest of rivers. Forty-five of the Rig Veda hymns shower praise on the Saraswati. No other river or geographical feature comes close in importance. The Ganga is barely mentioned twice and the Indus, although referred to as a mighty river, is not given the same reverence. In contrast, the Saraswati is called the mother of all rivers and 'great among the great, the most impetuous of rivers'. It is even called the 'inspirer of hymns' suggesting that the Rig Veda was composed on its banks.

The problem is that there is no living river in modern India that fits the description. This has led some historians to argue that the Saraswati is a figment of poetic imagination. Others have tried to identify it with the Helmand river in Afghanistan. However, the Rig Veda itself describes the geographical location of the river. In the *Nadistuti Sukta* (Hymn to the Rivers), the major rivers are enumerated from east to west starting with the Ganga. The hymn clearly places the Saraswati between the Yamuna and the Sutlej. There is no room for doubt. There is only one river that could fit this description— the Ghaggar. Its river bed may be dry today but satellite and ground surveys unequivocally tell us that it was once a mighty river. It is very difficult to escape the conclusion that the Rig Vedic people and the Harappans were dealing with the same river.

There is a further twist. Unlike later texts, the Rig Veda does not mention a drying Saraswati. Instead, it mentions clearly that the Saraswati entered the sea in full flow. This would suggest that the text was composed before 2600 BC! Even more intriguingly, the Rig Veda mentions poets and compositions from an even earlier age, although their works have not survived. So, we could be dealing with a culture that coincides with the early Harappan age. I know that not all scholars would agree with this—but it is important to keep this possibility in mind.

CAN ONE RECONCILE THE TWO ACCOUNTS?

The Harappan civilization and the Rig Veda coincide on many things—their time frames, their geography, the Bronze Age technology and even on the existence of the Saraswati river. Were they the same people? Combined with the genetic data discussed in the earlier chapter, it would seem that we are dealing with a population and culture that has continuously inhabited the subcontinent for a very long time. For some, especially archaeologists like B.B. Lal, the matter is settled. However, there are many scholars who remain sceptical. Let us look at many of the arguments usually put forward against identifying the Harappans with the Rig Vedic people. We will start with the weaker arguments and make our way to the more serious ones.

One of the oldest arguments is that the Rig Vedic people were nomads from Central Asia who could not have built the sophisticated cities of the Indus Valley. This is why, so the argument goes, the Rig Veda shows little knowledge of India's geography beyond the North West. This is a spurious argument because the Rig Veda neither mentions an invasion nor does it show any knowledge of Central Asia. All we can garner from the text is that these people were living in the area that corresponds roughly to modern Haryana, western Uttar Pradesh and Punjab (including Pakistani Punjab). They also knew about the Himalayas in the north, the seas in the south, the Ganga to the east and eastern Afghanistan to the west. It is entirely possible that they may have known about South India and/or Central Asia but the text tells us nothing about this.

Furthermore, the Rig Vedic people are clearly aware of

settled agriculture and of cities—both inhabited by themselves and those inhabited by their enemies. They are not wild nomads from the Steppes as has been suggested. Admittedly, the Rig Veda does not obviously reflect the Harappan obsession with municipal order but then it is a religious book and should not be expected to delve into the intricacies of sewage systems.

The second spurious argument is that the Rig Vedic people were iron-wielding 'Aryans' who were at constant war with their enemies called 'Dasas' (the latter being identified as the Harappans or aboriginal tribes). The term 'Arya' is commonly used in Sanskrit literature, but is never used in a racial sense. It refers to a cultured or noble person—which means that all groups like to refer to themselves as Aryan and to their enemies as non-Aryan. The use of the word in a racial sense occurs in ancient Iran and modern Europe, but not in India. Similarly, we need to be careful with the use of the word Dasa to denote non-Aryan enemies, especially when the greatest of the 'Aryan' chieftains mentioned in the Rig Veda is a Dasa himself: Sudasa, son of Divodasa (more on him later).[16]

In other words, the Rig Veda hardly gives us a consistent picture of Arya–Dasa conflict. It is rather a mish-mash of tribal feuds between clans whose ethnic background can no longer be discerned. Their technology is decidedly Bronze Age and the use of iron appears many centuries later in the Atharva Veda if at all.[17] By all accounts, iron smelting was an indigenously developed technology that arose in Central India from the plentiful iron ore found there. It could not have been an imported technological advantage that the invaders exercised over the locals.

In my view, the more serious argument against identifying

the Vedic Indians with the Harappans relates to the use of horses. The Rig Veda frequently mentions the bull and the horse. The former is a common theme in Harappan art but the horse appears to be conspicuously missing. I have not yet found a full explanation for this and perhaps the answer lies in the hundreds of unexcavated sites littered across India and Pakistan or in the thousands of bags of animal bones from earlier excavations that have not been examined for decades. Nonetheless, I would like to add two qualifications.

First, it is very likely that Harappans were at least familiar with the horse, even if it was not a commonly used animal. The horse was domesticated in Central Asia around 4000 BC and we know that a millennium later, the Harappans had a trading outpost on the Amu Darya. Surely they would have noticed how the locals had tamed an animal that could be so useful. In fact, it would not be surprising if they were there to procure horses. After all, the importation of horses remains a common theme throughout later Indian history. Thus, one could argue that it was the horse and not the Aryan who was imported. Indeed, there is independent evidence to suggest horses were familiar animals even in Central India from a very early stage. The stone-age rock paintings of Bhimbetka show horses. The Neolithic site of Mahagara on the Belan river has yielded horse bones—which may indicate a familiarity with the animal from a pre-Harappan era![18] In short, there may have been plenty of horses about, which fits with the fact that the so-called non-Aryan tribes in the Rig Veda also appear to have horses of their own.

Second, it is not entirely true that there are no signs of the horse in Harappan sites. While the horse is not depicted in any of the seals, there are at least two terracotta figurines that depict a 'horse-like' creature. The set of 'chessmen' found in Lothal, too, has a piece that looks like a horse's head. There are even claims that horse bones have been found in a few places and have been positively identified by leading scholars[19] although critics still argue that these remains are of asses/ donkeys and not of horses. I am not qualified to judge this but merely want readers to know that the absence of horses can no longer be evoked quite so easily to debunk the idea that the Harappans and the Vedic people were somehow related. In my view, the really interesting debate relates to lions and not horses. We will visit it in the next chapter.

On balance, the evidence appears to have tipped in favour of the archaeologists rather than the historians. New information—including genetic data—appears to be strengthening their hand. Over time, it is possible that the remaining controversies will be ironed out including that of the horse and the lion. My own sense is that the Harappans were a multi-ethnic society, rather like India today. The Rig Vedic people could well have been part of this bubbling mix.

Let us turn now to the geographical event on which the archaeology and the texts categorically agree—the drying up of the Saraswati. Whichever way one looks at it, one cannot escape the conclusion that the drying up of this river was a major event in the evolution of India's civilization.

WHAT HAPPENED TO THE SARASWATI?

The identification of the Saraswati with the Ghaggar is not new. A number of nineteenth-century British explorers and

cartographers identified the dry riverbed with the river
mentioned in old texts and legends. However, with modern
satellite data, the matter can now be said to be settled. As we
have seen, the Rig Veda talks incessantly about the great
Saraswati river, echoed by the later Vedas. However, texts of
the next generation repeatedly mention how the Saraswati
dried up. The *Panchavamsa Brahmana* tells us that the river
disappeared into the desert. There are many legends and folk
tales about how the river dried up or sank underground.
What was the cause of its downfall?

As already mentioned, physical surveys and satellite
photographs confirm that the Sutlej and the Yamuna were
once tributaries of the Saraswati. This would have made the
Saraswati a very impressive river with a flow that was larger
than that of the Indus and the Ganga. It is not surprising that
so many early Harappan settlements were centred around
this great river. Unfortunately, the river appears to have lost
the Yamuna, perhaps due to a major tectonic event. We have
seen how the Himalayas are notoriously unstable and prone
to major earthquakes. The earthquakes of 2600 BC may have
been especially large but there would have been other tectonics
movements as well. The loss of the Yamuna was not the end
of the Saraswati's misfortunes. It then lost the Sutlej, its other
major tributary, to the Indus. The Sutlej is a moody river and
has had many channels in its past. Its ancient name Shatadru
literally means 'Of a Hundred Channels'. At some point it
decided to swing west towards the Indus. The old channels
flowing east remain visible in satellite photographs.

The same process may even have cost the Saraswati its own
perennial source of glacial water. A Rig Vedic hymn hints that

it may have had three separate sources.[20] There is some research that argues that the Tons river, that is today a major tributary of the Yamuna, may have been one of the original sources of glacial water for the Saraswati, and that it flowed into the plains through the channel of the Markanda, which is yet another of the Ghaggar's tributaries.[21]

Without a perennial water source, the Saraswati must have become a rain-fed seasonal river. Even this became untenable as the climate became drier. Eventually, the river broke up into a series of lakes and then completely dried up. The dry riverbed of the Ghaggar is all that is now left although it does occasionally flow after an especially heavy monsoon season.

Nevertheless, the river was not forgotten. We find its memory echoed in legends, folk tales and place-names. Modern Hindus still worship the Saraswati as the Goddess of Knowledge, recalling the river's role as an 'inspirer of hymns'. In Haryana, one of the seasonal tributaries of the Ghaggar is called the Sarsuti. Farther south, a seasonal river called Saraswati rises in the Aravallis and flows into the Rann of Kutchh, not far from the estuary of the lost river. Deep in the deserts of Rajasthan, the Pushkar lake recalls many legends about the Goddess Saraswati. Where the Yamuna joins the Ganga at Allahabad, there is a legend that the Saraswati flows underground. Perhaps it is a way to remember the fact that the Yamuna was once a tributary of the lost river.

The shifting of the rivers may explain one of the mysteries of the subcontinent's wildlife: how the Gangetic and Indus river dolphins came to belong to the same species. Till the 1990s they were considered separate species but now they are classified as sub-species Platanista Gangetica Gangetica and

Platanista Gangetica Minor. The problem is that the two river systems are today not connected, and the dolphins obviously could not have walked from one to the other. The sea route too is unlikely since the mouths of the two rivers are very far apart. In any case, the river dolphins are not closely related to the salt-water dolphins of the Indian Ocean and must have evolved separately from them. One possibility, therefore, is that the shifting rivers allowed the dolphins to move from one river system to the other. Sadly, both sub-species are now under severe threat from pollution and the diversion of water into numerous irrigation projects.[22]

Standing on the banks of the Yamuna in Delhi, I ponder on the fate of a river killed by ill-advised civil engineering. Did the Harappans feel like this as they gazed on the dying Saraswati? The concern with water is echoed in the Vedas. The greatest feat of Indra, king of the gods, is to have defeated Vritra, a dragon, who had held back the river waters behind stone dams. Indra slays Vritra after a great battle, destroys the dams and sets the rivers free. It may be significant that the slaying of Vritra is specifically mentioned in a hymn eulogizing Saraswati. Perhaps the ancients too struggled with their inner demon—the suspicion that they may have somehow brought on their downfall by interfering with nature.

LAND OF THE SEVEN RIVERS

At the core of the Rig Vedic landscape was an area called Sapta-Sindhu (Land of the Seven Rivers). This is clearly the heartland of the Rig Veda, but the problem is that the text does not clearly specify the seven rivers. It is almost as if it was too obvious to be worthy of explanation. The hymns repeatedly describe the Saraswati as being 'of seven-sisters', so the sacred river was certainly one of the rivers, but the others are uncertain. The conventional view is that the seven rivers include the Saraswati, the five rivers of Punjab and the Indus. This would mean that the Sapta-Sindhu region included Haryana, all of Punjab (including Pakistani Punjab) and even parts of adjoining provinces. This is a very large area.

Having traversed much of this terrain and read and re-read the text, I have come to a somewhat different conclusion. The Vedas clearly mention a wider landscape watered by 'thrice-seven' rivers.[23] While one does not have to take it literally as referring to twenty-one rivers, it is obvious that the Sapta-Sindhu is a sub-set of the wider Vedic landscape. In my view, the Indus and its tributaries were not a part of the Sapta-Sindhu. The Indus has long been considered a 'male' river in Indian tradition and would have not been called a sister. Indeed, it is notable that the Indus and its tributaries are never described as 'of seven sisters'. My hunch is that the Sapta-Sindhu refers only to the Saraswati and its own tributaries. Take for instance the following stanza:

'Coming together, glorious, loudly roaring—
Saraswati, Mother of Floods, the seventh—
With copious milk, with fair streams strongly flowing,
Fully swelled by the volume of their waters'[24]

My reading of this stanza is that it talks of how six rivers emptied into the Saraswati, the seventh. There are several old river channels in the region, some of which still flow into the Ghaggar during the monsoon season. These include the

Chautang (often identified as the Vedic river Drishadvati) and the Sarsuti. The Sutlej and the Yamuna were probably also counted among the Saraswati's sisters.

If my hunch is right, it would mean that the Sapta-Sindhu was a much smaller area covering modern Haryana and a few of the adjoining districts of eastern Punjab. Incidentally, this area also corresponds to what ancient texts refer to as Brahmavarta—the Holy Land—where Manu is said to have re-established civilization after the flood. The texts define the Holy Land as lying between the Saraswati and the Drishadvati—again roughly Haryana and a bit of north Rajasthan, but excluding most of Punjab. So why was this small area so important? The people of the Sapta-Sindhu were obviously part of a cultural milieu that covered a much larger area. What was so special about these seven rivers? In my view the importance of the Land of the Seven Rivers probably derives from it being the home of the Bharatas, a tribe that would give Indians the name by which they call themselves.

THE BHARATAS

Although the Rig Veda is concerned mostly with religion, the hymns do mention one event that is almost certainly historical. This is often called the 'Battle of the Ten Kings' that occurred on the banks of the Ravi river in Punjab.[25] It appears that ten powerful tribes ganged up against the Bharata tribe and its chieftain Sudasa.[26] The confederacy appears to have mainly consisted of tribes from what is now western Punjab and the North West Frontier Province (both now in Pakistan). In contrast, the Bharatas were an 'eastern' tribe from what is now Haryana.[27] Despite the odds, the Bharatas crushed the confederacy in the battle. There are descriptions of how the defeated warriors fled the battlefield or were drowned in the Ravi.

As I stand on the edge of the Ghaggar river in Haryana, I imagine the Bharata tribesmen fording the river on their way to the great battle. As described in the Rig Veda, the warriors would have been dressed in white robes, each with his long hair tied in a knot on his head. There would have been horses neighing, bronze weapons shining in the sun and perhaps the rhythmic sound of sage Vashishtha's disciples chanting hymns to the gods. The Saraswati was a sizeable river then, not the stream that I see before me. Perhaps there would have been rafts ferrying men and supplies across the river. As I stand watching the river, a few soldiers from the nearby army camp wade knee-deep through the Ghaggar. They are Sikh soldiers, their hair knotted on top of their heads. There are no Vedic chants, but there is the soft rhythm of a diesel water-pump running in a farm somewhere.

So, how did the Bharatas single-handedly defeat the great confederacy? The political acumen and military tactics of Sudasa and his guru Vashishtha must have played a role. However, it is possible that it also had something to do with access to superior weapons, since the territory of the Bharatas included India's best copper mines. Even today, the country's largest copper mine is situated at Khetri along the Rajasthan–Haryana border. Armed with superior bronze and an energetic leadership, the Bharatas were a formidable force. A number of ancient 'copper hoards', some including weapons, have been discovered in recent decades in southern Haryana, northern Rajasthan and western Uttar Pradesh, and probably belong to this period.

Soon after the great victory, the Bharatas consolidated their position by defeating a chieftain called Bheda on the Yamuna.[28] They were now the paramount power in the subcontinent with an empire that stretched from Punjab, across Haryana to the area around Delhi–Meerut. Their command over the cultural heartland probably gave the Bharatas influence that extended well outside the lands they directly controlled. It is possible that they consciously consolidated their position by encouraging the compilation of the Vedas. The Rig Veda is full of praise for the Bharata–Trtsu tribe, its chief Sudasa and the sage Vashishtha, suggesting that the book was put together under the patronage of the victorious tribe, probably over several generations following the great battle.

The real genius of the Bharatas, however, may lie in the fact that the Vedas do not confine themselves to the ideas of the victors but deliberately include those of sages from other tribes, including some of the defeated tribes. Thus, the hymns of the sage Vishwamitra, the great rival of Vashishtha, are given an important place in the compilation. In doing so, the Bharatas created a template of civilizational assimilation and accommodation rather than imposition. It was a powerful idea and would allow, over time, for people in faraway places like Bengal and Kerala to identify with this ancient Haryanvi tribe.

This is why the Bharatas remain alive in the name by which Indians have called their country since ancient times: 'Bharat Varsha' or the Land of the Bharatas. In time it would come to denote the whole subcontinent. Later texts such as the Puranas would define it as 'The country that lies north of the seas and south of the snowy mountains is called Bharatam, there dwell the descendants of Bharata'. It remains the official name of India even today. Note that the name is also echoed outside India. In the Malay language, for instance, 'Barat' means West, signifying the direction from which Indian merchants came to South-East Asia.

Sudasa's achievements may also have triggered an imperial dream that would remain embedded in the Indian consciousness. After his victories, Sudasa performed the Ashvamedha or horse sacrifice and was declared a Chakravartin or Universal Monarch. The word 'chakravarti' itself means 'wheels that can go anywhere', implying a monarch whose chariot can roll in any direction. The spokes of the wheel symbolize the various cardinal directions. Over the centuries, the symbolism of the wheel would be applied to both the temporal and the spiritual. We see the symbol used in imperial Mauryan symbols, Buddhist art and in the modern Indian nation's flag.

Meanwhile, what happened to the defeated tribes? Some of the tribes would remain in Punjab, although much weakened. We know that the Druhya tribe was later chased away from Punjab to eastern Afghanistan. Their king Gandhara gave the region its ancient Indian name, which lingers on in the name of the Afghan city of Kandahar. The Puranas also tell us that the Druhyus would later migrate farther north to Central Asia and turn into Mlechhas (or foreign barbarians).[29] After that we hear nothing more of them. Another tribe called the Purus survived into the Mahabharata epic and probably accounts for King Porus who fought against the invading army of Alexander the Great in the fourth century BC.

Some of the tribes, however, appear to have fled further afield after the great battle. Two of them have names that suggest interesting possibilities: the Pakhta and the Parsu. The former are also mentioned by later Greek sources as Pactyians and one wonders if they are the ancestors of Pakhtun (or Pashtun) tribes that still live in Afghanistan and north-western Pakistan. This fits with the finding that, genetically speaking, the Pashtuns are related to Indians and not to Central Asians or Arabs as was previously thought.

Similarly, the Parsu are possibly related to the Persians because this is the name by which the Assyrians refer to the Persians in their inscriptions. This is not as fanciful a re-creation of events as may appear at first glance. There is a great deal of evidence that links the Rig Vedic Indians to the ancient Persians. The Avesta, the oldest and most sacred text of the Zoroastrian religion, is written in a language that is almost identical to that of the Rig Veda. The older sections of the Avesta—called the Gathas—are said to have been composed by the prophet Zarathustra himself. They can be read as Rig Vedic Sanskrit by making a minor phonetic change. The Avestan 'h' is the same as the Sanskrit 's'. Thus, the word Sapta-Sindhu becomes Hapta-Hindu.[30] A similar phonetic shift survives in the modern Indian language of Assamese and is easy to master.

The texts are clear that the Avestan people came to Iran from outside. Unlike the Rig Vedic Indians, they are much more self-consciously an ethnic group and call themselves the Aryan people. This makes sense because they were the outsiders in a foreign land and would have wanted to differentiate themselves. Moreover, they are aware of

Sapta-Sindhu but not of western Iran, suggesting that they entered the country from the east. Unlike the Vedas, the ancient Persians also talk of an original 'Aryan' homeland and even name the river Helmand in Afghanistan after the Saraswati (i.e. Harahvaiti). Indeed, the Persian identity as 'Aryans' was so strong that their country would come to be known as the Land of the Aryans or Iran. As recently as the late twentieth century, the Shah of Iran used the title 'Arya-mehr' or Jewel of the Aryans. Contrast this with the Indian identification with the Bharatas.

Another interesting indicator of the sequence of events is the use of the terms 'deva' and 'asura'. In the Rig Veda, the terms apply to different sets of deities and do not have clear connotations of good and bad. The god Varun, for instance, is described as an asura. However, in later Hinduism, the asuras would be identified as demons and the devas as the gods. In contrast, devas refers to demons in the Zoroastrian tradition of Persia while the word asura is transformed into Ahura Mazda—the Great Lord. Since the deva–asura dichotomy is not clear cut in the Rig Veda but becomes very distinct in later texts, it is reasonable to argue that these opposing sets of meaning came to be attached at a later date. What caused this separation? Did the Parsu have a religious dispute with the Bharatas? As they moved into the Middle East, was the Persian nomenclature influenced by the Assyrian god called Assur? One may never know for sure but these are some more intriguing possibilities.

There is a lot more evidence of Vedic-related tribes in the Middle-East in the second millennium BC. In 1380 BC, the Hittites signed a treaty with a people called the Mittani. This treaty is solemnized in the name of Vedic gods Indra, Varuna, Mitra and Nasatya. The Mittani appear to have been a military elite who ruled over the Hurrian people living in northern Iraq and Syria. There are records of their dealings with Egyptians, Hittites and the Assyrians. From their names and gods, we can tell that the Mittani were outsiders who had entered the region from the east. Yet again, we have evidence of a westward movement that confounds the traditional view that Vedic people moved eastward into India rather than the other way around. The peacocks that recur in Mittani art tell of a people who remember not just their gods but also the fauna of the land they left.

Amazingly, faint memories of these times remain alive among the secretive and much persecuted Yezidi people. The Yezidi are a tiny religious group of around 150,000 adherents who live among the Kurds of northern Iraq, eastern Turkey and parts of Armenia. Their religion has ancient pagan roots, albeit with an overlay of Islamic, Christian and Zoroastrian influence. They faced centuries of persecution, especially under Ottoman rule, for being 'devil worshippers'. Like Hindus, the Yezidis believe in reincarnation and avatars, they pray facing the sun at dawn and dusk, and have a system of endogamous castes. Their temples with conical spires look strikingly similar to Hindu temples. The 'Peacock Angel' (Tawuse Melek) plays a central role in the religion.[31] The peacock is a native to the Indian subcontinent and is not found naturally in Yezidi lands. Is it possible that the Yezidis have somehow preserved an ancient link to India? Indeed, the Yezidi themselves have a tradition that they came to the Middle East from India about 4000 years ago—around when the mature Harappan civilization would have begun to disintegrate or perhaps the Battle of the Ten Kings took place. Does one of these events explain the spread of R1a1, the genetic lineage that we discussed in the previous chapter?

The world of the Harappans and the Rig Veda dissolved as the Saraswati dried. No matter what one thinks of the Harappan–Vedic debate, two things are clear. First, geography and the forces of nature played an important role in the evolution of Indian history. Second, the subcontinent has witnessed a great deal of migration and churn. People, ideas and trade have moved in different directions at different points of time and for different combinations of reasons. It is very different from the conventional view that Indian history is only about unidirectional invasions from the north-west. We now turn to India's second age of urbanization, centred in the Gangetic plains and recalled in the great epics.

3

The Age of Lions

The Gangetic plain was the birthplace of the next cycle of urbanization. From 1300 to 400 BC, the area was made up of a network of small kingdoms and republics. Many of them were centred around towns. We come across place-names that are still in use, and remarkable socio-cultural continuities. Modern Indian children are still brought up on legends and bedtime stories that originate from this era. For the first time, we see an awareness of the whole subcontinent as a geographical and civilizational unit. It is also a time that we witness the growing cultural importance of the Asiatic lion— an animal that would come to occupy a central role in Indian symbolism. One of the most important cultural contributions of the period was the composition of the two great epics Ramayana and Mahabharata. They tell us a lot about how the geographical conception of India evolved in the Iron Age.

The Geography of the Epics

The great epics Ramayana and Mahabharata have long been central to Indian culture. From religious philosophy to art and common idiom, they remain a part of everyday life. Their depiction as a television serial in the late eighties brought the country to a virtual standstill whenever an episode was aired. A dispute over the birthplace of Rama, the central character of the Ramayana, fundamentally changed Indian politics in the early nineties.

According to tradition, the two epics are 'itihasa' or history. It is quite possible that that the central storylines, especially in the case of the Mahabharata, is loosely based on real events. However, in this book I am not concerned with the historical authenticity of the events described in the epics. My interest is in the expansion of geographical knowledge that we can discern from them.

The texts went through many changes over the centuries before they reached their current form, so one must not take all the information too literally. Nonetheless, in the understanding of the terrain there is a shift from the Vedic focus on the Sapta-Sindhu and neighbouring areas. Interestingly, the two epics have very different cardinal orientations. The geography of the Ramayana is oriented along a North–South axis while the Mahabharata is generally oriented on an East–West axis. This is not a total coincidence for they are aligned to two major trade routes. The Dakshina Path (or Southern Road) that made its way from the Gangetic plains though Central India to the southern tip of the peninsula while the Uttara Path (or Northern Road) that ran from eastern

Afghanistan, through Punjab and the Gangetic plains, to the seaports of Bengal.

As we shall see, these two highways have played a very important role in shaping the geographical and political history of India. The Uttara Path was a well-trodden route by the Iron

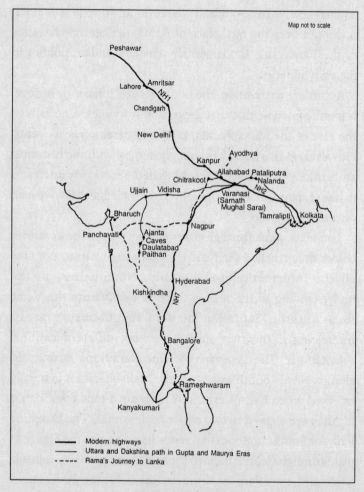

Ancient Highways

Age and formalized during the Mauryan Empire. Since then, it has been almost continuously rebuilt in some approximation to the original.[1] Sher Shah Suri, the Mughals, and the British invested heavily in maintaining it. The British called it the Grand Trunk Road and it was described by Rudyad Kipling as 'a river of life as never exists in this world'.[2] It survives today as National Highway 1 between Delhi and Amritsar and National Highway 2 between Delhi and Kolkata, and is part of the Golden Quadrilateral network.

In contrast, the path of the Southern Road has drifted over time although certain nodes remained important over long periods. During the early Iron Age, the Dakshina Path probably began near Allahabad where two navigable rivers, the Ganga and Yamuna, flowed into each other. It then went in a southwesterly direction through Chitrakoot and Panchavati (near Nashik) and eventually to Kishkindha (near Hampi, modern Karnataka). This would be the route followed by Rama during his exile.

The Ramayana is traditionally said to be the older of the two texts, although some scholars dispute this. There are several versions of the epic, including versions that remain popular in other parts of Asia. The most prestigious and possibly oldest version, however, is the one composed in Sanskrit by the sage Valmiki. He was a former brigand as well as an outcaste—someone we would today call a Harijan or Dalit (that is, a member of the lowest castes). It is interesting that this early example of Dalit literature would come to occupy such an important place in later orthodoxy.

Despite many differences, the various versions of the Ramayana do agree on the basic storyline: Rama is the young and popular crown prince of Ayodhya (now a small town in the state of Uttar Pradesh). However, he is forced to give up his claim to the throne and is exiled for fourteen years. Along with his wife Sita and younger brother Lakshman, Rama heads south, crosses the river Ganga near modern-day Allahabad and goes to live in the forests of Central India. After several years of living peacefully in the forest, Sita is abducted by Ravana, the powerful king of Lanka. Rama and his brother set out to find her. On the way, at a place called Kishkindha, they befriend a tribe of monkeys that promises to help them. Hanuman, the strongest of the monkeys, visits Lanka and discovers that Sita is being held captive in Ravana's palace garden. Together with the army of monkeys, Rama marches on Lanka but finds that the sea bars the way. So Rama and the monkeys build a bridge (more accurately a causeway) from Rameswaram to Lanka. A great battle ensues in which Ravana is defeated and killed, and Sita is rescued. Rama, Sita and Lakshman then return to Ayodhya and Rama regains his throne. Most versions of the story end here but some versions also tell of events after Rama's return to Ayodhya. (This bit appears to be have been added at a much later date.)

As one can see, the Ramayana is a journey from the Gangetic plains to the southern tip of India and on to Sri Lanka. It could be argued that the epic pre-dates geographical knowledge about South India and that the place-names were retro-fitted in later times to flow with the story. However, having visited some of the sites, I think this is unlikely. Take for instance Kishkindha, the kingdom of the monkeys. The site is across the river from the medieval ruins of Vijayanagar at Hampi. The terrain consists of strange rock-outcrops, caves with

Neolithic paintings, and bands of monkeys scampering over the boulders.

It is such an evocative landscape that it is likely that Valmiki either visited it or had heard detailed descriptions of it from merchants plying the Dakshina Path or Southern Road. There are small details that seem too much of a coincidence to be purely imaginary. The lake of Pampa, where Rama first meets Hanuman, is indeed a beautiful place with lotuses in bloom and a multitude of birds, surrounded by a ring of rocky hills. Not far away from this site is a sloth bear reserve that recalls Jambavan, Hanuman's sloth bear friend. Archaeologists have found the remains of several Neolithic settlements in the area. It is easy to believe that this setting was once populated by a Neolithic tribe that used the monkey as a totem and gave rise to the legend.

The same can be said of the bridge from Rameswaram to Lanka. There exists a 30-km-long chain of shoals and sandbanks that links India to the northern tip of Sri Lanka. Whether one believes that these are the remains of Rama's bridge or the result of a geological process, it cannot be denied that this is a remarkable feature. The true scale of the bridge is best seen in a satellite or aerial photograph. Again, the composer of the epic clearly knew about it.

Moreover, we can tell a lot about how Iron Age Indians perceived the geographical extent of their civilization from the way Ravana is depicted. He is the villain of the Ramayana but is not presented as a Mlechha (or barbarian). He is very much an insider: a learned Brahmin and a worshipper of Shiva. Whatever his failings, Ravana and his southern kingdom are categorically within the Indian civilizational milieu. Indeed, the Kanyakubja Brahmins of Vidisha claim Ravana as one of their own and still worship him![3] The exchange of goods and ideas along the Southern Road, therefore, had linked the north and the south of India long before political unification under the Mauryans in the third century BC.

The Mahabharata is 100,000 verses long and said to the longest composition in the world. According to tradition, it was composed by the sage Vyas but it appears to have been expanded over the centuries. We know that a shorter version of the epic was definitely in existence by the fifth century BC but it probably reached its current form centuries later. It is the story of the bitter rivalry between cousins—the five Pandav brothers and the Kauravs—for control over the kingdom of Hasthinapur. They initially agree to divide the kingdom and the Pandavs build a new capital called Indraprastha. The new capital was so beautiful that the Kauravs were filled with envy. They challenged the Pandavs to a game of dice that is fixed by their maternal uncle Shakuni. The Pandavs gamble away their kingdom and are exiled for thirteen years. During this time the Pandavs wander across India. However, when they return after thirteen years, the Kauravs refuse to return the kingdom.

The dispute culminates in the great battle of Kurukshetra in which virtually all the kingdoms of India are said to have taken sides. Krishna, leader of the Yadav clan and king of Dwarka, sided with the Pandavs and played an important role. The Pandavs win the war but at great cost. The Kauravs and their allies are almost all annihilated. The last act of the battle takes place away from the main battlefield. Bhim, strongest of the Pandav brothers, kills Duryodhan, the leader of the Kauravs, in single combat on the banks of the Saraswati. By now it would have dwindled to a shadow of its former self—perhaps no more than a rain-fed seasonal river.

Many of the places mentioned in the Mahabharata are located around Delhi. For instance, Gurgaon, now a modern boom-town full of gleaming office-towers and shopping-malls, was a village that belonged to Dronacharya, the teacher who trained the cousins in martial arts. The name Gurgaon literally means the 'Village of the Teacher'. The Pandav capital of Indraprastha is said to be located under the Purana Qila in Delhi. Similarly, the site of Hastinapur is identified with a site near modern Meerut. The battlefield of Kurukshetra is nearby, in the state of Haryana. Farther afield, we have the cities of Mathura and Kashi (or Varanasi) which remain very sacred cities for Hindus.

Some of the Iron Age sites have been excavated, starting in the 1950s and have thrown up remains of ancient settlements. For instance, there is a strong traditional belief that Indraprastha was located on the same site as the sixteenth-century Purana Qila (or Old Fort) in the middle of modern Delhi. The site even had a village called Indrapat till the nineteenth century. Excavation between 1954 and 1971 found that there was indeed a major settlement here that dates at least to the fourth century BC. Pottery shards suggest there may be an older Iron Age settlement somewhere close by. Sadly, the exploratory excavation of Mahabharata sites of the fifties and sixties was not properly followed up in later decades.

One of the more intriguing Mahabharata-related sites is that of Dwarka in the westernmost tip of Gujarat. It said to have been founded by Krishna as his capital after he led his people from Mathura to Gujarat. Thirty-six years after the Kurukshetra battle, the city is said to have been devoured by the sea. Underwater surveys near the temple-town of Dwarka and the nearby island of Bet Dwarka have come up with stone anchors, a sunken jetty and elaborate walls suggesting the existence of an ancient port in the area. Although I am not entirely convinced by all of the claims made about the site, it is yet another reminder of how the forces of nature have directed the course of history.[4]

All this does not confirm the events of the Mahabharata, but it strongly suggests that the composers of the epic were talking about real places. Such findings are not unique to India. Till the nineteenth century, the places mentioned in Homer's *Iliad* were considered to be mythical. However, Heinrich Schliemann's excavations in the late nineteenth century showed that Troy and many of the places mentioned in the Greek epics were real places. Similarly, Chinese legends about the ancient Shang dynasty (1600-1046 BC) have now been confirmed by modern archaeology. Inscriptions on oracle bones and bronze artifacts confirm much of what is mentioned in the ancient texts. Of course, there are gaps between the archaeological findings and the information in the texts[5], but this is only to be expected after such a long lapse of time.

As mentioned earlier, the Mahabharata largely has an East–West orientation unlike the North–South orientation of the Ramayana. Most of the action takes place around Delhi and the Gangetic plains but the eastern and western extremes of the subcontinent also play an important role in the unfolding events. The Kauravs' mother Gandhari is from the kingdom of Gandhar which is now eastern Afghanistan. Her devious brother Shakuni instigates his nephews against the Pandavs, fixes the game of dice and ultimately causes the war.

On the other geographical extreme, India's North East finds mention for the first time. Arjuna, the most dashing of the Pandav brothers, makes his way to remote Manipur during his years of exile. There he meets the warrior-princess Chitrangada. They fall in love and marry, albeit on the condition that Chitrangada would not have to follow Arjuna back to the Gangetic plains. Their son eventually becomes the king of Manipur and would defeat Arjuna in battle without realizing he was his father. The story goes that Ulupi, princess of the neighbouring Naga tribe, would then revive a dying Arjuna.

The people of the tiny Bishnupriya community that still lives in Manipur and neighbouring states trace their origins to the Mahabharata. They speak a language that is related to Assamese and has many Tibeto–Burman words, but still preserves several features of archaic Prakrit. Does the Chitrangada legend preserve the memory of an ancient migration into this area? The Bishnupriyas were a powerful clan in Manipur till the nineteenth century when a Burmese invasion scattered them. They now live in a few villages in Assam and Manipur, and there is a danger that their language and unique culture will get lost within a generation or two.[6]

Since the Kurukshetra battle is said to have involved all the tribes and kingdoms of India, the Mahabharata gives us long lists of kingdoms, clans and cities. Many of them were probably added to the text in later times. Nonetheless, it gives an idea of the Indian world view during the Iron Age. The name Mahabharata is itself interesting as it can be read to mean 'Greater India'. This would make sense for an epic that claims to tell the story involving all the clans of the subcontinent.

The text itself explains the name in terms of a primordial Emperor Bharata who is said to have conquered the whole country (but plays no important role in the central plot). The epic is therefore told as a history of the Bharata people. Since there is no independent evidence of an all-conquering Emperor Bharata, one wonders if this is an echo of the powerful Bharata tribe mentioned in the Rig Veda. Did Sudas's victory against the ten tribes create a dream of civilizational nationhood that gets echoed over the millennia?

There are interesting parallels with the Chinese view of civilizational nationhood. Long before the country was united into an empire by Qin Shi Huangdi in the third century BC, there was a strongly held belief that the country had once been united under the revered 'Yellow Emperor' and his four successors.[7] There is no archaeological evidence to support such a grand empire but it has been a very powerful idea throughout Chinese history. Indeed, it is embedded in the way China views itself even today.

The notion of a civilizational nation is not a simple one. It has meant different things to different people at different points in time. The Partition of India in 1947, for instance, was partly due to a fundamental divergence in views about the nature of India's civilizational nationhood. Still, it is important to recognize how Bronze Age ideas, honed in the Iron Age, gave shape to the way people have viewed themselves ever since.

The epics, furthermore, suggest a shift of political power to the eastern Gangetic plains during the Iron Age. It is more obvious in the Ramayana as the kingdom of Ayodhya is itself in the east. In the Mahabharata, most of the action takes place near Delhi in the north-west but, even here, we are told of the powerful kingdom ruled by Jarasandha in Magadh (modern Bihar). Indeed, even Krishna was forced to shift his people from Mathura to Gujarat because of the repeated raids of the Magadhan army. As we shall see, the rise of Magadh would have a pivotal role in later Indian history. So, why was Magadh so successful?

In my view it was geographical access to three important resources—rice, trade and iron. The kingdom not only had control over very fertile lands but was also served by a number of rivers including the Ganga itself. Thus, it would have had the agricultural muscle to support a large army. Moreover, the kingdom controlled the trade plying the Uttara Path between the North West and the emerging sea-ports of Bengal. Add to this, access to iron ore from what is now Jharkhand. In order to appreciate this conjunction of circumstances, consider the location of the kingdom's first capital, Rajgir (also referred to as Rajagriha or King's Home). Defended by hills, it sits strategically between the fertile farmlands to the north and the mines of the south. In short, Magadh was uniquely able to feed large armies and arm them with iron weapons. This explains why Magadh would be at the heart of the next stage in Indian history.

ENTER THE LION

India is the only country in the world where both lions and tigers co-exist. As discussed in Chapter 1, tigers evolved in East Asia and probably entered the subcontinent around 12,000 years ago. Soon, they had spread across the subcontinent.

They are commonly represented in Harappan art and seals. In sharp contrast, the Harappans appear to be ignorant of the lion! None of the main Harappan sites have thrown up any representation of the lion. This is very odd given the obvious appeal of the animal and its importance in later Indian culture. The tiger hunts by stealth in dense jungle and, therefore, is more of an object of fear. In contrast, the lion with its shaggy mane, its harem of lionesses, and its confident visibility is easily converted into a symbol of power.

Every culture that has encountered the lion has tended to give the animal a special status. Even in countries that have never had a lion population, such as Britain and China, the lion has been part of imperial symbolism. We know that lions were considered royal game in Mesopotamia in the second millennium BC and only the king could hunt them.[8] In ancient Egypt too, lion hunting was a royal prerogative. Amentohep III (1391-1352 BC) killed as many as 102 lions in the first decade of his rule. At Beital-Wali in Lower Nubia, a tame lioness is shown near the throne of Rameses II (1290–1224) with an inscription 'Slayer of his Enemies'. Five centuries later, the court records of the Assyrian king Ashurabanipal II (884–859 BC) recount:

> The gods Nemruta and Negral, who love my priesthood, gave me the wild animals of the plains, commanding me to hunt. Thirty elephants I trapped and killed, 257 great wild oxen I brought down with my weapons, attacking from my chariots, 370 lions I killed with my hunting spears.

The lion is also represented in a multitude of sculptures, friezes and paintings in Ancient Egypt and Mesopotamia. The Sumerian goddess Nana, the Assyrian goddess Ishtar and the

Persian goddess Anahita are all associated with the lion and sometimes depicted riding the lion—rather like the Hindu goddess Durga. It is obvious that the lion was an important animal in art, culture, royal symbolism and religion in the Middle East from a very early period. Why were the Harappans so lukewarm to an animal with such obvious charms?

The most likely reason is that the lion was not common in the subcontinent till after the collapse of the Harappan civilization. This should not be surprising. Before 2000 BC, north-west India was much wetter than it is today with higher rainfall and the Saraswati river flowing. The lion is an animal that hunts in open grasslands and could not penetrate the tiger-infested jungles that existed in the region. However, the balance shifted as the climate became drier and the Saraswati dwindled. There would have been a savannah phase when lions from Iran could have made their way through Balochistan and then into tiger territory, which would explain why the earliest artifact depicting a lion in the subcontinent, a golden goblet, was found in Balochistan. As Harappan urban centers were abandoned and populations migrated to the Gangetic plains, the lions would have taken over the wilderness. Over time they would penetrate as far east as Bihar and north-western Orissa, co-existing in many places with tigers. Eastern and southern India, nevertheless, remained the exclusive domain of the tiger.

Interestingly, the Rig Veda does mention the animal although it accords it far less importance than the horse or the bull. This poses the obvious problem of how the Vedic people knew of the animal if it did not yet exist in the Sapta-Sindhu heartland. One possible explanation is that the word for lion

('Singha'), at this stage of linguistic development, was also a generic word for big cats and was loosely used for both lions and tigers[9]. As we shall see, this dual use of the word is responsible for the naming of Singapore. However, Dr Divyabhanusinh Chavra, a leading expert on the Asiatic lion, still feels the Vedic description of a hunt suggests lions rather than tigers. Another explanation could be that while the lion was not common in the heartland, the Vedic people encountered it in lands to the west of the Indus (this would gel with the lion goblet found in Baluchistan). Yet again it must be admitted that we do not know enough about this period to be absolutely sure.

Whatever the exact circumstances of its entry, once the lion became a familiar animal in the subcontinent, it was quickly appropriated by Indian culture. As in the Middle East, it became the symbol of royal power and bravery. The word for 'throne' in Sanskrit and many Indian languages is 'singhasana' which literally means 'seat of the lion'. Similarly, Durga, the Hindu goddess of strength and war, is usually depicted as standing on a lion while slaying a demon. The Mahabharata repeatedly invokes the image of a lion to convey strength and vigour. To this day, communities that are proud of their martial tradition, such as Rajputs and Sikhs, commonly use Singh (meaning lion) as their surname

Interestingly, the lion plays an important role in the *Mahavamsa*, a Pali epic, that is the foundation myth of the Sinhalese people of Sri Lanka. According to the Mahavamsa, the Sinhalese people are the descendants of Prince Vijaya and his followers who sailed down to Sri Lanka in the sixth century BC from what is now Orissa and West Bengal. The story tells us that Prince Vijaya was the son of a lion and a human princess, which is why the majority population of Sri Lanka call themselves the Sinhala—or the lion people—and the country's national flag features a stylized lion holding a sword. Equally significant is the fact that the Tamil rebels of northern Sri Lanka chose to call themselves the 'Tigers'. The ancient rivalry between the two big cats remains embedded in cultural memory even as the animals themselves face extinction.

Sadly, there are now a mere 411 Asiatic lions left in the wild.[10] The Gir National Park in Gujarat is their last refuge. Less than two hundred years ago, this magnificent beast could be found around Delhi and were probably common in the Aravalli ridges south of Gurgaon. Now eight-lane highways roar though the lion's erstwhile lair. The last reported sighting of a lion in Iran was in 1942. In Iraq, the magnificent Assyrian friezes are all that remain of a beast last sighted in 1917.[11]

THE LATE IRON AGE

By the late Iron Age (eighth to fifth century BC), we find that a number of urban clusters are reaching scales that are comparable to the Harappan cities. Kausambi, near today's Allahabad, is said to have been founded after the king of Hastinapur, a descendant of the Pandavas, who was forced by a devastating flood to shift his capital further east. Spread over an area of 150-200 hectares, Kausambi had a population of around 36,000 people at its height.[12] Other major cities like Rajagir and Sravasti were on a similar scale. These are comparable to Mohenjodaro, the largest of the Harappan sites, which had a population of around 40,000. It is difficult to estimate the total population of the subcontinent at this time but it was probably in the range of 30 million.

The late Iron Age towns were fortified with moats and ramparts. Wood and mud-bricks were the common building material but the Harappan technology of kiln-fired bricks had not been forgotten. Kausambi, for instance, shows extensive use of kiln-fired bricks. The towns also have drains, soakage pits and other urban amenities, albeit of a design that is different from the Indus Valley era. However, the courtyard continues to be the basic prototype for houses while streets were systematically levelled to allow wheeled traffic.

Merchant boats would have plied the Ganga, especially between Kausambi, Kashi and Pataliputra (modern Patna). There were ocean-going ships as well. The legend of prince Vijaya in the Mahavamsa suggests coastal trade links along the Bay of Bengal extending from Bengal to Sri Lanka. Both the Uttara Path and the Dakshina Path would have been busy highways, with the people plying these trade routes carrying not just goods but also ideas, because this was also a time of great intellectual expansion. The philosophies of the Upanishads, Mahavira and Gautam Buddha are all products of this milieu.

The Buddha was born in Kapilavastu (on the Indo–Nepal border) but he attained enlightenment at Bodh Gaya, just south of the old Magadhan capital of Rajgir. However, he did not deliver his first sermon in Bodh Gaya, the nearby towns and villages or even in the royal capital of Rajgir. Instead, he headed west to Varanasi (also called Kashi). Why did he go all the way to Varanasi to spread his message?

According to historian Vidula Jayaswal, this was a natural

choice since Varanasi was an important place for the exchange of both goods and ideas because it stood at the crossroads between the Uttara Path and a highway that came down from the Himalayas and then continued south as the Dakshina Path. In some ways, this remains true to this day as the east–west National Highway 2 meets the north–south National Highway 7 at Varanasi. The latter then runs all the way down to the southern tip of India. The alignment of the modern north–south highway runs somewhat east of the ancient trade route but it is amazing how the logic of India's transport system has remained the same. Even when the British built the railways in the nineteenth century, they used Mughalsarai—just outside Varanasi—as the nerve-centre of the railway network.

When the Buddha went there in the sixth century BC, Varanasi was already a large urban settlement built on the Ganga. The city's name is derived from the fact that it was built between where the Varuna and the Asi streams flow into the sacred river. The Varuna is still a discernible stream but, sadly, the Asi has been reduced to a polluted municipal drain.

It was in a deer park at Sarnath, just outside the city, that the Buddha delivered his first sermon. As an important crossroads the place was already an established hub of commercial and intellectual activity by this time, which is precisely what attracted him to it. Tourists visiting the Buddhist archaeological site at Sarnath often do not realize that the spot is sacred to other religious traditions too. Just outside, the visitor will see a large Jain temple dedicated to the eleventh 'tirthankara'. Similarly, the archaeological museum next door contains many idols and artifacts of the Brahminical tradition.

The place is still sacred to the devotees of Shiva. In fact, the name Sarnath is a short form for Saranganath (meaning 'Lord of the Deer') which is another name for Shiva. This should not be surprising as Varanasi has long been, and remains, a very important hub for Hindus of the Shaivite tradition. It may explain why the Buddha found a park with sacred deer at this place. Even today, there is a temple dedicated to Saranganath, less than a kilometre from the archaeological site. It is a small village temple that almost no tourist visits and is a peaceful place to linger in.

The intellectual innovations of the age were not limited to religious philosophy. For instance, the period also witnesses the systematization of Ayurveda, India's traditional medical system. A compendium compiled by Sushruta, who also lived near Varanasi, contains a long list of sophisticated surgical instruments and procedures.[13] There are detailed descriptions of plastic surgery, ophthalmic couching (dislodging of the lens of the eye), perineal lithotomy (cutting for bladder stones), the removal of arrows and splinters and the dissection of dead bodies for the study of anatomy.[14]

Unfortunately, most of this knowledge would be lost in the medieval era. Nevertheless, some techniques survived in isolated pockets and were witnessed by European visitors in the eighteenth century. This includes the famous 'rhinoplasty' operation that took place in Pune in March 1793 that would change the course of plastic surgery in Europe and the world. Cowasjee was a Maratha (more likely Parsi) bullock-cart driver with the English army during its campaigns against Tipu Sultan of Mysore. He was captured and had his nose and one hand cut off. After a year without a nose, he and four others submitted themselves to an Indian surgeon who used skin from their foreheads to repair the noses. We know little about the surgeon but two senior British surgeons from Bombay Presidency witnessed this operation and sent back detailed descriptions and diagrams. The publication in Europe in 1816 of their account would give birth to modern plastic surgery.

Of course, all the cultural and intellectual activity of this period was not limited to the Gangetic heartland. Take for example Panini, the famous grammarian, who standardized the Sanskrit language during the fifth century BC. He is said to have been born in Gandhara (eastern Afghanistan) and to have lived in Taxila (near modern Islamabad). This part of the subcontinent was about to witness the first attempt by a European power to conquer India.

THE EMPIRE OF THE LION

The world of small tribal kingdoms described above went through a major shift in the third and fourth century BC. This happened almost simultaneously across the ancient world. It was not so much a change in technology as a shift in political ideology and ambition. Within a couple of generations, we see the idea of empire inspire a series of remarkable leaders around the world, whose conquests would redefine the political geography of the world.

The first of the empire-builders was Cyrus the Great of Persia in the sixth century BC, but it is only in the fourth century that we begin to see empire-building on a totally different scale. In China, King Hui of Qin began a cycle of conquest around 330 BC that would culminate in the first empire under Shi Huangdi a century later. At around the same time, Alexander the Great would take control of Greece, Egypt, the Levant, Mesopotamia, Bactria and Persia. Then in the winter of 327-326 BC he marched into India. Here he built an alliance with Ambhi, the king of Taxila. Together they defeated Porus on the banks of the Jhelum. It is possible that the name Porus refers to the Puru tribe that had inhabited the area since the Rig Vedic times.

Alexander wanted to push on eastwards but his troops were tired after years on the march. Also, there were stories about a large Magadhan army that would be mobilized against them in the Gangetic plains. With his army in virtual mutiny, Alexander was forced to turn back. However, he did not go back the way he had come but fatefully chose to sail down the Indus under the mistaken belief that the Indus constituted the upper reaches of the Nile. The Macedonians thought that if they just sailed down the Indus, they would end up in the Mediterranean! They had reached this conclusion because of the apparent similarities between the flora and fauna of India and those of the upper reaches of the Nile (Arrian mentions crocodiles and a certain variety of beans). As Alexander's army sailed down the Indus, it defeated many tribes and brutally destroyed several settlements. There is also a fascinating account of how a local chieftain entertained Alexander with a gladiatorial match between a lion and ferocious dogs (the Indians claimed that the dogs had been bred from tigresses).[15]

On reaching the sea, the Macedonians discovered their mistake. They were then forced to march along the dry Makran and Persian Gulf coast. This was the same route that early humans had used when they migrated east to the subcontinent. However, climatic conditions and the coastline had dramatically changed. Without proper maps, provisions and water, the desert exacted a terrible toll. Soldiers and pack animals died in large numbers from hunger and thirst. Much of the plunder accumulated over years of campaigning had to be abandoned for lack of horses and men. Alexander's army arrived back in Babylon undefeated but decimated. The conqueror himself died soon afterwards, possibly poisoned by followers who no longer believed in his leadership. Alexander's empire was divided up amongst his generals and his young son was murdered. The lack of geographical knowledge proved deadlier than the sword. As we shall see, when Europeans attempted to take control of India two millennia later, they would take great care to map it.

Alexander's invasion is not mentioned directly in Indian texts but the Macedonians have left us detailed accounts of their adventures.[16] Some of them includes fantastical tales about giant ants that were used to dig for gold. However, for the most part, their observations were accurate. Nearchus, Alexander's admiral, tells us that Indians wore clothes made from white cotton. The lower garment reached below the knee, halfway to the ankles. The upper garment was thrown over the shoulder and a turban was worn on the head. Nearchus was describing the dhoti and angavastra—clothes that have been worn since Vedic times and continue to be worn even today. He goes on to say that wealthy Indians wore ivory earrings and used parasols against the sun. They also wore leather sandals with elaborate trimmings and thick soles to make themselves look taller!

Although Alexander's invasion did not make much of a dent in the Indian heartland, it did trigger a chain of events that led to the founding of India's first great empire, that of the Mauryas. The empire was created by two extraordinary characters: Chanakya (also called Kautilya[17]) and his pupil Chandragupta Maurya. The Persian, Chinese and Macedonian Greek empires were created by princes and warriors. In contrast, Chanakya was a professor of Political Economy in Taxila. When Alexander entered into an alliance with the king of Taxila, the Brahmins of the city opposed this. Plutarch tells us that Alexander had several of them hanged to death.[18]

According to legend, Chanakya then travelled east to Pataliputra (modern Patna), capital of the powerful kingdom of Magadh to ask for help against the Greeks. However, he was insulted and thrown out by the king of the Nanda dynasty. Chanakya decided to return to Taxila to plot his revenge. On the way he met a boy called Chandragupta Maurya. There are some interesting tales—impossible to verify—about how they met. Chanakya took the boy back with him and began to train him for future kingship. He also wrote the *Arthashastra* (Treatise on Prosperity), a detailed manual on how to run the future empire.

When Alexander died, there was a power vacuum in north-west India. Chanakya and his protégé used the opportunity to put together a band of rebels. However, their initial efforts at unseating the Nanda king of Magadh appear to have failed. There is a legend that tells of how Chandragupta had to flee into the forests to escape the Nanda king. Overcome with fatigue he collapsed and fell into a deep slumber. However, a lion appeared and licked him clean. Then it stood guard till the future king awoke. When Chandragupta realized what had happened, he saw it as a good omen and renewed his efforts to unseat the Nandas. The story may have been spread by later Mauryan propagandists but, yet again, it emphasizes the symbolic importance of the lion.

After several years of effort, Chanakya managed to cobble together a large army, possibly with the help of the hill tribes of Himachal. He and Chandragupta slowly took control of the north-west of the country. Then they steadily encroached into the Gangetic plains. Around 321 BC, they defeated the Nanda king of Magadh and emerged as the paramount power in the subcontinent. Astonishingly, Chanakya did not take the throne for himself but crowned his pupil. Then they spent over a decade establishing control over central India.

By around 305 BC, Chandragupta felt confident enough to directly confront the Macedonians. One of Alexander's most talented generals, Seleucus Nikator, was in control of the conqueror's Asian domains, including Persia and Central Asia. He also laid claim to the Indian territories conquered by Alexander. However, judging from the terms of a treaty between the two in 303 BC, the Mauryan army decisively won the war. Chandragupta gained control over Balochistan and Afghanistan. Seleucus also gave his daughter in marriage to a Mauryan prince, perhaps Chandragupta himself.

For three generations, the Mauyran empire would cover the whole subcontinent from the edge of eastern Iran to what is now Bangladesh. Only the southernmost tip of India would remain outside its direct control. At its height, it was the largest and most populous empire in the world, dwarfing both Alexander's domains and those of Shi Huangdi in China.

Furthermore, unlike the empires of Alexander and the first Chinese empire, the Mauyran empire lasted at least three generations as a complete unit.

Yet, both Chanakya and Chandragupta were very unlike the other two empire-builders. Chanakya was happy to remain a minister and, according to one version, may have gone back to teaching in Taxila once the empire had been stabilized.[19] In 297 BC, Chandragupta placed his son Bindusara on the throne, gave up all worldly possessions and became a Jain monk. He took the Dakshina Path and travelled down to Sravana Belagola (in Karnataka) and, according to Jain tradition, starved himself to death to cleanse his soul.

The hill on which he spent his last days meditating and fasting is still called Chandragiri in his honour.

The renunciation of power remains a powerful theme in later Indian history. When India became independent in 1947, Mahatma Gandhi refused all positions of power and made way for his protégé Jawaharlal Nehru to become modern India's first prime minister. Civilizations have long memories, both conscious and sub-conscious, and the legendary deeds of ancient heroes can echo down the centuries. We see this in China too where Mao Zedong liked to have himself compared to Qin Shi Huangdi.

The second Mauryan emperor Bindusara ruled from 297 to 272 BC. His reign appears to have been a period of relative calm and consolidation. We have records of how the Mauryan emperor exchanged ambassadors and trade delegations with Alexander's successors in the Middle East. There is a tale that the second emperor, Bindusara, asked Antiochus of Syria for figs, wine and a Greek teacher of rhetoric. Antiochus sent the figs and the wine but refused the last request on grounds that Greek law did not permit the sale of scholars![20]

There appears to have been a succession struggle on Bindusara's death. The winner of the fratricidal struggle was Ashoka who was crowned in 268 BC. He was not his father's chosen successor but would rule the empire for forty years. In 260 BC, Ashoka would expand the empire for one last time to include Kalinga (roughly modern Orissa). He now ruled the whole subcontinent except for the small kingdoms of the extreme south with whom he had friendly relations. They are mentioned by name: Chola, Pandya, Keralaputra and Satiyaputra. Note the longevity of the names. The Cholas would remain a powerful clan for the next one and half millennia and would head a powerful empire of their own in the tenth and eleventh century AD. We will revisit them in a later chapter. The name of the Keralaputras has proven even more persistent, and the state at the south-western tip of the Indian peninsula is today called Kerala in their memory.

OF IMPERIAL PILLARS AND EDICTS

Ashoka is the first Indian monarch who has left us artifacts that indisputably belong to his reign. To be absolutely accurate, the name Ashoka does not appear on any major edict inscription. The edicts were issued by a king who called himself 'Beloved of the Gods', Piyadassi. However, there is strong circumstantial evidence that link Piyadassi to Buddhist legends about a great king called Ashoka. The link was discovered from dynastic lists in the Puranas, Hindu religious texts, that describe a king called Ashoka as Chandragupta's grandson.

Best known of Ashokan artifacts are a series of edicts engraved on rocks and on stone pillars scattered across the empire. These pillars and inscriptions have been found across the subcontinent from Afghanistan in the north to Karnataka in the south, Gujarat in the west to Bengal in the east. They are also scattered across the northern plains, including one in Delhi (near Greater Kailash). Given the lapse of time, it is safe to assume that there were many more pillars and inscriptions that did not survive. Still, what remains is impressive and gives us a sense of the scale and extent of the Mauryan empire.

The edicts and inscriptions have elicited a great deal of interest ever since they were deciphered in the nineteenth century. This is not surprising given their age as well as the sentiments they express. Ashoka openly regrets the invasion of Kalinga and the bloodshed it caused. He exhorts his subjects to be good citizens, while underscoring his own commitment to their welfare. Below is an example of one of his edicts:

> When he had been consecrated eight years, the Beloved of the Gods, king Piyadassi, conquered Kalinga. A hundred and fifty thousand people were deported, a hundred thousand were killed, and many times that number perished[21]. Afterwards, now that Kalinga is annexed, the Beloved of Gods very earnestly practiced Dhamma, desired Dhamma, and taught Dhamma[22]. On conquering Kalinga the Beloved of the Gods felt remorse, for when an independent country is conquered the slaughter, death and deportation of the people is extremely grievous to the Beloved of Gods and weighs heavily on his mind. . . . Even those who were fortunate to have escaped and whose love is undiminished suffer from the misfortunes of their friends, acquaintances, colleagues and relatives. The participation

of all men in suffering weighs heavily on the mind of the Beloved of the Gods'.

—Major Edict XIII.
Translated by Romila Thapar[23]

The Kalinga campaign was clearly brutal, with 150,000 deported, a direct death toll of 100,000 and even larger numbers dead from wounds and famine. India's population at this stage would have been around 65 million[24] and casualties on such a scale would have been devastating for a small province like Kalinga. Excavations at Kalinga's capital of Tosali reveal structures that still bear marks of a devastating assault. The large number of arrowheads found embedded in a small section of the ramparts tell of a blizzard of arrows. Ashoka appears to have regretted his decision because of the suffering it caused— very unusual for any era and in stark contrast to the brutal rule of the First Emperor of China at about the same time. Nonetheless, one should always take statements made by politicians with a pinch of salt. The edicts are, after all, what Ashoka wanted us to remember of him. Notice that Ashoka expresses regret but does not offer to free Kalinga and its inhabitants.

Although the inscriptions are very interesting, I think historians have focused too much attention on the noble sentiments expressed in them and not enough on the overall impact of the pillars. Around 40–50 feet high, the stone columns are impressive structures often capped by a lion (or lions), an animal that was associated with the Mauryas since Chandragupta's time. In some of the pillars, the lions are accompanied with the 'chakra' or wheel. Historians often associate this with the Buddhist 'dharma-chakra' but, in my view, they could just as well be interpreted to symbolize the 'Chakravartin' or Universal Monarch. The pillars and the lions are a clear expression of imperial power. They were the Mauryan way of marking territory.

Remember that Ashoka's average subject would have been illiterate and would have been unable to read the noble sentiments in the inscription. He/she, however, would have been left in no doubt about the real message regarding the power of the sovereign. The use of columns to signal imperial might is not unique to the Mauryans or even to India. The ancient Egyptians and the Romans used them as well. In India, the imperial successors of the Mauryas would raise their own columns as well as insert their own inscriptions on the Ashokan columns.

The Mauryan lions and pillars were mostly made from sandstone quarried at Chunar, near Varanasi, where the Ganga nudges the Vindhya range. We now know the exact location of the quarries to the south-west of Chunar fort, close to the famous Durga temple. Stone is still quarried here, and one can also see some of the ancient quarries as well as cylindrical blocks of unfinished stone abandoned by the ancient stone-cutters. Some of them bear inscriptions that identify the era when the stone was originally quarried.

It appears that the Mauryans rolled the stones to the river and then transported them by boat to workshops near Varanasi, in much the same manner as the ancient Egyptians transported stone blocks down the Nile to construct their temples and pyramids. Although various irrigation projects these days have drastically reduced the water-flow in the Ganga, it is still possible to make the journey by boat from

Chunar to Varanasi. Archaeologists have found remains of workshops along the river where this stone was carved and polished.[25] As the river turns, the ancient ghats of Varanasi come into sight and, for a moment, one can imagine oneself as a Mauryan boatman transporting Chunar stone to the imperial workshop.

The stone used to carve the Sarnath lions, modern India's national symbol, would have made this journey from quarry to workshop and then to Sarnath. I found several stone-carvers who still work the Chunar sandstone in and around Varanasi. Some of them were carving lions to adorn homes and temples. Somehow, the new sculptures all have the characteristic 'grin' that one sees on the Mauryan lions. Is this conscious choice or just the unconscious weight of history?

Later rulers understood the symbolic meaning of the Mauryan columns and were always keen to appropriate them. This is why the emperors of the Gupta and Mughal dynasties, went out of their way to put their own inscriptions next to those of Ashoka. Feroze Shah Tughlaq, the fourteenth-century sultan of Delhi, even had two of the pillars shipped to his newly built palace complex. Therefore, it should not be surprising that, when India became independent, Mauryan lions and the chakra became the country's national symbols. The founding fathers of the Indian Republic intuitively understood that the lions and the wheel stood for the power of the State. Indeed, Ashoka himself may have appropriated pre-existing symbolism. There are legends that associate Ashoka's grandfather with lions. Scholars like John Irwin argue that some of the Ashokan columns may actually have been put up by his predecessors and that Ashoka had merely added his inscriptions to them![26]

Ashoka ruled till he died at the age of seventy-two in 232 BC. The Mauryan empire collapsed soon after. Many arguments have been put forward to explain why the empire collapsed so quickly after Ashoka. There are those who feel that the emperor's growing infatuation with Buddhist philosophy sapped the morale of the army and the administration. It is very difficult to say what exactly happened, but there is evidence that the empire had already begun to crumble in Ashoka's later years. There are many stories about intra-family intrigues and feuds that left the ageing monarch increasingly powerless. In my view, the real problem was that Ashoka held on to power for too long. Despite his protestations about following the path of righteousness, he was unable to give up the trappings of power even when he was too feeble to rule effectively. Contrast this with the attitude of his grandfather and Chanakya, the founders of the empire. The problem of ageing rulers would haunt India through the centuries.

OF CITIES AND HIGHWAYS

By the time the Mauryan empire was established, the second cycle of India's urbanization had been underway for a millennium. Taxila in the north-west was not just a vibrant city but an important intellectual hub. In the east, Tamralipti was established as a major port; it is likely that Emperor Ashoka sent his son Mahindra on a mission to Sri Lanka from there. The site is located across the river from Kolkata and is not far from the port of Haldia. The name 'Tamralipta' means 'full of copper' and may have originally been linked to export of copper goods. Archaeological excavations have revealed punch-marked coins from this period. As we will see in the next chapter, the port would evolve into an important international trading hub in subsequent centuries.

The imperial capital of Pataliputra, of course, was the most important city in the empire. Megasthenes,[27] the Macedonian ambassador to Chandragupta, tells us that Pataliputra was surrounded by massive wooden palisades with 64 gates and 570 watch-towers. The city was shaped like a parallelogram 14.5 km in length and 2.5 km in breadth. Even if one does not take the numbers literally, they imply a very large city. Tower-bases and stockades found from excavations corroborate this. The main gates had wide timber-floored walkways with bridges across a moat system. The moat system, fed by the Son river, was almost 200 metres wide on the landward side. Along the Ganga, wooden piles were sunk into the mud to protect against inundation. Brick and stone were used to construct buildings inside the walls, especially for important structures. However, wood was a common building material and fires were a major hazard.[28] Megasthenes tells us that he had seen all the great cities of the east, including Susa and Ecbatana, but that Pataliputra was the greatest city in the world. Unfortunately, further excavations have become increasingly difficult as the growth of modern Patna has now covered the site.

What was it like to live in a Mauryan city? Kautilya's *Arthashastra* has a long list of municipal laws that give us a good insight into the civic concerns of the times.[29] For instance, there were traffic rules stating that bullock-carts were not allowed to move without a driver. A child could only drive a cart if accompanied by an adult. Reckless driving was punished except when the nose-string of the bullock broke accidentally or if the animal had panicked.

The *Arthashastra* also contains instructions for waste-disposal, building codes, the maintenance of public spaces like parks and rules against encroachment into a neighbour's property. We know that Kautilya did not approve of nosy neighbours as there is even a rule against interfering in the affairs of a neighbour. Very interestingly, there are specific injunctions against urinating and defecating in public spaces. The *Arthashastra* specifies fines for urinating or defecating near a water reservoir, a temple and a royal palace. One wonders why today's Indian cities do not enforce the ancient example.

The municipal laws specified in the *Arthashastra* clearly reflect a society that has a sophisticated understanding of urban life. Was this all relearned in the Iron Age or do they contain vestiges of the Harappan way of life? Of course, the majority of the people in the Mauryan empire lived in villages and Kautilya attaches a great deal of importance to agriculture, animal husbandry and land revenue. He also gives detailed instruction on the management of forests, especially those that supplied elephants. Summer was deemed a good time to catch elephants and twenty-year-olds were considered of the ideal age. At the same time, the capture of pregnant or suckling females and of cubs was strictly forbidden.

The establishment of the Mauryan empire appears to have created a stable environment that encouraged internal and external trade. There were major imperial highways crossing the country. The most important of these imperial highways extended from Taxila to the port of Tamralipti in Bengal. The

Mauryans were merely formalizing the Uttara Path that had already existed for a thousand years. The Macedonian ambassador Megasthenes very likely used it to visit the imperial capital of Pataliputra. As discussed earlier, this highway survives as NH1 between Amritsar and Delhi and as NH2 between Delhi and Kolkata. During Mauryan times, the section through Bihar would have taken a somewhat northerly route through Patna in order to accommodate the imperial capital.

The Dakshina Path also remained an important highway, especially given the extensive Mauryan conquests in the south. However, it appears that the trajectory of the road had shifted somewhat eastwards since the Iron Age. The new route passed through Vidisha and then made its way to Pratishthana (modern Paithan in Aurangabad district of Maharashtra). It is likely that, by the Mauryan period, a branch of the southern highway already connected Ujjain to the ports of Gujarat although this route would become more important during the Gupta period.

Meanwhile, the sea routes were gaining in importance. We know that, by Mauryan times, there was coastal shipping between Tamralipti in Bengal and Sri Lanka. Links with South East Asia were also being established. It is likely that the ships initially hugged the coast but, as we will discuss in the next chapter, nautical skills and shipbuilding technology were soon advanced enough to allow merchants to directly cross the Arabian Sea and the Bay of Bengal.

A Sense of History

By the time the Mauryans created their empire, Indian civilization was already well developed and conscious of itself.

It also had a developed sense of history as evidenced by the long lists of kings preserved in the Puranas and elsewhere (this is a comment about their intent, not necessarily their accuracy). The Mauryan empire was drawn from this pre-existing milieu and used its symbols—including the idea of the Chakravartin or Universal Monarch. However, the Mauryans introduced an important innovation—the use of columns and rock inscriptions to record their presence. As already discussed, these were meant to mark territory and impress the subjects but, I suspect, they were also meant to speak to us. Like monarchs around the world, Ashoka wanted to be remembered. He wanted future generations to be impressed by his power and to think well of him.

There is nothing wrong in this, it is only human. What is interesting is that later rulers instinctively understood what the Mauryans were trying to do. As we shall see in the following chapters, they not only created their own edifices but also systematically tried to link themselves to the Mauryans. Moreover, they continued to do this centuries after the Brahmi script had been forgotten and the original edicts could no longer be read. It is remarkable how this chain was deliberately sustained not just by Indian kings but also by rulers of foreign origin. It is as if these kings were conscious that they were just a moment in the history of a very ancient people and they wanted to record their place in it.

One of the best places to experience this is Girnar hill in Junagarh, Gujarat. At the foot of the sacred hill, there is a rock outcrop with an Ashokan edict. More than three centuries later, a Saka (i.e. Scythian) king called Rudradaman added his own inscription next to it. The second inscription records the restoration of the Sudarshana reservoir. We are told that the reservoir was originally constructed by Pushyagupta, Chandragupta Maurya's provincial governor, and that it was completed during Ashoka's time by Tushaspa, an official of possibly Greek origin. The inscription goes on to say that the reservoir was severely damaged by a great storm and floods in the year 72 (probably 150 AD). This was considered a catastrophe by the local people, but Rudradaman proudly tells us that he had the lake restored within a short time and without resorting to forced labour or extra taxes.

This is not the end of the story. Another three hundred years later, the Sudarshana lake burst its banks again. There is a third inscription on the rock that tells us that this time it was repaired by Emperor Skandagupta of the Gupta dynasty in 455-56 AD. If this is not a sense of history, what is?

Girnar is remarkable not just for these inscriptions. It is one of those places where fragments from India's long history sit piled up on top of each other. To experience this, climb up the hillock behind the rock inscriptions and above the picturesque Kali shrine. On one side, you will see Girnar hill with its multitude of ancient Hindu–Jain temples. On the other side is Junagarh fort and town. The fort is one of the oldest in the world and, according to legend, the upper citadel was built by Krishna's army. Indeed, the very name Junagarh literally means old fort. Over the centuries, Saka, Rajput, and Muslim kings would rule over it. As we shall see, Junagarh would be the focus of important events when India gained independence in 1947. Barely half an hour's drive away is Gir National Park, the last refuge of the Asiatic lion.

4

The Age of
Merchants

With the collapse of Mauryan hegemony, the outer edges of the empire dissolved into smaller kingdoms. A rump empire continued under the Shunga dynasty. It was still a substantial realm and the northern and southern trade routes continued to flourish. The imperial court continued to maintain international diplomatic relations as evidenced by a stone pillar raised by Heliodorus, the Greek ambassador in Vidisha, a major pit-stop on the Dakshina Path. Nonetheless, the north-western parts of the subcontinent were steadily occupied by Indo-Greek kingdoms that evolved a culture based on a mix of Indian, Greek and Bactrian elements. However, climate fluctuations would again play an important role in the chain of events.

In the first century BC, a severe famine caused by excessive snow affected the area that we now call Mongolia.[1] This was an area inhabited by fierce tribes of nomads called the Xiongnu. It is uncertain exactly who these people were but they were probably forerunners of the Mongols. These tribes had been the bane of early Chinese civilization and had prompted the First Emperor to build the earliest version of the Great Wall. The great drought caused the Xiongnu to migrate into the lands of another Central Asian tribe called the Yueh-Chih. In turn, the Yueh-Chih displaced the Sakas (Scythians), the Bactrians and Parthians. One by one, these groups were forced into the subcontinent. Thus, Afghanistan and North West India saw a succession of invasions and migrations.

Of course, it was not all warfare and invasion. There were relatively peaceful periods when trade and culture flourished. Taxila remained a centre of learning and new urban centres appeared, especially under Kushan rule. Buddhist ideas made their way into Central Asia and then eventually to China. Nonetheless, it is fair to say that the North West was unsettled for several centuries after the decline of the Mauryas. The heart of Indian civilization had already shifted from the Sapta-Sindhu region to the Gangetic plains during the Iron Age. Now, the action shifted to the coasts due to a boom in maritime trade. We see this all along the coast from Gujarat in the west to Kerala in the south-western tip and then all along the eastern seaboard up to Tamralipti in Bengal.

Maritime trade was not new to India. As we have seen, the Harappans traded actively with Mesopotamia. In the Iron Age, centres like Dwarka may have maintained these links. We know that by the time of the Mauryans, Tamralipti was a thriving port with links as far as Sri Lanka. We also know that the empire had diplomatic and trade links with the Greek kingdoms of the Middle East. However, it was from the second century BC that we see trade with both the Graeco–Roman world and South East Asia jump an order of magnitude. A Tamil epic from this period, the *Silapaddikaram*, tells us about the story of two lovers—Kannaki, daughter of a captain, and a merchant's son Kovalan. This how the epic describes the great port of Puhar (or Kaveripatnam):[2]

> Great and renowned kings envied the immense wealth of the seafaring merchants of the opulent city of Puhar
>   Ships and caravans from foreign lands poured in abundance rare objects and diverse merchandise
>   Its treasure would be untouched by the entire world, bound by the roaring seas

The literature of this period is full of references to trade. This is especially true of the *Sangam* anthologies. These collections of early Tamil poetry appear to have been put together in a series of ancient conferences. Exact dates are not available, but they probably took place between the third century BC and the sixth century AD. Madurai appears to have been the venue for most of these gatherings. However, it is said that the tradition began in an even earlier city, also called Madurai, that was built along the coast and that, like Dwarka, was swallowed by the sea.

This collection of poems was almost entirely lost and forgotten by the mid-nineteenth century. Luckily, a few scholars like Swaminatha Iyer dedicated their lives to painstakingly collecting the old palm-leaf manuscripts from old temples and remote hamlets. In the process, Iyer uncovered ancient religious practices that have survived in isolated pockets in a continuous chain to this day. Still, a significant portion of the corpus appears to have been lost, probably forever.

Sadly, much of the scholarship around Sangam literature is focused on trying to use the corpus to discern the roots of pristine Dravidian culture, unsullied by 'Aryan' influences from the north. This is ridiculous at many levels. First, the society described in the poems is full of trade and exchange with the rest of India as well as foreign lands. It is a world that is busily absorbing all kinds of influences and clearly revelling in it. Looking for signs of a pristine past misses the point about the people who composed the anthologies. Secondly, the composers of the *Sangam* poems clearly show strong religious and cultural links with the rest of the country. This includes knowledge of Buddhist, Brahminical and Jain traditions that are of 'northern' origin. Even when 'local' gods like Murugan (Kartik) are mentioned, they are depicted not as separate but as obviously part of the overall cultural milieu.

The point is that by the late Iron Age, the people in southern India were not just aware of the rest of Indian civilization but were comfortably a part of it. Goods and ideas were flowing along the coast as well as the Dakshina Path. For some odd reason, Indian historians see cultural influences flow only from the North to the rest of the country. The reality was of back-and-forth exchange. We see this in how the 'northern' Sanskrit language evolved over the centuries by absorbing words from other languages. Contrary to popular perception, Sanskrit was never a 'pure' language and its success was largely due to its ability from the earliest times to absorb ideas and words from Tamil, Munda and even Greek[3]. Many of the words that are generally considered as Sanskrit words used in modern Tamil are actually ancient Tamil words that found their way into Sanskrit. We will see how such exchange continued into subsequent centuries as with the spread of Shakti worship emanating from the east or with Shankaracharya's ideas from the far south. Of course there are significant regional variations, but these are small compared to what is shared with India's wider civilization.

Instead of using it to split hairs over regional differences, I would say that Sangam literature is far more remarkable for the extraordinary continuities it shows us that remain alive today. For instance, one of the Sangam poems gives us a glimpse of Madurai as it was under Pandyan king Neduchelyan. We are told of the stalls near the temple selling sweetmeats, garlands of flowers and betel paan. The bazaars were full of goldsmiths, tailors, coppersmiths, flower-sellers, painters and vendors of sandalwood. It is astonishing, two thousand years later, how well this would describe a temple-town of today.

THE WORLD OF THE *PERIPLUS*

The world described above was at the heart of a mercantile network that extended from the Mediterranean to the South China Sea. The single most important factor that allowed this boom in trade was an understanding of monsoon-wind patterns, a discovery that Greek sources credit to a navigator called Hippalus. The discovery allowed merchant fleets to sail directly across the Arabian Sea rather than hug the coast. As a result, Greek, Roman, Jewish and Arab traders flocked to Indian ports even as Indian merchants made their way to the Persian Gulf, the Red Sea and even down the East African coast. We know a significant amount about these trade routes because an unknown Greek writer has left us a detailed manual called the *Periplus Maris Erythraei*.[4]

According to the *Periplus*, the port of Berenike was a key hub in the trading network. It was located on the Red Sea coast of Egypt and had been established by the Ptolemies, the Greek dynasty that was founded in Egypt by one of Alexander's generals. Archaeological excavations in the nineties have confirmed its location.[5] Goods from India landed here and were then taken overland to the Nile. Then they were transported down the Nile in boats to Alexandria. There were other routes as well. Some fleets, for instance, sailed all the way up the Red Sea to Aqaba. Goods would then have been transported by camel and donkey caravan through desert towns like Petra to Mediterranean ports like Tyre and Sidon.

There is a story that Cleopatra, when defeated by the Romans, had hoped to escape with her family to India. When Octavian attacked Egypt in 30 BC, she sent Caesarion, her seventeen-year-old son by Julius Caesar, to Berenike with a great deal of treasure. Before she could escape, however, she was captured in Alexandria and famously committed suicide by snake-bite. Meanwhile, Caesarion had reached Berenike and could easily have escaped to India. Unfortunately, he was convinced by his tutors, almost certainly bribed, to return to Alexandria for negotiations. Octavian promptly had his cousin murdered. Cleopatra's Alexandria, like Dwarka and old Madurai, now lies under the sea.

The *Periplus* tells us that ships sailing from Berenike to India went down the Red Sea to Yemen and then, dodging pirates, to the island of Socotra. The island had a mixed population of

Arab, Greek and Indian traders. Even the island's name is derived from Sanskrit—Dwipa Sukhadara (Island of Bliss). This may explain why many Yemenis carry genes of Indian extract. From here, there were two major routes to India. The first made its way north to Oman and then across the Arabian Sea to Gujarat. Ships were advised to make this journey in July to take advantage of the monsoon wind.

There were many ports in Gujarat but Barygaza (modern Bharuch) appears to have been the most important. The port-town is at the estuary of the Narmada river. Treacherous shoals and currents made it difficult for ships to sail up the river. Therefore, the local king had appointed fishermen to act as pilots and to tow merchant ships to Barygaza port which was several miles upriver. The author of the *Periplus* almost certainly visited the area because he describes in great detail the impact of a ferocious bore tide in the estuary.

Imports into Barygaza are listed by the *Periplus* and include: gold, silver, brass, copper, lead, perfumes and 'various sashes half a yard wide'. Italian and Arabian wine was also imported in large quantities. The Indian love of imported alcohol is clearly not new. Furthermore, the manual informs us that the local king 'imported' luxury items such as good-looking women for his harem. Exports included spikenard, ivory, onyx stone, silk and, most importantly, cotton textiles. Cotton textiles have remained a major export from this area till modern times.

The second route to India was a more southerly one that went across from Socotra to the Kerala coast. The most important port in this area was Muzaris (or Muchheri Pattanam) that is mentioned frequently in both Graeco–Roman and

Indian texts. A variety of goods were traded in Muzaris but the most important item of export by far was pepper, a spice that is native to the southern tip of India. It must have been exported in very large quantities because it was commonly available as far as Roman Britain.

For a long time historians had debated the exact location of this great port of antiquity. Excavations between 2004 and 2009 have identified it with a village called Pattanam, 30 km north of Kochi. Archaeologists have dug up a large number of Roman coins, amphorae and other artifacts in the area. It would remain a major port till it was destroyed by a big flood on the Periyar river in 1341 AD. The main trading hub then shifted to Kochi, but the Muzaris area retained enough strategic importance for both the Portuguese and the Dutch to maintain a fort there. When I visited the site in October 2011, the fort was being excavated by the Archaeological Survey. The oldest extant structure, however, is the Kizhthali Shiva temple that is said to have been built by the Chera dynasty in the second century BC. The dragons carved into the steps in front of the shrine strongly reminded me of the temples of South East Asia. Has this style made its way from Kerala to Java or the other way around?

During ancient times, an overland trade route from Muzaris and other Kerala ports made its way through the Palghat Gap (a gap in the Nilgiri mountain range near Coimbatore) to inland cities like Madurai or further on to ports on the eastern coast. Some Greek and Roman products would then have been re-exported to Bengal and South East Asia.

According to another ancient Greek geographer, Strabo, around 120 ships made the year-long trip to India and back in the first century AD[6]. This probably excludes Indian merchant ships that also made the trip in reverse. We know that, for most of this period, India ran a large trade surplus with the Graeco–Roman world. This resulted in a constant one-way flow of gold and silver coins. Roman writer Pliny (23–79 AD) wrote: 'Not a year passed in which India did not take fifty million sesterces away from Rome.' This is corroborated by the fact that many hoards of Roman coins have been found in India. In a world where money was based on precious metals, this one-way flow of gold and silver would have been equivalent to severe monetary tightening. At one point, the drainage of gold became so serious that Roman Emperor Vespasian was forced to discourage the import of Indian luxury goods and ban the export of gold to India. Nonetheless, as a result of centuries of trade surpluses, India accumulated a large store of gold and silver. It is estimated that even today 25–30 per cent of all the gold ever mined is held privately by Indians even though the country itself has very few gold mines of its own.

Over the centuries many groups of people came to India's western coast to trade or find refuge. Their descendants continue to live here and, in many instances, preserve ancient customs and traditions to this day. Not many people realize that India is host to one of the oldest Jewish communities in the world. It is believed that the earliest Jews came to India to trade in the time of King Solomon but, after the destruction of the Second Temple by the Romans in 70 AD, many refugees settled in Kerala. St. Thomas the Apostle is said to have landed in Muzaris at around this time and lived amongst this community. One can visit the spot where the saint is said to have landed. The descendants of his converts survive as the Syrian Christian community.

For fifteen centuries, this Christian community continued to observe old practices, including the use of Syriac, a dialect of the Aramaic language. Aramaic is the language that would have been used by Jesus Christ himself and it is astonishing that it survived in isolation for so long in India[7]. Unfortunately, the Portuguese tried to forcibly eradicate Jewish customs, including the language, and replace them with Catholic ones in the sixteenth century. Nonetheless, some ancient traditions live on in the Syrian Christian community.

As one can see, the legacy of the ancient trade-routes is still very much alive and is yet another example of India's astonishing ability to maintain civilizational continuities. If Cleopatra had made good her escape, we would probably have a group that directly traced its origins to the Egyptian queen and Julius Caesar. It is still possible to experience the atmosphere of those times in the older parts of Kochi (Cochin). Pepper, ginger and other spices are still warehoused and traded in the bylanes. Deals are sometimes negotiated using a system of hand signals, hidden from onlookers by a cloth, that evolved centuries ago. Sitting in the toddy-shop, I watch modern ships ply in the harbour. I imagine myself as Hippalus, the ancient Greek mariner, enjoying his first drink after months at sea. Not far is 'Jew Town' where a tiny Jewish community lives clustered around a sixteenth-century synagogue. The Jews must have been held in high esteem by King Rama Varma for he allowed the construction of the synagogue right next to his palace. Sadly, the community has been sharply depleted in recent decades by emigration to Israel.

To the Island of Gold

Even as the western coast traded with the Middle East and the Graeco–Roman world, the eastern coast of India saw a similar boom in trade with South-East Asia and all the way to China. There were dozens of ports all along the coast including the great port of Tamralipti in Bengal, the cluster of ports around Chilka lake in Orissa (recently renamed Odisha), the Pallava port of Mahabalipuram and the Chola port of Nagapattinam. Note that I am generalizing about a very long period of time and the relative importance of the various ports waxed and waned over the centuries.

From these ports, merchant fleets set sail for Suvarnadwipa (the Island of Gold or Sumatra) and Yavadwipa (Java). Some of them sailed on further to what is now South Vietnam. It is here, thousands of miles from the Indian mainland, that we see the rise of the first Indianized kingom in South East Asia. Chinese texts tell us of the Hindu kingdom of Funan that flourished in the Mekong delta in the second century AD.[8] According to a legend told both by Chinese sources as well as by local inscriptions, the kingdom was founded by the Indian Brahmin, Kaundinya, who married a local princess of the Naga (Snake) clan. Together they founded a dynasty that ruled Funan for a hundred and fifty years. The Naga or snake motif would remain an important royal symbol in this part of the world.

The capital of Funan was Vyadhapura, now the Cambodian village of Banam and its main port was Oc Eo. In the early twentieth century, French colonial archaeologists found the remains of a large urban agglomeration of houses built on stilts along a network of canals extending 200 kilometers. There were irrigation canals as well as big canals that were navigable by ocean-going vessels. This is why it was possible for Chinese travellers to talk about sailing across Funan on their way to the Malayan peninsula.

Over the next thousand years, Funan's legacy would evolve into the great Hindu–Buddhist kingdoms of Angkor in Cambodia and Champa in Vietnam. Strongly Indianized kingdoms and cultures evolved in other parts of South East Asia as well. In Sumatra and the Malay peninsula, the Srivijaya kingdom prospered on trade between India and China. In Java, a succession of Hindu kingdoms culminated in the powerful Majapahit empire in the fourteenth and fifteenth centuries.

Significantly, Indian civilization exerted this influence on South East Asia almost exclusively through trade and, with the exception of the Chola raids on Srivijaya in the eleventh century, there is no record of Indian military intervention in the region. Contrast this with successive Chinese emperors who repeatedly tried to impose a tributary relationship with these kingdoms. Although they sometimes succeeded in gaining temporary submission, often backed by military threats, they failed to match India in making civilizational inroads till the voyages of Admiral Zheng He in the fifteenth century.

The cultural impact of this era lives on in South-East Asia. It may be most obvious in the Hindu island of Bali, but, throughout the region, the influence of ancient India is alive in the names of places and people as well as the large number of Indian-derived words used in everyday speech. The national languages of both Malaysia and Indonesia are called 'Bahasa', and both are full of Sanskrit words. Indeed, the name itself is derived from the Sanskrit word *bhasha* meaning language. From Myanmar to Vietnam, Buddhism remains the dominant religion. To this day, the coronation of the king of Buddhist Thailand and other royal ceremonies must be done by Hindu priests. There are more shrines to the god Brahma in Bangkok than in all of India.

India's influence is civilizational rather than narrowly religious, and it extends all the way to the Korean peninsula. The prestige associated with ancient Indian civilization, for example, is recalled in the national myth of Korea. According to the *Samguk Yusa*,[9] Princess Huh Hwang-ok of Ayodhya sailed all the way to Korea to marry King Suro in the fourth century AD. They had ten sons and together founded Korea's earliest dynasty. The Gimhae Kim clan claims to be direct descendants of this union and remains influential (former President Kim Dae Jung was from this clan).

It is amazing how the essence of a civilization can survive over large distances in space and time. Watching the Ramayana performed in the Javanese style against a backdrop of the ninth-century Prambanan temples in Java, one is struck by how the landscape of a far-off time and a faraway land is evoked. The stone temples transform themselves from scene to scene—sometimes they recall the rocky outcrops of Kishkindha, sometimes Ravan's palace in Lanka. A couple of hours' drive away, the sunset seen from the top of the Buddhist stupa at Borobodur retains its magical effect even if Buddhist chants have now been replaced by the Islamic call to prayer.

In India, too, cultural traditions continue to recall the ancient trade routes. For instance, in the state of Orissa, the festival of Kartik Purnima still celebrates the day when Sadhaba merchants set sail for South-East Asia. People light lamps before sunrise and set them afloat on small paper boats in rivers or in the sea. The festival is held in early November when the monsoon winds reverse. At the same time, in the town of Cuttack, a large fair takes place—called 'Bali-Yatra' (literally meaning 'the voyage to Bali'), scholars feel it marks the departure of merchant fleets for the island of Bali.[10] These festivals echo a culture that celebrated its entrepreneurs and risk-takers.

Further south, the seventh-century stone temple of Mahabalipuram still stands on the shore as if waiting for merchant fleets to come home. The town, 60 km south of modern Chennai, was a thriving port under the Pallava dynasty from the seventh to the ninth century AD. According to local legend, the existing temple complex was only one of seven such temple complexes that once existed. It was said that the sea swallowed up the other six temples as well as numerous palaces, bazaars and other grand buildings. Local fishermen had tales of how their nets would often get tangled in underwater structures. Serious historians, however, used to dismiss these stories as mere myth.

On 26 December 2004, a massive earthquake devastated the Indonesian province of Aceh and triggered a tsunami across the Indian Ocean. The event is estimated to have killed 230,000 people. The tsunami struck India's south-eastern coast as well. However, before the waves crashed in, the sea withdrew a couple of kilometres. The residents of Mahabalipuram reported seeing a number of large stone structures rising from the seabed. Then the sea returned and covered them up again. Since then, divers have confirmed that there are a large number of man-made structures out in the sea although they have not yet been systematically mapped. The tsunami also shifted the sands along the shore and uncovered a number of other structures, including a large stone lion.[11] Archaeologists also found the foundations of a brick temple from the Sangam period that may have been destroyed by a tsunami 2200 years ago. A second tsunami may have hit this coast in the thirteenth century. Yet again, folk memory has been proved to have been based on historical fact even if one cannot exactly confirm if there indeed were another six temples in Mahabalipuram.

SAILING ON STITCHED SHIPS

As we have seen, the boom in maritime trade made India both an economic and a cultural superpower. According to Angus Maddison, the country accounted for 33 per cent of world GDP in the first century AD. India's share was three times that of western Europe and was much larger than that of the Roman empire as a whole (21 per cent). China's share of 26 per cent of world GDP was significantly smaller than India's[12]. He also estimates India's population at 75 million (compared to today's 1.2 billion).

What did the merchant fleets plying the Indian Ocean look like in this era? There were a wide variety of vessels, ranging from small boats for river and coastal use to large ships with double masts for long sea voyages. There were also regional variations. As shown in the panels of Borobodur, the

Indonesians preferred a design with outriggers. However, they all seem to have shared a peculiar design trait: they were not held together by nails; they were stitched together with rope! Throughout the ages, travellers from outside the Indian Ocean world have repeatedly commented on this odd design preference. The technique persisted into modern times—locally built vessels were being stitched together well into the twentieth century. A survey of the Orissa coast by Eric Kentley in the 1980s found that boats called 'padua' were still being made by sewing together planks with coir ropes.[13] I am told that there are boat-builders who continue using this approach into the twenty-first century. Like the Harappan ox-cart, it is another example of how ancient technologies live on in India even as it adopts new ones.

It is unclear why the shipbuilders in the Indian Ocean region had such a strong preference for this peculiar technique when they had access to iron nails from an early stage. It has been suggested that it may have been the result of a superstition that magnetic lodestones in the sea would suck in ships with iron-nails, but this is a very unlikely explanation. More likely, it was a response to the fact that these ships sailed in waters full of atolls and reefs, and had to be beached in many places due to the lack of sheltered harbours or due to the rough monsoon sea. All this required a hull that was a bit flexible and would not break-up easily. The stitched technique provided this flexibility although it would later limit the ability of Indian ship-building to match Chinese and then European design innovations.

So, how did it feel to sail in these ships? A Chinese scholar Fa Xian (also spelled Fa Hien) visited India in the fifth century and has left us a fascinating account of his return journey by the sea route.[14] Fa Xian came to India by the land route through Central Asia. He spent several years in northern India studying and gathering Buddhist texts. He then made his way to the port of Tamralipti. The site of this famous port of antiquity, now called Tamluk, is not far from modern Kolkata. It is close to where the Rupnarayan river joins the Gangetic delta, but the old channel that served the port has silted up and is no longer navigable. Except for a 1200-year-old temple dedicated to the goddess Kali, there is little there to hint at a glorious past as a successful hub of commerce. Indeed, Tamluk is close to the infamous village of Nandigram where a dispute over land acquisition in 2007 led to a bloody clash between the state government and locals that left scores dead. It is now considered a hotbed of Maoist rebels.

In 410 AD, however, Fa Xian would have found a port town bustling with activity. He tells us that he boarded a large merchant ship bound for Sri Lanka. The voyage was during the winter months when the monsoons winds would have been blowing south. The ship sailed in a south-westerly direction for just fourteen days before arriving in Sri Lanka. Fa Xian calls it the Land of the Lions—a clear reference to the mythical origins of the Sinhalese people (there were never any real lions in Sri Lanka).

The Chinese scholar spent two years in Sri Lanka studying Buddhist texts before setting sail for South East Asia. He tells us that it was a large vessel that could carry two hundred people. It was accompanied by a smaller ship that carried extra provisions and could help in an emergency. Unfortunately, after two days at sea, the ships were caught in a major storm and the larger ship sprang a leak. Suddenly there was panic. Many of the merchants wanted to shift to the smaller vessel immediately, but its crew panicked when faced with a virtual stampede. They cut the cables and sailed off. This further increased the state of panic. The merchants were now forced to throw most of their goods overboard. Fa Xian tells us that he too threw away his water-pitcher, wash-basin and other possessions. He was afraid that the merchants would also throw out his precious cargo of books, but fortunately this did not happen.

Finally, after thirteen days, the storm cleared up. The crew beached the ship on a small island, possibly one of the Andaman and Nicobar islands. The leak was found and repaired before they set sail again. We are told that the mood remained tense because the area was notorious for pirates and the crew was not quite sure about their location. In the end, however, they regained their bearings and set a course for Java.

The ship arrived in Java after ninety days at sea. In common with other Chinese pilgrims who visited India to study Buddhism, Fa Xian saw the world in largely religious terms. The only thing he has to say about Java is that its people were Hindus and not Buddhists (also not entirely accurate given the evidence of Borobodur). After staying in Java for five months, he set sail for China on a very large merchant ship.

The vessel must have been enormous since the crew alone numbered 200. Fa Xian comments that he was very comfortable on this ship. It is possible that ships of this size had private cabins. For over a month, the ship made good progress till it, too, hit a major storm. Yet again, there was panic. Fa Xian tells us that some of his fellow passengers accused him of bringing bad luck. They had probably heard of the storm on his previous voyage and thought that this was too much of a coincidence! Luckily an influential merchant defended him and the matter was settled.

Meanwhile, the ship's crew realized that they had been blown off-course and were lost. They had been at sea for seventy days by now and were running dangerously short on food and water. Given the desperate situation, some of the more experienced merchants decided to take control of the ship and set a new course. After sailing for yet another twelve days, the ship finally arrived on the Chinese coast. Thus ends one of the earliest accounts of a sea journey between India and China. It reminds us that Indian Ocean voyages were dangerous and that these ancient merchants ran enormous risks when they set sail for foreign lands.

REBUILDING THE IMPERIAL DREAM

When Fa Xian visited India, much of the country was under the sway of the Gupta Empire, the second of India's great empires. The first of the Gupta emperors was Chandragupta I (320–335 AD) who established control over the eastern Gangetic plain with his capital in Pataliputra (now Patna). However, it was his son Samudragupta who dramatically expanded the empire over his forty-year rule. He first ensured that he had control of the entire Gangetic plains. Then he led a campaign deep into southern India where he reduced the kings of the region, including the Pallavas, to tributary status. Having proved himself as the most powerful monarch in the subcontinent, he performed the Vedic ritual of the

Ashwamedha Yagna and proclaimed himself the Chakravartin or Universal Monarch.

Samudragupta's successor Chandragupta II (also called Vikramaditya) next expanded the empire westward to include Malwa and Gujarat by defeating the Sakas (or Scythians) who had ruled this area for several generations. Many of the small kingdoms and republics of north-west India were also reduced to tributary status. Thus, the Guptas established effective sway over much of India. In North and Central India, this control was exercised directly, while in peninsular India and in the north-west it was exercised indirectly through tributaries and close allies like the Vakatakas.

There is strong evidence to suggest that the Guptas consciously modelled themselves on the Mauryans and set out to recreate the empire of their predecessors. Not only did two of their emperors share a name with Chandragupta Maurya, but the Guptas went out of their way to put their own inscriptions next to Mauryan ones. For instance, much of what we know about the conquests of Samudragupta is from inscriptions carved on an Ashokan pillar that is now housed in Allahabad fort. Similarly, Skandagupta, fifth of the Gupta emperors, placed his own inscription in the vicinity of a Mauryan edict in Girnar, Gujarat. In art and literature too we find an echo of the Gupta fascination with the Mauryas. A well known Sanskrit play of this period, *Mudrarakshasa*, is based on the story of how Chanakya and Chandragupta Maurya defeated the Nandas and built their empire.

Many well-known scholars take the view that ancient Indians did not have a sense of history and that the extraordinary continuities of Indian history are somehow accidental or unconscious. It is modern arrogance to think that ancient people were somehow incapable of comprehending their place in history. As we can see, the Gupta monarchs clearly wanted to establish a link not just with the Mauryans but back as far as the Bronze Age. This is why at least two of the Gupta emperors conducted the 'Ashwamedha Yagna' or Vedic Horse Sacrifice—a ritual that was considered ancient even in the fourth century AD. By declaring themselves as Chakravartins, the Guptas were sending the same signal as the Mauryans did through the symbol of the so-called chakra or wheel. At the same time, the Guptas wanted to create a link to the future. The rust-free Iron Pillar in Delhi is usually remembered as an example of advanced metallurgy, but it was not meant as a technological wonder. Its real purpose was to provide a permanent record for posterity. What better way to do this than to inscribe on a solid iron pillar that would never rust?[15]

LIFE IN A GUPTA CITY

Despite the numerous conquests, the Gupta empire was significantly smaller than that of the Mauryas. However, it made up for this in economic and cultural vigour. The two centuries of Gupta rule coincided with the mercantile boom described earlier in this chapter. With ports on both coasts and control over major internal highways, the Gupta economy witnessed a period of exceptional prosperity. This is corroborated by Fa Xian's diaries. Indeed, the country must have been very well governed because, in his many years of solo wanderings, the Chinese scholar does not appear to have ever been robbed or cheated. This cannot be said of foreign travellers who visited India in subsequent centuries. Later visitors like Xuan Zang and Ibn Batuta would all have to face armed bandits. Even today, backpacking alone like Fa Xian can be unsafe for a foreigner in many parts of the country.

The Gupta emperors invested heavily in intellectual and artistic excellence. It was under their rule that the astronomer-mathematician Aryabhatta worked out that the earth was spherical and that it rotated on an axis. He argued that the phases of the moon were due to the movement of shadows and that the planets shone through reflected light. He even worked out a remarkably accurate estimate of the circumference of the earth and of the ratio Pi. All this a thousand years before Copernicus and Galileo.

Not far from his capital Pataliputra, Emperor Kumaragupta founded Nalanda University, which would go on to become a world-renowned hub for Buddhist studies. Further west, the Guptas established a secondary capital in Ujjain. The city not only became an important commercial node in the Southern Road but also an important centre of learning for the Hindu tradition. It was probably here that Kalidasa, often called India's Shakespeare, composed his famous works. Ujjain is today a small town in Madhya Pradesh, undistinguished except for a number of ancient temples. In the fifth century AD, however, it was a lively hub of commercial and intellectual exchange. Late on a monsoon night, when the cool moist breeze blows, it is still possible to imagine Kalidasa composing the *Meghdoota*, the Messenger of the Clouds.

So what was it like to visit one of these cities? Fa Xian tells us that cities of the Gangetic plains were exceptionally large and prosperous.[16] When he visited Pataliputra, he saw the

ruins of Ashoka's palace that still stood in the middle of the
city after six centuries. He was so impressed by the sheer scale
of the stone walls, towers and doorways that he declared that
they could not have been built by human hands—they must
be the work of supernatural creatures.

While in Pataliputra, he witnessed a festival where the
people built gigantic four-wheel wagons and then erected
towers on them that were five storeys high. They then covered
the towers in fine white linen and decorated them with
canopies of embroidered silk. Fa Xian tells us that the people
placed idols of their gods within these structures and images
of the Buddha on the corners of the wagons. On the day of the
festival, twenty such wagons were pulled through the city in a
grand procession. Devotees from all walks of life, ranging
from the royal family to the poor, participated in the festivities.
They offered prayers and flowers to the gods and lit lamps in
the evening. The whole city became like a fair ground with
amusements and games. We are also told that, on this day,
the rich made generous donations to the poor and physicians
even held free health clinics for them.

The festival described above is clearly the Rath Yatra or
Chariot Festival that is still celebrated by Hindus in many
parts of the country. The most famous is the one held in
honour of Lord Jagannath in Puri, Orissa. From Fa Xian's
description, the festival has survived almost unchanged since
Gupta times. The only significant difference is that Buddhists
used to actively participate in this event. Indeed, it appears
that the popular practice of Buddhism and Hinduism
overlapped significantly despite doctrinal disputes between
scholars, and were seen to be part of the same spectrum. This

relationship remains alive in the Indic family of religions. Nepali Hindus routinely worship at Buddhist shrines just as Buddhist Thais commonly pray to the Hindu god Brahma and Punjabi Hindus visit Sikh gurudwaras.

Not everything written in this period was about high literature, science or religion. One of the most famous books of this age is the *Kamasutra*, the Treatise on Love. It is best known for its long lists of complicated sexual positions, but it also tells us a lot about the social mores of that time. The book suggests that at least urban attitudes were surprisingly liberal. Although obviously written by a man, the *Kamasutra* is quite sensitive to the female perspective and even hints at a female readership. Most interestingly for our purposes, it paints a vivid picture of the life of a rich and idle *nagaraka* or 'a man-about-town'.[17]

The *Kamasutra* advises the nagaraka to live in a big city if possible. On getting up in the morning, the book tells us, the nagaraka should have an oil-massage, bathe, shave, apply perfumes and, most importantly, clean the sweat from his armpits (the author is quite insistent on this). After lunch, he should entertain himself by teaching his parrot to talk, or by attending a cock-fight or ram-fight. Then, after a nap, it was time to dress up and head for the salon. The *Kamasutra* tells us that the evenings would be full of music, singing and drink. By late evening, the nagaraka and his friends would withdraw to a private room, decorated with flowers, where women could rendezvous with them. The courtesans are colourfully described as 'women who love all men equally'. They would share wines and spirits made of grapes, honey and sugarcane. The *Kamasutra* advises the men to engage the women in 'gentle conversation and courtesies that charm the mind and the heart'. Presumably the evening did not end just in conversation.

Picnics too are described in the same way. The men would get ready early in the morning and head for the countryside on horseback accompanied by friends, servants and courtesans. They would while the day away in gambling, cock-fights and theatrical performances. In the summer, the picnickers would enjoy water-sports in specially built pools designed to keep crocodiles out (very sensible in my view; it can really spoil your day to have a limb bitten off while frolicking in the pool with the ladies).

The *Kamasutra*'s description of the lifestyle of a fourth-century man-about-town is fascinating, and finds an echo in much later periods. The lives of the idle nawabs of nineteenth-century Lucknow and the Bengali zamindars of early-twentieth-century Kolkata have been common themes in literature and film, but some of these characters would have not been out of place if they had been transported back fifteen centuries to imperial Pataliputra. Like other aspects of Indian culture, this tradition too lives on in the world of 'Page 3' socialites in cities like Delhi and Mumbai.

So what did all these people and their world really look like? Despite the long passage of time, we have carvings and paintings that give us a visual insight into this world in the Ajanta and Ellora caves in Maharashtra. These were constructed under the rule of the Vakatakas, close allies of the Guptas. The paintings are obviously stylized but they give us a sense of what Indians of this period idealized. One of the things that strikes me is that most of the people in the paintings are very dark-skinned. It appears that ancient Indians had a preference for dark skin. This is supported by a lot of other evidence. For instance, the epitome of male handsomeness in the Hindu tradition is Krishna who is clearly dark. His name literally means 'The Dark One' (his depiction as 'blue-skinned' is merely a medieval artistic innovation). Similarly, the beautiful Draupadi, the common wife of the Pandava brothers in the Mahabharata, is also described as being very dark.

This preference for dark skin appears to have survived well into the medieval period. Indeed, Marco Polo specifically mentions this in his comments about India: 'For I assure you that the darkest man is here the most highly esteemed and considered better than others who are not so dark. Let me add that in very truth these people portray and depict their gods and their idols black and their devils white as snow.'[18] One only needs to look at the idol of Lord Jagannath in Puri to see what Polo meant.

It is unclear when and why this preference switched, but it shows that the traditional Indian aesthetic was very different from how we now perceive it. This may be somewhat inconvenient to those who sell skin-whitening creams to modern Indian consumers. Of course, Indians are not the only ones subject to changing tastes. Just five generations ago, Europeans considered pale white skin so attractive that Victorian women were willing to risk poisoning by using an arsenic-based compound to whiten their skin. Today, their descendants risk skin cancer from too much sun-bathing. Basically, you cannot win.

BATHING IN HOLY WATERS

By the first half of the sixth century, the Gupta Empire began to gradually crumble in the face of internal frictions and repeated attacks by Hunas (White Huns) from the North West. Taxila, the famous centre of learning where Chanakya had once taught, was sacked by the Hunas around 470 AD. Over the next few decades they pushed the Gupta defences back into the Gangetic valley. A rump empire would remain for several generations, but the glory days were gone.

In the centuries that followed, a number of powerful kingdoms rose and fell in northern India—the Palas of Bengal, Harsha of Thaneshwar and so on. The city of Pataliputra slowly went into decline and was replaced by Kannauj (now a small town in Uttar Pradesh). Nonetheless, most things drifted along. Both Nalanda and Ujjain remained important centres of learning. Thinkers like Bhaskara and Varahamihira made great contributions to mathematics and astronomy. Chinese scholars continued to visit India to study Buddhism. The most prominent of these scholars was Xuan Zang who visited India in the seventh century, more than two hundred years after Fa Xian.

Like his predecessor, Xuan Zang (also spelled Hiuen-Tsang) made his way to India through Central Asia, which was then inhabited primarily by Buddhist and pagan Turks. He spent over a decade in the subcontinent during which he criss-crossed the Gangetic plains and went as far east as Assam. He even spent two years studying at Nalanda, which was then at the height of its fame.

One of the places he visited on these travels was Allahabad

(then called Prayag). This town is near one of the most sacred sites in Hinduism—the 'Triveni Sangam' or the Mingling of Three Rivers. Two of the rivers are obvious: the sacred Ganga and the Yamuna. However, the factor that gives this spot a special significance is that the Saraswati is also said to flow underground and join the other two at this place. In this way, a primordial memory of the vanished river is kept alive. For a Hindu, the sins of a lifetime are washed away by taking a dip in the confluence of these rivers. It is especially auspicious to do this at the time of the Kumbh Mela, which is held here every twelve years.[19] This is part of a four-year cycle by which this event is held in turn in Ujjain, Haridwar, Nasik and Allahabad. However, it is the great Kumbh Mela of Allahabad that is the largest and most prestigious. The last time this festival was hosted in Allahabad in January–February 2013, an estimated 80 million people participated over fifty-five days—the largest human gathering in history.

Xuan Zang tells us that large numbers of people participated in the festival in the seventh century including the rulers of different countries and even Buddhists. Most interestingly, he describes the rituals of the sadhus (ascetics). Evidently, a large wooden column was erected in the middle of the river and the sadhus would climb it. At sunset they would hang from the column with one leg and one arm while stretching out the other leg and arm into the air. Thus would they stare into the setting sun. The wooden pole and the particular ritual are no longer around, but, considering the ash-covered sadhus who still congregate at the Kumbh Mela, the ritual seems entirely in character.[20]

Despite these outward signs of continuity, one does get the

feeling that the economic and cultural centre of gravity steadily shifted to the south. Even militarily, the southern kings could more than hold their own against the kingdoms of the Gangetic plains. When Xuan Zang visited India, the northern plains had been welded into an empire under Emperor Harsha, but he was roundly defeated by the Chalukya king Pulaksen II when he attempted to extend his empire into the Deccan.

The source of southern power was trade—both with the flourishing Indianized kingdoms of South East Asia as well as with the Persians and Arabs who had replaced the Romans in the west. The kingdoms of the south were aware of the importance of commerce and actively encouraged it. When necessary, they were not afraid to use military might to keep the trade routes open. The most famous examples of this are the Chola naval expeditions to South-East Asia in the eleventh century.

The Cholas were an ancient dynasty and are even mentioned in Ashokan edicts. In the ninth to the eleventh century AD, they created an empire that covered most of peninsular India and briefly extended to the banks of the Ganga. Unusually for an Indian empire, however, it also had a maritime empire that included Sri Lanka and the Maldives. For the most part, they also had very good relations with kingdoms of South-East Asia. Inscriptions on both sides show the existence of large merchant communities and that the kings exchanged emissaries and gifts. For instance, we have an inscription that tells us that Sri Mulan, the agent of the Srivijaya king of Sumatra, Malaya, had donated several lamp-stands to be installed at the Shiva temple in Nagapattinam.

The problem probably arose because the Cholas began to

create direct trade links with the Song empire in China. Records show that Cholas and the Chinese exchanged a number of trade delegations in the early eleventh century. Indo–Chinese trade relations were not new. We know from Chinese sources that a large Indian merchant community had long been established in Guangzhou and that there were three Hindu temples functioning there. However, Song–Chola diplomacy appears to have led to a further boom in Indo–Chinese trade.

Unfortunately, the Srivijaya kings probably felt that their role as middlemen was being threatened by such direct linkages. They reacted by tightening controls and imposing heavy taxes on ships passing through the Straits of Malacca. A contemporary Arab text tells us that the Srivijaya kings were demanding a levy of 20,000 dinars to allow a Jewish-owned ship to continue to China.[21] This was a serious matter and the Cholas felt that they had to react. This led to a naval raid against Srivijaya in 1017 AD and then a more substantial expedition in 1025. These represent very rare examples of Indian military aggression outside of the subcontinent. The hostility was fortunately not long-lasting and a few decades later we find the Cholas and Srivijaya sending joint embassies to the Chinese.

I do not want to leave the reader with the impression that India's relationship with South-East Asia was one of cultural, economic and, occasionally military, domination. Indian trade and civilization clearly had a very large impact on this part of the world, but it was a two-way flow. For instance, the university of Nalanda may have been founded by the Guptas, but its subsequent growth was partly due to the strong financial support extended by the Srivijaya kings. Moreover, South-

East Asian kingdoms like Angkor, Majapahit and Champa took the Indian input and built on it. These people were not blindly copying Indian prototypes but innovating and indigenizing.

In fact, the Indonesians independently conducted their own maritime expeditions. From the third to the sixth century AD, they crossed the Indian Ocean in their outriggered ships and settled in Madagascar in large numbers. Thus, the first humans in Madagascar came from distant Indonesia rather than nearby Africa. The descendants of the Indonesian settlers still form a significant proportion of the population of the island country and the Malagasy language retains the strong influence of dialects from Borneo!

A Chain of History

It is commonly argued by scholars that ancient Indians only wrote one formal history—Kalhana's *Rajatarangini* or River of Kings, a history of the kings of Kashmir written in the twelfth century. This is then put forward as proof that Indians did not have a sense of their history or of the continuity of their civilization. This is simply not accurate and it is important to recognize the degree to which this sense of continuity is deliberately maintained over generations. Even if one ignores works like Bana's *Harshcharita* as being royal eulogies, there are numerous examples, such as the Vanshavali tradition of Nepal or the Burunjis of Assam, where lengthy genealogical records were meticulously maintained. There is obviously a very developed sense of historical continuity.

Kashmir's Kalhana too saw himself as a link in a chain, and

he tells us that he read the works of eleven earlier historians as well as inspected temple inscriptions and land records. He even criticizes fellow historian Suvrata for leaving out details and making his history too concise.[22] Most of these other works may have been lost but they all clearly existed. Moreover, Kalhana is followed by three other works that continue the chronicle down to the time of Mughal emperor Akbar. When Akbar conquered Kashmir in the sixteenth century, he was given a copy of Kalhana's *Rajatarangini* that was translated into Persian for his benefit. A summary was then included in the *Ain-i-Akbari*, the chronicles of Akbar's own rule, in order to link him back to the historical chain.

Kalhana's history is not just about kings and battles but contains an interesting account of how human intervention altered the landscape of Kashmir. He tells of the minister Suyya who carried out a number of major engineering works during the reign of Avantivarman in the ninth century. We are told that landslides and soil erosion had led to a great deal of rubble and stone being deposited in the Jhelum, which was impeding the flow of the river. The rubble was dredged and embankments were built. The landscape was restructured to human use as dams created new lakes while old lakes were drained to clear the way for cultivation. It is even suggested that Suyya may have significantly altered the courses of the Jhelum and Indus rivers.[23] It appears, therefore, that much of the beautiful 'natural' landscape of Kashmir may be due to thousands of years of human intervention!

5

From Sindbad to Zheng He

At about the same time that Emperor Harsha was consolidating his empire and Xuan Zang was setting off on his long pilgrimage, a former merchant called Muhammad had set in motion a chain of events that would dramatically change the political and religious landscape of Arabia and eventually of the world. By the time Prophet Muhammad died in 632 AD, he already controlled much of the Arabian peninsula. However, within a century, his followers created an empire that stretched from the Iberian peninsula to Central Asia. In the eighth century, the Arabs established a toehold in Sindh by defeating Raja Dahir.

The Muslim conquest of Sindh, however, did not seem to have impacted the Indian heartland. Arab attempts at further expansion appear to have been fended off by the Rashtrakuta and the Gurjara–Pratihara kingdoms (the latter gave their name to the state of Gujarat). Arab chroniclers specifically wrote about the excellent quality of Indian cavalry. Indeed, the emerging Rajput military class appears to have made counter-raids of its own and much of Afghanistan continued to be ruled by the Hindu Shahis well into the tenth century. Thus, for the first several centuries of Islam, India's interaction with Islam was defined not by conquest but by trade.

THE AGE OF SINDBAD

Arabs had been actively involved in trade with India from pre-Islamic times. In the early seventh century, the ports along the western coast were regularly visited by Byzantines, Persians, Yemenis, Omanis, and even Ethiopians. There were merchants from the Mecca region too; Muhammad would have personally known several merchants who had visited India. The Cheraman Juma mosque in Kerala claims to have been established in 629 AD. If true, this would not just make it India's oldest mosque but also the second oldest in the world![1] While exact dates are difficult to prove, there is no doubt that the mosque is very old and was built in the very early years of Islam. It stands close to the site of ancient Muzaris. Old photographs show that the building was originally an adaptation of local temple architecture. Sadly, during renovations in 1984, the old structure was replaced with one sprouting domes and minarets in order to conform to a more 'conventional' view of Islamic architecture. It was an inexcusable act of vandalism. Now there is talk of recreating the old structure to attract tourists, but it is never quite the same thing.

With the creation of the Islamic empire, with its headquarters in Baghdad, the Arabs came to control a vast trading network. Arab merchants sailed the Mediterranean, criss-crossed the Sahara in camel caravans, traded for Chinese silks in the bazaars of Central Asia and made their way down the East African coast in search of slaves. This was the age of Sindbad the Sailor. Even if the tales of the *One Thousand and One Nights* are fictional, they retain the colourful spirit of the times.

The Iraqi port of Basra became the most important trading hub of the empire because of its proximity to the capital. Indian goods and merchants so dominated the trade that the Arabs spoke of Basra as 'belonging to al-Hind'.[2] The merchandise included perfumes, spices, ginger, textiles and medicinal substances. After the Arab conquest of Sindh, large numbers of slaves were also brought in from the province[3]. Interestingly, the most important Indian export of the period was the steel sword. The country was famous at that time for the quality of its metallurgy, and the swords used by the early Muslim armies were often of Indian origin.[4] This remained true even at the time of the Christian Crusades and the famous 'Damascus Sword' was either imported directly from India or was made using Indian techniques.

Just as in South-East Asia, there was a large diaspora of Indian merchants along the ports of the Arabian Sea and the Persian Gulf as well as in inland trading towns. Abu Zayd reports in the ninth century that 'Hindus came to Siraf and when an Arab merchant invites them to a feast, their numbers often approach or exceed a hundred'.[5] Similarly, Arab merchants came in large numbers to the ports along

India's western coast. The famous Arab historian and geographer Masudi tells us that Indian kings welcomed the traders and allowed them to build their own mosques. He tells us of a particularly large settlement of ten thousand Muslims in the district of Saymur where immigrants from Oman, Basra, Siraf and Baghdad had permanently settled. Farther south, there were a number of Arab settlements in Kerala where they mixed with local converts. Their descendants, called the Moplahs or Mappilas, account for a quarter of the state's population today.[6] By a reversal of fortune, since the 1970s, they have been going in large numbers to work in the oil-rich Arab states. Thus, the churn of people continues.

Meanwhile, farther north, Gujarat came to host the last remnants of the once-powerful Zoroastrian tradition. As discussed in Chapter 2, the origins of this tradition are closely linked to the Rig Vedic people. For fifteen hundred years or more, Zoroastrianism was the dominant religion of Persia. However, it went into sharp decline after the Islamic conquest. A small group escaped persecution and sailed to Gujarat in the eighth century. According to the *Qissa-i Sanjan*,[7] the local Hindu king allowed them to settle on the condition that they adopt the local language (Gujarati) and cease to bear arms. They were otherwise allowed full freedom in religious matters. Their descendants, known as Parsis, migrated to Mumbai in the nineteenth century to repair and build ships for the British. Some of them sailed to British-controlled Hong Kong and made large profits from participating in the opium trade with China. The Parsis then ploughed the money back into building large commercial and industrial businesses back in Mumbai.

They remain one of the country's most successful business communities.

In addition to slaves and merchants, there were several other Indian groups in the Middle East during this period, including mercenaries. According to the oral tradition of the Mohyal Brahmins of Punjab, some of their ancestors died fighting for Hussein in the Battle of Karbala, Iraq, in 680 AD. This is why this group of Hindus, also known as Husseini Brahmins, still join Shia Muslims during the ritual mourning of Muharram every year.[8] Such are the complex twists and turns of human history.

At about the same time, another group from central India travelled west, across the Middle East, to Europe. We know them today as the Gypsies or the Roma. The link between the Roma and India has long been debated on linguistic and cultural grounds, but genetic studies have now confirmed it.[9] We do not know why this group left the subcontinent, but it is possible that they were a group of stranded soldiers from the Gujara–Pratihara armies fighting the Turks and Arabs in Sindh. Alternatively, they may have always been a nomadic group that the circumstances of history caused to drift ever westwards. In 1971, at the World Romani Conference near London, the Roma adopted a blue and green flag for their nomadic nation. At the centre of the flag, they placed a wheel— the symbol of the Chakravartin. In some ways, the Roma have the greatest claim to this symbol, for their wheels can truly roll in all directions.

Of course, the exchange of goods, people and ideas was not just with the outside world. There was a great deal of internal exchange, with several examples of how ideas emanating from one part of India spread quickly across the rest of the country during this period. The eighth-century philosopher Adi Shankaracharya, for instance, was from Kerala in the extreme south, but he travelled all over the country. His ideas would become very influential across the subcontinent and beyond.

Similarly, the Shakti tradition associated with the worship of Goddess Durga and her incarnations originated in ancient times in the eastern provinces of Bengal and Assam. However, by the medieval period, the distribution of the fifty-two shakti-peeths[10] (i.e. pilgrimage sites related to this tradition) came to be spread across the subcontinent—from Kamakhya in Assam to Hinglaj in Baluchistan, and from Jwalamukhi in Himachal Pradesh to Jaffna in Sri Lanka. There are even Shakti temples in South East Asia. The ninth-century Prambanan temple complex in central Java, Indonesia, has a shrine dedicated to the Goddess Durga slaying the demon Mahishasura. The exquisitely carved idol would not look out of place, twelve centuries later, at the annual Durga Puja festival in modern Kolkata.

THE TURKIC INVASIONS

In many ways, life in the subcontinent till the beginning of the eleventh century remained more or less a continuation of earlier times. Maritime trade continued to flourish in the southern ports even as foreign scholars continued to flock to Nalanda to study. There had been changes in architecture, technology and style, but the cities of the subcontinent would have been broadly familiar to a visitor from a thousand years earlier. However, the country was about to experience a major shift.

In the late tenth century, waves of Turkic invasions began to erode the Hindu–Buddhist kingdoms of Afghanistan. In 963 AD, the Turks captured the strategically important town of Ghazni. From there they steadily ate away at the Hindu Shahi kingdom of Kabul and pushed them into Punjab. The Shahis doggedly fought back for decades but, on 27 November 1001, they were routed by Mahmud of Ghazni in a battle near Peshawar. The Shahi king Jayapala was so distraught that he abdicated in favour of his son and committed suicide by climbing on to his own funeral pyre.[11] The Shahis would continue to fight the Turks, but they were now a spent force.

Over the next quarter-century, Mahmud would make seventeen raids into India, many of them directed at wealthy temple towns such as Mathura and Nagarkot. His most infamous raid was against the temple of Somnath, Gujarat, in 1026 AD. It is said that this single attack left over fifty thousand of its defenders dead and yielded twenty million dirhams worth of gold, silver and gems. Although the Somnath temple would be destroyed and rebuilt many times, it is the raid of Mahmud Ghazni that is still remembered most vividly.

The temple that stands on the site today was built in the early 1950s. Its symbolic importance can be gauged from the fact that its reconstruction was one of the first major projects initiated by the Indian Republic. Standing right on the sea-shore, the temple is a wonderful place to watch the sun set even as the sound of the evening 'arati' drifts across from the inner sanctum. Yet, something of the horror of that medieval massacre seems to linger in the air. Barely half a kilometre away is the spot where the Pandav warrior Arjun is said to have conducted the last rites of Krishna. Three rivers meet the sea here—one of them named after the Saraswati.

The Turkish raids were no doubt inspired partly by religious zeal and partly by the lure of plunder. However, it is often forgotten that one of their most important motivations was the capture of slaves.[12] Over the next few centuries, hundreds of thousands of Indian slaves—particularly from West Punjab and Sindh—would be marched into Afghanistan and then sold in the bazaars of Central Asia and the Middle East. Unused to the extreme cold of the Afghan mountains, they died in such large number that the range would come to be known as the Hindukush meaning 'Killer of Hindus'.

Despite the shock of Mahmud Ghazni's raids, however, there was no equivalent to the Mauryan or Gupta responses to foreign invasion. The last great Hindu empire of North India—that of the Gujara–Pratiharas—was in steep decline and the creative heart of Indic civilization had shifted south of the Vindhyas. The most powerful Indian kingdom of that time, the Cholas, ruled in the far south and would not have been concerned with the gathering clouds in the North West. Meanwhile, freed from the political and cultural domination of the Gangetic plains, Central India experienced a cultural and economic boom. This was the age of the remarkable Raja Bhoj, the warrior-scholar who ruled much of Central India and of the Chandelas of Bundelkhand who built the temples of Khajuraho.

Academic historians tend to ignore Raja Bhoj but the oral tradition of Central India is full of stories and ballads about him. It is difficult to ascertain the veracity of all these tales but one cannot deny the geographical importance of this king. He rebuilt the Somnath temple, repulsed a number of Turkish raids and constructed one of the largest forts in the world at

Mandu in Madhya Pradesh. However, his most visible legacy is the huge lake that he created using an earthen dam in Bhopal, a city that is also named after him. Before the infamous industrial accident of 1984, the city of Bhopal was best known for this body of water. It is a testimony to the skills of the medieval engineers that the lake still exists a thousand years later. It is proof that big dams work well in the Malwa plateau. Tectonics and silt often make them unwise in the rest of India.

Farther north, the Chandelas of Bundelkhand were originally feudatories of the Gujara–Pratiharas but carved out a small but vigorous kingdom for themselves when the latter went into decline in the tenth century. They celebrated their successes by building the famous temples of Khajuraho, a UNESCO World Heritage Site. The Kandariya Mahadev temple, the largest in the complex, is said to have been built after the Chandelas succeeded in fending off Mahmud Ghazni himself.

All discussion about Khajuraho tends to focus on the erotic sculptures that adorn some of the temples. However, if one actually visits the temples, it is quickly apparent that the most striking sculptures depict lions or lion-like dragons. Several of them are shown locked in mortal combat with a Chandela king or warrior (occasionally women warriors). Just like the Mauryan emperors, the Chandelas liked to use the lion as a symbol of their power. Equally telling is the total absence of tigers in the sculptures. I found this particularly intriguing given that Panna Tiger Reserve is barely a twenty-minute drive away from Khajuraho. Was this lion country during medieval times? Or, was the tiger simply not considered a worthy symbol of royal power?

For a century and half after Mahmud's raids, the Turks were largely restricted to West Punjab. If anything, there was a sense of complacency. That changed in 1192 when Muhammad Ghori defeated Prithviraj Chauhan, the Rajput king of Delhi and Ajmer, in the Second Battle of Tarain (150 km from Delhi in the modern state of Haryana).

The Turks occupied Delhi and then embarked on a series of conquests that radically changed the political, social and urban geography of India. By 1194, Varanasi and Kannauj were captured and sacked. The latter, then the largest city in northern India, would never really recover. Within a few years, the university of Nalanda was destroyed by Bakhtiyar Khilji, its library was torched and most of its scholars put to death. The scene was chronicled by Minhaj-ud-din, a judge from Ghor, who had accompanied the invading army:

> The great number of the inhabitants of that place were Brahmans . . . and they were all slain. There were a great number of books there; and when all these books came under the observation of the Mussalmans they summoned a number of Hindus that they might give them information respecting the import of these books; but the whole of the Hindus had been killed . . .[13]

While there were many Brahmin scholars at Nalanda, the bulk of those massacred were probably Buddhist monks. A few survivors would linger, but most would flee to Tibet where their traditions would be kept alive till the Chinese take-over of the mid-twentieth century. After Nalanda, Bakhtiyar Khilji attacked and completely destroyed Vikramshila, another famous Buddhist university. The practice of Buddhism in the subcontinent, already in decline, would collapse after these devastating attacks. In 1235, Sultan Iltutmish laid waste Ujjain—once the secondary capital of the Gupta empire and a major centre for mathematics, literature, astronomy and Hindu philosophy. It is worth noting that at exactly the same time as these universities were being destroyed, the University of Oxford was being established on the other side of the planet.

By the end of the thirteenth century, armies led by generals like Malik Kafur would be making raids into the deep south. It was a very bloody period in Indian history—ancient cities, universities and temples were laid waste and hundreds of thousands, probably millions, were massacred. Anyone who doubts this should read the *Tarikh-i-Farishtah*.[14] Thus ended the second cycle of urbanization that had begun in the Gangetic plains during the Iron Age.

A few sparks of the classical period would remain alive in the city of Vijaynagar in the far South and in the even more faraway kingdoms of South East Asia. However, India was embarking on a new cycle of urbanization that derived many of its elements from Central Asia and Persia. This book is not meant as a comprehensive history of empires, individuals and events. I will, therefore, deal with this cycle of urbanization largely through the evolution of its most prominent city— Delhi.

THE MANY CITIES OF DELHI

The area in and around Delhi has been inhabited by humans from the Stone Age—stone implements have been found scattered in the ridges of the Aravalli range. The Rig Vedic people would also have been familiar with the region since it falls in the eastern corner of the Sapta-Sindhu landscape. There are even scattered remains of small settlements from the late Harappan age. Perhaps, this was one of the places where the Harappans settled as they abandoned the drying Saraswati and shifted to the Gangetic plains.

Since then, cities have been built, abandoned, pillaged and rebuilt many times on this site. Depending on how you count, between eight and sixteen Delhis have been built through history. Thus, the terms 'Old Delhi' and 'New Delhi' have meant different things at different points in time. So when William Sleeman visited the city in 1836, he referred to Shahjehanabad, what we now call Old Delhi, as New Delhi[15]. To him, Old Delhi referred to the ruins that were scattered from Mehrauli to Purana Qila—the area that is now occupied by what we call New Delhi. Nevertheless, the current cycle of expansion is remarkable even by standards of the city's long history. After Delhi was sacked by the British in 1858, its urban population fell to a mere 154,417 as per the 1868 census.[16] Today, the urban system of Delhi, the National Capital Region, is home to almost twenty million people and it continues to grow and evolve rapidly.

As we have already discussed in Chapter 3, many of the events of the Mahabharata relate to the area around Delhi. Indraprastha, the capital of the Pandavas, is said to have been situated in Delhi along the banks of the Yamuna. According to a strong tradition, its site was under the sixteenth-century fortress of Purana Qila (literally Old Fort). The tradition was given credence by the fact that a village called Indrapat used to occupy the mound. Archaeological excavations inside the fort have revealed a significant Late Iron Age settlement that continued to be occupied till the Gupta period. There is a small museum in Purana Qila that shows photographs and artifacts from the excavations. However, it is impossible to prove if this was indeed the city mentioned in the epic. Nothing has been found so far that obviously matches the descriptions of Indraprastha—no palace or audience hall that would have attracted the envy of the Kauravas. Perhaps the remains lie hidden under a later building or perhaps they were swept away by a flood on the Yamuna. It is impossible to say. Nonetheless, we can see that Delhi was an important settlement for many centuries. An Ashokan rock inscription was found near the Kalkaji temple in 1996, suggesting that Delhi may have included several habitations in addition to that at Purana Qila.

The first Delhi of which we have definite historical knowledge was built by the Tomar Rajputs, who made it their headquarters in the eighth century. Their first settlement was at Suraj Kund in the extreme south of Delhi. Then, as now, the water supply was a major concern, and a large stone dam built by the Tomars still stands. The nearby village of Anangpur recalls the name of Raja Anang Pal. A stream from the dam feeds a stepped tank that was probably linked to a temple dedicated to the Sun God—hence the name Suraj Kund (Pool of the Sun). Unfortunately, the lake is often dry now because urbanization and illegal quarrying have disrupted the water-catchment.

In the eleventh century, the Tomars moved to a more defensible position farther west and constructed a large fort—Lal Kot, meaning Red Fort. Thus, Shah Jehan's seventeenth-century Red Fort was not the first to bear that name. To mark his place in history, Anang Pal also added his name to the Iron Pillar.

A century later, the Chauhans of Ajmer took control of the city and substantially expanded it. Now renamed Qila Rai Pithora, this was the capital of Prithviraj Chauhan. I was pleasantly surprised to find that large sections of the walls of this city have survived, although almost no one visits them. Anyone interested can drive to the northern end of Mehrauli village and will find them just past Adam Khan's tomb. The approach is not pretty and is used as an open toilet by a nearby slum. The visitor is therefore advised to walk through one of the shanties and climb on top of the walls. The walk on top of the nine-hundred-year-old ramparts is beautiful. As one leaves the village behind, one is surrounded by a thick forest of thorny Kikar trees. The walls extend a couple of kilometres and along the way one can distinguish towers and other structures including a major gateway. Perhaps Prithviraj used this gate as he bade farewell to the beautiful Samyukta as he rode out to face Muhammad Ghori. The urban landscape of Delhi can just be discerned beyond the trees even as the Qutub Minar looks sternly on.

When the Turks captured Rai Pithora, they made it their Indian headquarters and began to remodel it for their own use. The Qutub Minar complex, a UNESCO World Heritage site, has some of the oldest Islamic buildings in northern India. At its centre is the mosque built by Ghori's slave-general Qutubuddin Aibak. An inscription on the east gate of the mosque tells us that it was built by demolishing twenty-seven Hindu–Jain temples.[17] Defaced idols can still be discerned amongst the columns. Interestingly, the Iron Pillar was allowed to continue standing on one side of the mosque courtyard. Perhaps it was an effort by the new rulers to appropriate ancient symbols of power. It is also possible that Qutubuddin wanted to let it stand in the shadow of his own great column, the 72.5m-high stone tower of the Qutub Minar, a medieval example of 'mine is bigger than yours'. It is a truly impressive structure even by modern standards. When the Moroccan traveller Ibn Batuta visited Delhi over a century later, he was impressed by both the spectacular height of the tower and the unique metallurgy of the pillar.[18] He also tells us of how a later sultan wanted to build a tower twice as high but the project was abandoned. The remains of Alauddin Khilji's failed attempt can still be seen nearby.

At the beginning of the fourteenth century, Alauddin Khilji built the new fort of Siri at the site of a military camp north-east of the existing city. The main urban cluster continued to be in the old city but the sultan, who was paranoid about assassins, probably felt safer in the new fort. Unfortunately, within a few years of it being built, Siri fell to a Mongol raid. Alauddin managed to push the invaders back and then took care to strengthen the fortifications. This was a wise move because the Mongols were soon back. This time they captured the main city and pillaged it. However, Alauddin held out in Siri for months till the Mongols decided to go back. There are only a few stretches of walls and other buildings that remain of Siri. Its site is now occupied by the urban village of Shahpur Jat. It is one of the many villages that live on in the urban fabric of modern Delhi and is home to numerous small offices and designer workshops. The rest of Siri is covered by the

Asian Games Village that was built to house athletes for the event in 1982.

Water supply has always been a major issue for Delhi. In order to supply the expanding city, Alauddin Khilji built a large reservoir called Hauz Khas. It still exists and is surrounded by a beautiful park, a wonderful place to go for a walk on a sunny winter afternoon. Overlooking the waterbody are the remains of an old Madrassa (Islamic religious school) built by a later sultan and the urban village of Hauz Khas. Since the1990s, this village has transformed itself into a warren of expensive boutiques and trendy bars. This is ironic because Alauddin was a severe man who strictly controlled the prices of all goods and forbade the consumption and sale of alcohol.[19] Such is the revenge of history.

The Khilji dynasty barely survived a few years after Alauddin and was replaced by another Turkic dynasty, the Tughlaqs. They also decided to build a new city, called Tughlaqabad, and chose a location to the east of the existing city. It is unclear why the first Tughlaq Sultan wanted to build yet another city and why he chose the specific location. Perhaps it was just to satisfy his ego. Ibn Batuta tells an interesting story that may or may not be true. Evidently, when the Sultan was just a nobleman serving the Khiljis, he had suggested to the king that this would be a good place to build a city. The incumbent had sarcastically replied, 'When you are Sultan, build it.' Thus, it was one of the first building projects of the Tughlaqs.

Although overgrown and encroached upon, the extensive fortifications and other remains of Tughlaqabad are very impressive. Excavations in the 1990s revealed a secret passage connected to the palace, with elaborate passageways, hidden storage rooms and disguised entrance and exit. The exit is a small opening on the outer wall that looks like an innocuous drain. However, despite its rather solid appearance, the city was only occupied for a few years before being abandoned, probably because its water-supply was not secure.

Muhammad Tughlaq was the second sultan of the dynasty. He decided to shift the capital a thousand kilometers south to Daulatabad in 1326 AD. The fort held a strategic position on the Southern Road or Dakshina Path, and was ideally located for making raids into southern India. Therefore, the Sultan's decision was understandable but for the fact that Muhammad insisted that every single inhabitant had to move with him. We have a macabre tale about how an old beggar was too feeble to make the journey. The Sultan had him tied to a cart and dragged along for forty days. Only his feet arrived in Daulatabad.

However, the Sultan soon changed his mind and the entire population was made to trudge back to Delhi. Muhammad now decided to expand the recently repopulated city and invited settlers from the rest of his empire and from Central Asia. He built a set of walls that connected the old city of Lal Kot with the Khilji fortress of Siri. This enclosed a very large area that would be the next city of Delhi—Jahanpanah. Note that the older cities continued to be inhabited. Even some parts of the abandoned Tughlaqabad were used for storage and to house garrisons. Thus, Jahanpanah was probably not entirely built up but contained open areas and even farming communities within the walls. Nonetheless, a massive new palace-complex was built. It is this patchwork of urban settlements that Ibn Batuta saw when he visited Delhi.

Ibn Batuta is one of the greatest travel writers of all time. Originally from Tangier in Morocco, he was a near-contemporary of Marco Polo, and travelled across the known world through North Africa, the Middle East, Central Asia and India, and eventually to China. He then made his way back to Morocco before dictating the story of an adventure that had lasted almost three decades. When he arrived in Delhi, Muhammad Tughlaq ruled from his new palace in Jahanpanah. This was a time when the erratic despot was trying to build up the prestige of his court by importing learned Muslim scholars. Ibn Batuta soon found himself a lucrative position and spent several years in the city.

He has left us a very vivid description of the Tughlaq court. He tells us that one had to pass through three gates to enter the Sultan's audience hall. There was a platform in front of the first gate where the executioners sat. When a man was sentenced to death, he would be executed outside this gate and his body would be left there for three days as a warning to others. The first gate also had a number of trumpeters and pipe-players. Whenever a notable arrived, they would blow the trumpets and loudly announce the person's name. Between the first and second gates, Ibn Batuta tells us, were platforms occupied by large numbers of palace guards.

At the second gate sat the royal ushers in gilded caps, the chief usher wielding a golden mace. Inside this gate was a large reception hall where people could sit as they awaited their turn. The visitor would then walk up to the third and final gate where scribes entered the person's name, time of arrival and other details. A nobleman who had failed to attend the court for more than three days without a valid excuse was not allowed beyond this point except by the Sultan's explicit permission. Beyond this gate was the main audience hall, a large wooden structure of 'a thousand pillars'.[20]

The Sultan sat on a raised throne supported by cushions. An attendant stood behind the king and flicked a flywhisk to chase away the flies. (Well, you cannot leave dead bodies lying around on the front porch for days and not expect flies.) In front of the Sultan would be members of the royal family, the nobility, the religious establishment, the judiciary and so on. Each person was accorded a position according to his status. We are told that when the Sultan arrived and sat down, the whole court rose and shouted 'Bismillah!'. A hundred of his armed personal guards stood on either side of the throne. Clearly the Sultan was taking no chances.

Most of the nobility and senior officials would have been foreigners—Turks but also Khurasanis, Egyptians, Syrians and so on. Ibn Batuta tells us that Muhammad Tughlaq systematically gave high positions to foreigners. He was not unusually biased. The Turks would have considered themselves as an army of occupation and Indians—both Hindus and local Muslims—would have been treated with contempt. Indeed, there were periods when Indians would have been tolerated within the walls of medieval Delhi only as slaves, menial workers and other service providers. This attitude only changed under the Afghan Suris in the mid-1500s and was institutionalized under Mughal Emperor Akbar. It was a slow transformation. As Percival Spear points out, even under Akbar, most of the nobility was foreign-born.[21]

Ibn Batuta tells us that from time to time, the Tughlaq Sultan held banquets. All the guests would be seated by rank.

Each person was first given a cup of 'candy-water' that they were expected to drink before they ate. Then, the food would be brought from the kitchen in a procession headed by the Chief Usher holding a golden mace and his deputy holding a silver mace. As they walked by, they would cry out 'Bismillah!'. The food consisted of rounds of unleavened bread, roast meats, chicken, rice, sweets and, interestingly, samosas. After the meal, each person was given a tin cup of barley water to settle the stomach. Finally, everyone was served paan (betel leaves and areca-nuts). When the meal was finished, the chamberlains cried 'Bismillah!' and everyone stood up.

We are not sure exactly where Muhammad Tughlaq's palace stood but the most likely site is the enigmatic ruins of Bijay Mandal, very close to IIT Gate. Very few tourists visit the site and it appears to be used mostly by the teenage boys of nearby Begumpur village to steal a forbidden drink—there are empty beer bottles everywhere. Just behind the Bijay Mandal complex is the impressive Begumpur Mosque which may have once served as the imperial mosque but, again, is rarely visited by tourists. I found the place entirely to myself on a sunny winter afternoon and sat there thinking about Ibn Batuta and the unpredictable Sultan.

Ibn Batuta grew to fear the volatile Sultan over time. He would eventually get himself assigned to an embassy to China and flee. We are told that, as the embassy made its way south, it was repeatedly attacked by bandits. Ibn Batuta tells us that he was captured and nearly killed before being set free. The fact that even an imperial embassy could not safely travel on a major highway shows us the degree to which the interiors of the country had been plunged into chaos by the Turkic invasions.

After many more adventures, Ibn Batuta did eventually make his way to China. Despite his fame in the Arab world, his adventures are barely remembered in India outside of the world of specialist historians and scholars. His memory is now limited to a mention in a somewhat inane but popular Hindi song about his shoe!

One would have thought that after having built three capitals—Tughlaqabad, Daulatabad and Jahanpanah—the Tughlaq dynasty would have grown tired of building. Not so. Muhammad's successor Feroze Shah Tughlaq was an even more enthusiastic builder. He built many new structures as well as repaired many old ones. He also extended the city northwards by building a fortified palace-complex along the Yamuna called Feroze Shah Kotla. We know that the older Delhis were still inhabited, so it is possible that this was just a royal suburb like Versailles.

The enigmatic ruins of Feroze Shah Kotla are near the busy ITO crossing and just behind the offices of India's leading newspapers. They were repeatedly cannibalized for building material by builders of later Delhis. Nonetheless, the site contains a three-storeyed pavilion topped by the Ashokan pillar that had been carefully brought there by the Sultan. The complex is said to be inhabited by djinns and people, mostly Sufi Muslims, visit the site to light lamps to assuage and petition them. One will see small offerings and walls blackened by the smoke from the lamps. Some of the faithful tie colourful strings to the grill put up by the Archaeological Survey to protect the Ashokan pillar. Thus we have the impossible combination of modern Indians paying their respects to an ancient imperial pillar in order to petition medieval spirits.

Feroze Shah ascended the throne in middle-age and ruled till he died after several years of illness at the age of eighty-one. As with Ashoka, his empire was already weakening while he was alive and, after his death, there was a quick succession of ineffective rulers. The Turko–Mongol marauder Taimur the Lame (also known as Tamerlane) saw his opportunity and swept into the country from Central Asia in 1398. He defeated the Sultan's army with ease and entered Delhi. Exclusively Muslim enclaves were spared, everything else was pillaged and the entire Hindu population was either massacred or taken away as slaves.[22] Taimur later wrote in his diary, 'I was desirous of sparing them but could not succeed as it is the will of God that this calamity should befall this city'. Somehow, I am not convinced.

Not surprisingly, after this episode, Delhi went into a period of decline. For the next one and a half centuries, the most important city in India would be Vijaynagar in the far south. We will return to it later. Meanwhile, the Tughlaqs were replaced by a succession of minor dynasties. Although the empire was much diminished, Delhi's patchwork of urban habitations continued to be a political and economic hub of some importance. Like all dynasties that have ruled this city before and after, the rulers of this period also built grand memorials to themselves. One can visit some of them at Lodhi Gardens in the heart of New Delhi, one of the most beautiful city parks in the world. The rich and powerful of modern India come here for their walks and to discuss the affairs of the world. It is also a good place to watch the extraordinary variety of birds that inhabit Delhi.

In 1526, a Turko–Mongol adventurer called Babur defeated

the Sultan of Delhi in what is known as the First Battle of Panipat. We know a great deal about Babur because he has left us a fascinating account of his life in the form of a diary written in Turkish, the *Tuzuk-i-Baburi*. He was a shameless opportunist, but comes across as a loveable rogue. His enemies may not have seen him as loveable though—I suppose there are some advantages to writing your own history.

Babur had impeccable lineage. He was a direct descendant of Ghengis Khan from his mother's side and from Taimur the Lame on his father's side. However, Taimur's empire had disintegrated by the time Babur was born. At the age of twelve, he inherited a tiny kingdom in the beautiful Ferghana valley in Central Asia. Babur tells us that it could barely support an army of three to four thousand men.[23] This did not deter him from repeatedly trying to capture Taimur's capital of Samarkand. He even succeeded briefly, but could not hold on to it. Eventually, the Uzbeks chased him out and he made his way south with a tiny band of followers. Ever the adventurer, he won and lost many battles along the way till he gained control of Kabul. It was then that he saw the opportunity of making a raid into India.

It was an audacious plan because his army was much smaller than the Sultan's, but Babur had a secret weapon—matchlock guns. This was the first time that guns would be used in North India. (South India had already tasted Portuguese artillery a few decades earlier.) Babur decisively defeated the Sultan and quickly went on to beat off all other rivals, including the Rajputs. Thus was born the Mughal (i.e. Mongol) empire in India. Note that the dynasty did not use this term to describe itself. Rather, the Mughals preferred to call themselves

'Gurkhani'. This is after the title of 'Gurkhan' meaning 'son-in-law' that Taimur liked to use after he was married to a princess from Ghengiz Khan's dynasty.

Although Babur had finally conquered a significant kingdom, he always hankered for Samarkand. His opinion of India is rather unflattering: 'Hindustan is a place of little charm. There is no beauty in its people, no graceful social intercourse, no poetic talent or understanding, no etiquette, nobility or manliness. The arts and crafts have no harmony or symmetry. There are no good horses, meat, grapes, melons, or other fruit. There is no ice, cold water, good food or bread in the markets'. At least, Babur was very candid about why he was in India: 'The one nice aspect of Hindustan is that it is a large country with lots of gold and money'.[24]

Babur died less than five years after he came to India. His empire was inherited by his son Humayun, who started construction on the next Delhi—Dinpanah. Built just south of Feroze Shah Kotla, along the river Yamuna, it included a citadel that we now know as Purana Qila (or Old Fort). As we have already discussed, it was said to be the site of ancient Indraprastha. There is nothing to suggest that this historical association had anything to do with the choice of location. In addition to the citadel, there was a fortified city. Unfortunately, very little has survived of the city of Dinpanah except one of its impressive gates—the Lal Darwaza (or Red Gate). One can see this imposing structure across the road from Purana Qila and Delhi Zoo.

Humayun did not complete either Dinpanah or Purana Qila. He was chased out by a group of Afghan rebels led by Sher Shah Suri and escaped with his family to Persia. It was

Sher Shah who completed Purana Qila. He was also a
remarkable administrator who carried out many key reforms
during his short reign. He re-organized tax collection, minted
the first silver Rupiya (precursor to the modern Rupee), and
revived the ancient city of Pataliputra (Patna). He also rebuilt
the ancient Uttara Path highway from Punjab to Bengal.
Known as 'Sadak-e-Azam' (or Great Road), it would be a
major artery of the Mughal period; the British would know it
as the Grand Trunk Road and it is now part of the Golden
Quadrilateral highway network.

If Sher Shah Suri had lived longer, it is possible that we
would not remember Mughal rule as anything more than one
more Central Asian raid. However, he died in a gun powder-
related accident after just five years on the throne and
Humayun was able to come back and re-occupy Delhi.
Humayun too did not enjoy the Purana Qila for long, dying in
a curious incident. He had gone to watch the rise of Venus
from the roof of his library. One his way down the steep stairs,
he tripped on his robe and died from the fall. Humayun's
library building survives in Purana Qila. The stairway,
however, is not open to the public and visitors trying to re-
enact Humayun's last moments will be disappointed.

A thirteen-year-old Akbar now became the new ruler. He is
usually called the third Mughal Emperor but, in reality, it was
he who created the foundations of a stable empire. He not
only continued Sher Shah's reforms but also institutionalized
a more liberal relationship with the country's Hindu majority.[25]
This was a major step in the evolution of Indian civilization.
Although it is today considered politically incorrect to see it in
these terms, it is difficult to deny that, before Akbar, there was

a 'clash of civilizations' element to Hindu–Muslim interaction in North India. This is evident from both the writings of Muslim authors of that time as well as from the Hindu response to the Turkish invaders.

Take for instance the dogged resistance to the Turks by the Rajput-ruled kingdom of Mewar in southern Rajasthan. The rulers of Mewar did not see themselves merely as kings but explicitly as the custodians of Hindu civilization embodied in the temple of Eklingji, a manifestation of Shiva. The deity was considered the real king of Mewar and this is why its rulers did not use the title of Maharaja (which means Great King) but that of Rana (i.e. Custodian or Prime Minister). It is important to recognize this if one is to understand why Mewar kept up continuous resistance to the Sultans despite suffering extreme hardship over centuries. On three separate occasions, its capital Chittaur was defended to the last man and, even after it fell, the struggle was sustained in the hills. One cannot explain away this behaviour merely in rational political terms.

In order to comprehend this state of mind, one must visit the shrine of Eklingji, less than an hour's drive from Udaipur. It is a thousand-year-old temple complex wedged into a hillside. If one walks around in the surrounding Aravalli hills, it becomes obvious that they are heavily fortified. The fortifications of Chittaur, Kumbhalgarh and even Udaipur are within a few hours' drive. Mewar must have been the most militarized place in the medieval world. It tells of a population that considered itself under siege and was prepared to hold out to the end.

By the time Akbar appeared on the scene, however, centuries of conflict had left both sides exhausted. Thinkers like Guru

Nanak, the founder of the Sikh tradition, had already put forward arguments for civilizational accommodation. Emperor Akbar probably had a naturally liberal disposition, but his thoughts also evolved with time. The tipping point may have been the siege of Chittaur, the capital of Mewar, in 1568. The fort fell after many months. The defenders fought literally to the last man and the womenfolk committed ritual suicide (*jauhar*). Akbar massacred an additional twenty thousand non-combatants. Like Ashoka, eighteen centuries earlier, he may have been shocked by his own savagery.

We now see Akbar laying greater emphasis on reconciliation between the two cultures. In 1555, the Mughal nobility or Omrah, consisted of fifty-one foreign-born Muslims (Uzbeks, Persians, Turks, Afghans). By 1580, the number had jumped to 222 but included forty-three Rajputs and a similar number of Indian Muslims.[26] Not everyone was convinced. On one hand, the orthodox Muslims were very unhappy with the emperor's liberal attitude. On the other hand, the rulers of Mewar would continue to view him with suspicion and keep up their resistance (perhaps not surprising given their recent experience). The ballads of how Rana Pratap and his army of Bhil tribesmen fought the Mughals can still be heard in the Aravallis of Mewar. His coat of armour and that of his horse Chetak are prominently displayed in the Udaipur City Palace Museum. It would be more than a generation before Mewar would accept a non-antagonistic relationship with the Mughals.

Sadly for Delhi, Akbar shifted the capital south to Agra and then to a newly built city called Fatehpur Sikri. The latter took fifteen years to build but it was abandoned after only fourteen years because, like Tughlaqabad, its water supply was deemed unreliable. The capital moved back to Agra. Meanwhile, Delhi remained an important city but would have to play second fiddle to Agra till Akbar's grandson built Shahjehanabad (Old Delhi) a century later. Akbar did, however, make one important addition to Delhi's skyline— the tomb of his father. Humayun's tomb is a grand affair and

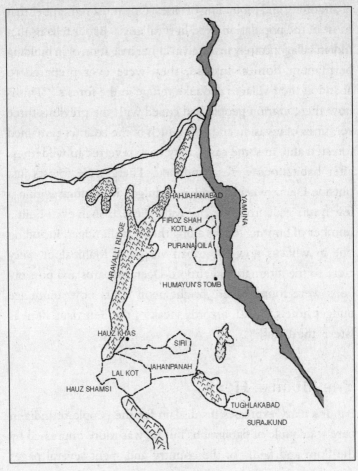

Medieval Delhi

an architectural precursor to the Taj Mahal. Since it is not usually mobbed by tourists like the Taj, it is a much more satisfying place to linger and retains the air of an emperor's tomb.

I do not want to leave the reader with the impression that medieval India was only about the building, pillaging, abandoning and rebuilding of cities. One must remember that most of the population lived in rural areas. Babur tells us that Indian villagers rarely invested in either irrigation or in building permanent homes. Instead, they were ever prepared to abandon their villages and take refuge in the forests.[27] This is how the common people had coped with the previous three centuries of invasion and war. Much of the country remained forested and, in some cases, may have reverted to wilderness after habitations were abandoned. There were forests just outside Delhi, where its rulers indulged in hunting within a few hours' ride from the city walls. Feroze Shah even built a number of hunting lodges along the Aravalli ridges, including one in what is now the urban village of Mahipalpur, very close to the international airport. Deer, leopards and possibly lions were found where bright neon lights now announce budget hotels. British records speak of the 'Hurriana lion' as late as the 1820s.[28]

THE MUGHAL HUNT

Babur's diary expresses his disdain for the people of India in barely a couple of paragraphs but he was more impressed by the flora and fauna of the country and spent several pages describing them. Babur tells us about peacocks, elephants and river dolphins. He was particularly intrigued by the rhinoceros that he encountered in forests near Peshawar. It is interesting that rhinos were found so far to the west in the sixteenth century. They are now found only in the swampy grasslands of Assam, North Bengal and Nepal's Terai regions. Oddly, Babur does not mention the big cats. It is possible that he had encountered lions and cheetahs in Afghanistan and north-eastern Iran and did not think of them as uniquely Indian.

The Mughals were enthusiastic hunters whose expeditions are recorded in numerous writings and in paintings. They hunted a wide array of animals including nilgai, blackbuck, birds and, of course, lions. Note that there are relatively fewer accounts and paintings related to hunting tigers. This may merely reflect the fact that the Mughals did most of their hunting in the north-west of the country, which was lion, rather than tiger, country. We know that there were important hunting grounds near Agra, Delhi, and Bhatinda in Punjab. Most of these areas are now densely populated and intensively farmed but Bernier tells us that there were large expanses of uncultivated land near Delhi and Agra as well as on the road to Lahore. It is estimated that barely 27.5 per cent of Agra suba, at the heart of the empire, was cultivated in 1600.[29] The human population of India at that time was around 116 million. This means that there were large areas that were available to wildlife and several tracts were reserved exclusively for the royal hunt. The association of the lion with the power of the State remained. The hunting of lions was reserved for the king and the royal family and was closed to others, except by special permission.

There are many stories about Emperor Akbar's lion hunts.

On one occasion in 1568, Akbar went hunting in the Mewat region near Alwar, south of Gurgaon. A lion emerged and was quickly slain by a hail of arrows shot by his companions. Akbar was annoyed and ordered that should another lion emerge, he would tackle it himself. At that very moment, another lion did emerge and the emperor shot it in the eye with an arrow. The enraged animal charged but Akbar could not get a good shot even though he had dismounted from his horse. In the excitement of the moment, one of the courtiers shot an arrow that infuriated the lion who mauled the man. The animal had to be finished off by other courtiers.[30]

As one can see, Akbar was quite ready to take personal risks and, in his younger days, would hunt on horseback or even on foot. His main indulgence was the use of a large number of trained cheetahs to help him in the chase. Later in life he would keep a stable of a thousand of these beasts. Over time, however, the emperors grew used to hunting from the relative safety of an elephant's back and to the use of increasingly accurate guns. In a single hunting expedition to Rupbas near Agra in February–March 1610, Akbar's successor, Jehangir, and his companions killed seven lions, seventy Nilgai, fifty-one blackbuck, eighty-two other animals, 129 birds and 1023 fish—all this within a fifty-six day period. It was still a risky activity as illustrated by a story from the same year.

On a hunt in 1610 in Bari near Agra, one of Emperor Jehangir's courtiers, Anup Rai, came across a half-devoured cow and traced a lion in the thicket. The animal was surrounded and the emperor was informed. Jehangir rushed to the spot and set up his musket on a stand. He fired twice and missed. The lion charged and the emperor's retinue bolted and, according to him, even trampled on him in the panic! Anup Rai saved Jehangir's life by battling the lion to the ground with his bare hands till Prince Khurram killed the animal with a sword. That a Hindu Rajput was not just accompanying the royal family on a hunt but was willing to risk his life for a Muslim king—Taimur's direct descendant, no less—shows how the relations between Hindus and Muslims had evolved over the preceding half-century. Jehangir gave Anup Rai the title Ani Rai Singhdalan, meaning Commander of Troops and Lion Crusher.[31]

A few years after the above events, the first English ambassador arrived at the Mughal court. Sir Thomas Roe was a distinguished diplomat and was in India from 1615 to 1619. He became a close friend of Emperor Jehangir and was even his drinking partner on several occasions. However, this does not mean that he was given blanket permission to freely kill lions. In 1617, a lion and a wolf made nightly raids on Roe's camp near Mandu and killed a number of his sheep and goats. However, it was forbidden for him to hurt the animals and had to send for the monarch's special leave. It was eventually granted but the lion escaped. The wolf was not so lucky.[32]

Roe tells us that the lion was a very important part of royal imagery and one of the royal standards had a lion and the rising sun. This symbolism was shared with both the Shahs of Iran as well as the indigenous Hindu tradition. The Mughals were conscious that they were inheritors of an ancient imperial dream and Emperor Jehangir inserted his own inscription in Persian on the Mauryan pillar in Allahabad. Thus, the column has inscriptions by three of India's most powerful emperors—Ashoka, Samudragupta and Jehangir—a continuity maintained over eighteen centuries! What is going on? Whether one takes Jehangir's inscription on the Mauryan pillar or the effort to link Akbar to Kalhana's history of Kashmir, the Mughals were trying to build the foundations of their empire in India within the framework of India's civilization. Therefore, they were systematically inserting themselves into civilizational memory. Notwithstanding Feroze Shah Tughlaq's interest in Mauryan pillars, this was a radical shift away from how earlier Delhi Sultans saw themselves.

THE VOYAGES OF ADMIRAL ZHENG HE

While northern India was suffering from waves of invasion from Central Asia, the world of Indian Ocean trade continued to flourish. Both Marco Polo and Ibn Batuta were witness to this. However, under the surface, the role of Indians in the network began to change from the end of the twelfth century. Indian merchants had once been explorers and risk-takers who criss-crossed the oceans in their stitched ships. They could be found in large numbers in ports from the Persian Gulf to China. Buddhist and Brahmin scholars sailed in large numbers to South-East Asia where they were in great demand. Suddenly, a little over a century after the Chola naval raids on Srivijaya, they almost all disappeared. What happened?

The proximate cause for this change was the enforcement of caste rules prohibiting the crossing of the seas. However, the caste rules were merely a reflection of a wider malaise. As I have argued in an earlier book, *The Indian Renaissance*, there appears to have been a shift in India's cultural and civilizational attitude towards innovation and risk-taking.[33] This is not the place to discuss the root causes of this transformation, but there are many independent signs of the closing of the mind. Sanskrit, once an evolving and dynamic language, stopped absorbing new words and usages and eventually fossilized. Sanskrit literature became obsessed with purity of form and became formulaic. Similarly, scientific progress halted as the emphasis shifted from experimentation to learned discourse.

It is interesting that foreigners who visited India at that time noticed the change and wrote about it. Al-Biruni, writing at the same time that Mahmud Ghazni was making his infamous raids, commented that contemporary Indian scholars were so full of themselves that they were unwilling to learn anything from the rest of the world. He then contrasts this attitude with that of their ancestors.

Given this cultural shift, Indian merchants became increasingly shore-based, while shipping passed mostly into the hands of Arabs. However, there were also Jews, Persians and even the Chinese. Ibn Batuta saw a number of Chinese ships in Calicut (Kozhikode) and he describes a military junk that must have accompanied a merchant fleet. It was large enough to accommodate a thousand men, six hundred sailors and four hundred men-at-arms. In other words, Ibn Batuta was exploiting a very active trading network on his journeys. It is testimony to the vigour and sophistication of this network that Ibn Batuta met a man from Ceuta, a city very close to his home town of Tangier, first in Delhi and then, accidentally, again in China.[34] Ibn Batuta may have been the one to write about his travels but the routes he took were well known to the world of Arab merchants.

Nonetheless, the spirit of ancient India was kept alive for

several more centuries by the kingdoms of South East Asia. Angkor continued to be the capital of the Khmer empire till it was sacked by the Thais in 1431. Its ruins must be seen to be believed. Lesser known but equally interesting are the remains of the kingdom of Champa in Vietnam. The kingdom flourished till its capital Vijaya was sacked by Viet troops in 1471. A smaller Cham kingdom would limp along till it, too, was overrun in the late seventeenth century. Hindu temples built by the Chams are scattered across Vietnam—a few are still used by the tiny Balamon Cham community that continues to practise Hinduism (they number around 30,000). Sadly, the most important cluster of Cham temples in My Son was heavily bombed by the Americans during the Vietnam war. The site is now designated a UNESCO World Heritage site but frankly there is very little to see. The small museum at the entrance has some pre-war photographs that provide an idea of its former glory.

Perhaps the most vigorous of the India-inspired cultures, however, was that of Java. In the fourteenth century, the Majapahits of Java had established direct or indirect control over much of what is now Indonesia. As they expanded, they pushed out the ancient Srivijaya kingdom based in Sumatra. A naval raid on the Srivijaya capital of Palembang in 1377 finally eliminated their main rival in the region.[35]

Faced with the Javan threat, one of the Srivijaya princes, Sang Nila Utama, is said to have sought refuge in the Riau cluster of islands, just south of the Malay peninsula. One day, so the story goes, he had gone hunting on the island of Temasek, where he is said to have seen a lion. So, when he built a settlement here, he named it Singapura (Sanskrit for Lion-

City). This is how Singapore got its name—although the prince had almost certainly not seen a lion but a Malayan tiger. The last wild tiger of Singapore was killed in the 1930s in the neighborhood of Choa Chu Kang.

One of Sang Nila Utama's successors, Parmeswara, appears to have found Singapore untenable due to local rivalries and the continued threat of the Javans. He moved farther north and established his headquarters at Melaka (also spelled Malacca). This is what South-East Asia looked like when Admiral Zheng He arrived with the Chinese 'treasure fleet'.

Zheng He was an unlikely admiral for the Chinese fleet. He was a Muslim eunuch from land-locked Yunnan who had been brought as a boy prisoner to the Ming court and castrated. Yet, he led seven major naval expeditions between 1405 and 1433 that visited South-East Asia, India, Sri Lanka, Arabia and East Africa. The 'treasure fleets' were of an astonishing scale, with over hundred ships and tens of thousands of men. Chinese naval technology at this stage was centuries ahead of the rest of the world. In recent years, some authors have argued that Zheng He may even have visited the Americas. He certainly had the technology, but I am not convinced that he actually made the journey across the Pacific.

The naval expeditions had many objectives including trade and exploration. However, the main goal was to project Chinese power and to cement its geo-political position. The Chinese had overthrown Mongol rule just a few decades earlier, and they were very keen to establish their place in the world. If the sheer size of the fleet did not overawe the locals, Zheng He was prepared to make military interventions as he did in a civil war in Sri Lanka.

When Zheng He was making his voyages, there already existed a number of Chinese settlements in South East Asia but the Majapahit empire of Java was the most powerful in the region.[36] Indeed, a century earlier, the Javans had militarily beaten back Chinese–Mongol attempts to establish control in the region. In 1378, the Ming emperor had sent envoys to try and instal his candidate on the Srivijaya throne. The Majapahit had, not surprisingly, seen this as interference in their sphere of influence and had killed the envoys.[37]

Zheng He would have been aware of this history. The Chinese admiral, therefore, decided to create a counterweight by supporting Parmeswara's nascent kingdom in Melaka. A large Chinese settlement was created in Melaka and Parmeswara personally visited the Ming court. Most interestingly, the Chinese encouraged the Melakans to convert to Islam. Zheng He and many of his commanders were Muslims, but this policy is unlikely to have been driven merely by religious zeal. By most indications, Zheng He had a pragmatic view of religion. It is probable that Chinese support of Islam in South East Asia was more of a geo-political strategy to create a counterweight to the Hindus of Java.

It is even possible that the Chinese wanted to diminish the outside risk of an Indian revival re-exerting its influence on the region. The Chinese of this period were very conscious of themselves as a civilizational nation and wanted to establish themselves as the civilizational top dog. In any event, the Chinese strategy set in motion the steady Islamization of South East Asia.[38] Melaka boomed while the Majapahit slowly withdrew till the last of the Majapahit princes sought refuge in the small island of Bali, where their descendants have kept alive their culture. The network of Chinese merchants survived European colonization and they are still an important part of business in the region.

The Chinese domination of the seas, however, came to an abrupt end. The mandarins decided that the voyages were not worth the expense. The treasure fleets were allowed to rot and their records suppressed. Like India, China turned inward and slipped into centuries of decline. Technological superiority could not save China from the closing of the mind. For a while, it seemed that the Indian Ocean would revert to the Arabs but that was not to be. In December 1497, a small Portuguese fleet rounded the Cape of Good Hope and sailed boldly into the Indian Ocean.

6

The Mapping of India

As we saw in Chapter 3, geographical awareness jumped sharply between the Vedic Age and the Iron Age. The epics clearly show knowledge of the far corners of the subcontinent. They certainly had a fairly detailed knowledge of the terrain by the time of the Mauryan empire. But, did ancient Indians try to map their country? Over centuries of maritime trade, they would have come to know quite a lot about the geography of the Indian Ocean rim, even as far as the Chinese coast in the west and of the Red Sea in the east. At the same time, they were also quite used to diagrammatic representation of ideas, including architectural plans. Thanks to Aryabhatta, by the time of the Guptas, Indians were aware that the world was spherical and even had a fairly accurate estimate of its circumference. All the ingredients of cartography were there—one would have expected the Indians to pull together this knowledge to systematically map their country and the surrounding oceans. Similarly, one would expect that there would be maritime manuals equivalent to the Greek *Periplus* to help merchants and seamen.

Yet, there is nothing to prove that ancient Indians ever attempted to map their country or systematically write down geographical knowledge. A seaman's manual written in the Kutchhi dialect of Gujarat has been found, but it exists as a relatively modern copy and nothing is known of its history.[1] Of maps there are none. Of course, it is entirely possible that such things existed but have been lost. What survives is a cosmological scheme centred around 'Jambudwipa' or the Continent of the Rose Apple that was really not meant as a cartographic description.[2]

I am not suggesting that ancient Indians did not have a sense of geography. If anything, they were very strongly conscious of the layout of the subcontinent and, given their maritime activities, of the Indian Ocean rim. Thus, when the famous eighth-century philosopher Adi Shankaracharya set up four monasteries, he chose sites in the four corners of the country—Puri in the east, Dwarka in the west, Sringeri in the south and Joshimath in the north. This is clearly not a random distribution. Nonetheless, it does seem that cartography as a science did not flourish in ancient India.

In contrast, the Arabs wrote several books on geography during the medieval period. They also preserved some of the works of classical scholars like Ptolemy of Alexandria at a time when Christian Europe would have dismissed such knowledge as pagan. In the twelfth century, the famous Moorish geographer, Al Idrisi, drew a map that combined his own knowledge with that of Ptolemy. It showed the Indian Ocean as landlocked, an idea that suited Arab interests by discouraging any attempt by Europeans to find a sea route to the east. By the fourteenth century, the Persians were drawing maps that show the Indian peninsula. Nonetheless, the quality of cartography remained quite basic. The real experts of medieval cartography were the Chinese. They had long been drawing maps of their own country. By the time of Admiral Zheng He, or perhaps as a result of his voyages, they had good strip-maps of shipping routes through South East Asia and even of parts of the East African coast. These are mostly in the nature of sailing instructions rather than accurate representations of the physical geography, but they are surprisingly detailed and far in advance of anything possessed by other people.

Meanwhile, Europe was literally in the dark about the geography of Asia. The Arabs appear to have been able to enforce an information blockade over centuries. With the works of classical geographers lost and memories of pre-Islamic trade with India fading, Europe was hostage to garbled information and even blatant charlatans. One of the most famous of the charlatans was Sir John Mandeville, an Englishman who wrote a book full of fantastical tales called simply *The Travels*. He set off from St. Albans in 1322 and returned to England thirty-four years later claiming to have visited India, China, Java, Sumatra and many other places. Geographers, kings and priests studied the book in detail and it was translated into virtually every important European language. His importance can be gauged from the fact that 300 handwritten copies of *The Travels* have survived in various libraries, four times as many as Marco Polo's book.[3]

Some writers like Giles Milton have argued that Mandeville's stories about the Eastern Mediterranean have an element of truth in them, but it cannot be denied that his writings about Asia are outrageous. He talks of women with dogs' heads, one-eyed giants, geese with two heads, giant snails, men with testicles that dangled between their knees, and cannibal pagans who ate their babies. He embellished the widely-held medieval belief that India was ruled by a powerful Christian king called Prester John. Mandeville tells us that he arrived in India after an arduous overland journey but was pleased to find the rich and populous kingdom of Prester John. He goes to some length to describe the palace and the liberal use of precious stones. We are told that the emperor ruled over a massive kingdom and was waited upon by seven kings, seventy-two dukes and 360 earls—all Christian. Every time he went to battle, he was accompanied by three huge crosses of solid gold. Each cross was protected by 10,000 men-at-arms and 100,000 foot soldiers.[4] All this was lapped up by Europeans pleased to hear that there was a potential Christian ally in the east.

Despite everything, Mandeville's book had a very profound impact on the history of the world. He claimed that his travels had proved that the world was round and his book popularized the idea that it was possible to reach India by sailing west. Columbus planned his 1492 expedition after reading *The Travels*, and explorers like Raleigh read the book very carefully. Thus, one of the greatest discoveries of history was based on an elaborate lie!

Not all reports by European travellers, however, were fictional. With the sudden expansion of the Mongol empire in the thirteenth century, the Arab stranglehold was finally broken and a few Europeans did genuinely travel to the east. The best known of these is Marco Polo. He is today remembered for his travels along the Silk Route to China and his stay at the court of Kublai Khan. However, he returned home by the sea route through South East Asia around 1292. On the way, he visited the ports of southern India and has left us extensive descriptions of what he saw. He tells us of bustling ports that exported pepper and imported horses, of Hindu temples and rituals, of diving for pearls, of a royal harem with 500 concubines, and even of a popular and wise queen who ruled an inland kingdom that produced diamonds (probably Kakatiya queen Rudrama Devi of Golkonda).[5]

Polo's facts and Mandeville's fiction both fired the European imagination. As the Renaissance took hold in the fifteenth century, European scholars opened their minds to the knowledge of classical civilizations. The works of Ptolemy were revisited and there were attempts to draw maps of India based on his descriptions. The Ptolemaic maps are a strange construct. Since no maps had survived from classical times, they were drawn purely by reading a text. Therefore, the Ptolemaic maps miss out on basic facts that would have been so obvious to Ptolemy himself that he did not dwell on them in his text. For instance, the maps do not show India's coastline as a peninsula but as a long east–west coast. Furthermore, the texts were over a thousand years old by the time they were being used to re-construct India's geography. Thus, they prominently mark places like Taxila that had disappeared over a millennia earlier. Such was the state of knowledge when the Portuguese decided to look for a way around Africa.

FOLLOWING VASCO

The Portuguese were the first European country to invest heavily into the systematic mapping of the world's oceans. Prince Henry the Navigator, the king's younger brother, became a patron of cartography and exploration. Through the fifteenth century, the Portuguese explored the west coast of Africa and established trading posts and refuelling points. Imagine their indignation when Spain backed a maverick called Columbus who sailed west, based on patchy and erroneous data, and made one of the greatest discoveries of history. Incensed, they lobbied with the Pope to divide the world into Spanish and Portuguese spheres of influence. As per the Treaty of Tordesillas 1494, Spain was awarded a claim to all lands west of a meridian of longitude 370 leagues west of the Cape Verde islands. All lands discovered to the east of the line belonged to Portugal.

When it soon became clear that Columbus had not found a westward route to India, the Portuguese must have heaved a sigh of relief. They knew from an earlier voyage led by Bartholomeu Dias that Africa could be rounded. A new expedition was prepared in 1497 under Vasco da Gama. It comprised of three ships—the flagship *San Gabriel*, the smaller *San Rafael* and the traditional caravel *Barrio*.[6] An unarmed supply-ship also accompanied them part of the way. Note that these ships would have been quite small and unsophisticated compared to those of Admiral Zheng He, but the Chinese had already withdrawn into an inward-looking shell and were no threat to the Portuguese.

The fleet set sail on 8 July 1497 and rounded the Cape of

Good Hope by November. After this point Vasco was in uncharted waters. As they sailed up the Mozambique coast, the Portuguese began to encounter Arabic-speaking people. Vasco must have been very pleased to see this because it proved that he was indeed in the Indian Ocean. The Arabs had long established slaving ports along this coast and some of them had grown into sizeable habitations. However, no one in this world expected to come upon a European fleet. Indeed, it appears that the Arabs initially thought that these fair-skinned foreigners were Turks. The Portuguese had the advantage of having several Arabic speakers amongst them as the Iberian peninsula had only recently been liberated from Moorish rule. Thus, they were able to converse with the locals and pretend to be fellow-Muslims. When asked by a local sheikh for his copy of the Koran, Vasco lied that he had left it behind in his homeland near Turkey.[7]

The deception could not last for ever and was eventually discovered. The Portuguese fended off an attack and hastily sailed farther north in search of Kilwa, an island-city and port that was important enough to be known in Europe. However, they got lost and instead found themselves in Mombasa which was another important port-city. Unfortunately, news of their deception had already made its way up the coast and the Portuguese narrowly escaped being lured into a trap by the sultan of Mombasa.

Vasco da Gama pushed farther north. Along the coast, he made inquiries about Christians and about the kingdom of Prester John. At last he found himself in the harbour of Malindi, a port that had been visited by the Chinese treasure fleet eighty years earlier and was the source of two giraffes that had been taken back to China. The ruler of Malindi was under no illusions about the identity of his guests but was in need of allies against Mombasa. He, therefore, opted to welcome the Portuguese.

Alvaro Velho, one of Da Gama's soldiers, has left us a description of the part-Arab, part-African world of the Swahili coast. The larger port-towns like Mombasa and Malindi had houses built of stone and lime. The population was mainly black African, with a ruling class of Arab extract. The merchants were mainly Arab but some Indians continued to visit these parts despite the caste restrictions. Vestiges of this world can still be seen in the Stone-Town of Zanzibar, Tanzania. The island of Zanzibar remained a major source of slaves bound for the Middle East till the nineteenth century. It continued to be ruled by an Omani Arab dynasty, under British protection, till as recently as 1963.

A community of Indian merchants had long visited Zanzibar but, under British protection, many more went to settle down there. By the early decades of the twentieth century, there was a thriving Indian community on the island. The singer Freddie Mercury was born here into a Parsi family in 1946. His name at birth was Farrokh Balsara and the house where he spent the first few years of his life still stands in Stone-Town. In a bloody revolution in 1963, however, the Arab dynasty was overthrown, thousands of Arabs and Indians were killed and the island soon became a semi-autonomous province of Tanzania. Still, a small Indian community lives in the narrow lanes of Stone-Town, speaking the Kutchhi dialect of Gujarat and worshipping in the few remaining temples. There was something about the atmosphere of Zanzibar that reminded me strongly of the old parts of Kochi and even of old Ahmedabad on the other side of the Indian Ocean. Perhaps it was the food, the smell of spices sold in the open, sailing-dhows bobbing in the sea or just the weight of centuries of trade with India.

In early 1498, Vasco da Gama had been trying to get a good pilot to guide his fleet across the Indian Ocean but was having difficulty finding one. In Malindi his luck changed and the sultan provided him with an experienced pilot described as a 'Moor from Gujarat'. There is considerable debate about the identity of this pilot and some scholars have argued that it may have been the famous Arab navigator Ibn Majid. In reality we know very little about the man except that Velho called him by the name Malema Cana.

Both the pilot and the weather proved to be good, and the Portuguese fleet reached the Indian coast in barely twenty-three days. The open harbour of Kozhikode (also called Calicut) was filled with vessels of different sizes and the beach was lined with shops and warehouses. Further inland was a large and opulent city. The Portuguese ships were a novelty and we are told that the locals rowed up to them, women and children in tow, to have a closer look.

The ruler of Calicut was the Samudrin or Lord of the Sea (often mispronounced as Zamorin). He lived in a large palace and was protected by ferocious warriors of the Nair caste. The majority of the people were Hindu, but the Portuguese initially thought of them as debased Christians. Their confusion may have been partly derived from the legends of Prester John and partly from the presence of communities of genuine Christians. They would correct their view later. The

Portuguese would have also noticed that maritime trade was dominated by a large and powerful community of Arab merchants who would not be pleased to see them.

Vasco knew that he had to get back to Lisbon as soon as possible to report his findings. The longer he stayed, the more likely that the Arabs would find a way to trap him or turn the local ruler against him. He presented himself to the Samudrin and tried to make the best possible impression with gifts and protestations of peace. Although the Arabs did instigate some Nair guards to briefly hold Da Gama captive, he was soon freed and was heading back to Europe. Not surprisingly, he was given a hero's welcome in Lisbon. King Manuel lost no time in writing to the Spanish monarchs to inform them that the Portuguese half of the world contained India. He also assured them that India was full of Christians 'although not yet strong in faith and possessed of a thorough knowledge of it'.[8]

The Portuguese lost no time in following up on their discovery. A fleet of thirteen ships and 1200 men was dispatched under the command of Pedro Alvares Cabral. They were heavily armed with cannons and guns, still unknown in the Indian Ocean. By now the Portuguese had worked out that winds and ocean currents made it more efficient to first sail south-west and then turn east rather than hug the coast of Africa. The fleet swung so far west that they landed on the Brazil coast and claimed it for Portugal. Note that only a small part of Brazil actually fell within the Portuguese sphere as per the Treaty of Tordesillas, but cartographic ambiguity would allow the Portuguese to grab more than their share. The Spanish would have their revenge by taking the Philippines which was clearly in the Portuguese sphere. Soon, the papal division would completely break down as other Europeans joined the race.

On reaching Calicut, Cabral presented the Samudrin with many lavish gifts before putting forward the demand that he expel the Arabs and trade exclusively with the Portuguese. The Samudrin was understandably taken aback. While these negotiations were going on, a Meccan ship loaded with cargo prepared to leave for Aden. The Portuguese seized it and triggered riots in which a number of Portuguese men were killed. Cabral responded by lining up his ships and firing broadside after broadside into the city. The Samudrin was forced to flee from his palace. A number of merchant ships were seized and their sailors were burned alive in full view of the people onshore. Thus began the European domination of the Indian Ocean that would last till the middle of the twentieth century.

Within a few decades, the Portuguese used their cannons to establish a string of outposts in the Indian Ocean. Control over Socotra and Muscat allowed them to control the Red Sea and Persian Gulf respectively. In 1510, they conquered Goa. A year later, a fleet sent out from Goa took over Melaka and established control over the key shipping route to the Spice Islands. Soon, they had trading posts in Macau and Nagasaki. The Portuguese maintained control over the seas with an iron fist and, even by the standards of the time, gained a reputation for extreme cruelty and religious bigotry. They destroyed numerous Hindu temples, persecuted the Syrian Christians and harassed ships carrying Muslims for the Hajj, on occasion burning the ships mid-sea with the pilgrims still on board.

Perhaps no one suffered more from Portuguese repression than the Sri Lankans, both Tamils and Sinhalese. Much of the island was in a state of almost constant war for one and a half centuries. One can only be grateful that the Portuguese lacked the resources to attempt a full-scale conquest of the subcontinent.

Portuguese control over the Indian Ocean was based on a network of forts along the coast. The best preserved of these forts is in Diu, a small island just off the Gujarat coast. I recommend climbing the ramparts to see the beautiful views of the Arabian Sea and the impressive array of sixteenth- and seventeenth-century cannons. There are few places in the world where one can see and touch such a large number of early cannons, their solid wood wheels weathered by centuries of rain and sun. In 1538, the Portuguese were able to defend Diu against a combined attack by the Sultan of Gujarat and a large fleet sent by the Ottoman Turks. A huge Ottoman cannon, cast in 1531 in Egypt, is the only remnant of the failed Turkish expedition and can still be seen in Junagarh fort. The Portuguese would manage to hold on to Diu till as recently as 1961. The last of the outposts in Asia, Macau, was handed back to the Chinese in 1999. The Portuguese had been the first Europeans to come to this part of the world and they were the last to leave.

THEATRUM ORBIS TERRARUM

When Vasco da Gama landed in India, it had a population of around 110 million. At that time, China had an estimated population of 103 million, the United Kingdom 3.9 million and Portugal just 1 million.[9] India was still a major economic power with a share of 24.5 per cent of world GDP. Nonetheless, this was smaller than the one-third share of world GDP that it had enjoyed in the first millennium AD. Around 1500, the Chinese economy bypassed the Indian economy in terms of size for the first time. Moreover, per capita income in India fell below the global average. After having lagged behind India for centuries, most European countries enjoyed higher per capita incomes by 1500. The richest country in Europe, Italy, had a per capita income that was twice the Indian level. The individual brilliance of rulers like Akbar and Krishnadeva Raya may have created periods of prosperity, but it did not reverse the trend. In short, the glittering Mughal court of the sixteenth and seventeenth century hid the fact that India was already in relative decline.

As argued in my previous book, *The Indian Renaissance*, the problem was a growing technological gap between the Europeans and everyone else. The most cutting-edge technology of that time was cartography—the technique of making maps—and the Europeans were simply miles ahead by the beginning of the sixteenth century. The discoveries of the Portuguese were put down on hand-drawn maps and these charts were considered top secret. Before each voyage, the captain was allowed to make a copy from the royal library and was expected to return it with new discoveries marked out when he got back.[10] Not surprisingly, the maps were the focus of international espionage. In 1502, Alberto Cantino, an agent of the Duke of Ferrera, stole a chart from Lisbon and took it to Italy. It is preserved in the Biblioteca Estense of Modena and shows that the Portuguese had quickly worked out that India was a peninsula although many elements of Ptolemaic geography were still retained.

The first map showing the Indian peninsula to be published publicly was by Johan Ruysch in Rome in 1508. It shows India as a peninsula and marks a few of the ports on the coast but shows little knowledge of the country's interiors. The Indus and the Ganga are the only two Indian rivers marked but their courses are essentially arbitrary. It also shows the Malay peninsula and marks Melaka (spelled *Malacha* on the map). A well-known map by Waldseemüller in 1513 has a broadly similar layout. Over the next century, more maps were published and the level of knowledge improved, albeit not always linearly. Mistakes were common and often perpetuated by cartographers copying information from each other. Empty spaces were decorated with drawings, often echoing the fantastical creatures of Mandeville. Nonetheless, geographical knowledge went through a major shift in the sixteenth century. At the centre of the cartographic revolution were two individuals, Gerardus Mercator and Abraham Ortilius, contemporaries from the Low Countries.

Mercator was born in 1512 near Antwerp and was an accomplished engraver of maps and charts by the time he was twenty-four. Although he does not seem to have ever travelled to the faraway lands that were being newly discovered, he was able to systematically assimilate all the information available about them. In 1538, he published his first world map that is one of the earliest to bear the names North and South America. He also showed Asia and America to be separate continents long before the discovery of the Bering Strait proved it to be a fact.

Mercator lived in a time of great religious and political ferment. An innovator who asked too many questions was always suspect and, in 1544, he was arrested as a heretic. If he had not been rescued by influential friends a few months later, it is likely that he would have been beheaded or burned at the stake by the Inquisition. A few years later, Mercator would shift east to Duisburg where he would produce his most famous work. In 1569, he produced his world map with the legend 'New and Improved Description of the Lands of the World, amended and intended for the use of Navigators'.[11] The map did not just have richer information than earlier maps; it used a novel system of projecting the curved surface of the world on a flat surface. This was a major innovation in cartography. The 'Mercator Projection' is still the most commonly used format for a world map even though it is based on a distortion that squeezes the countries near the equator and stretches those near the poles. This is why countries like Norway and Sweden look much larger than they are in reality while India and Indonesia look much smaller.

It was with Mercator's encouragement that Ortilius produced the first atlas in 1570 in Antwerp. The first edition of the atlas had seventy sheets and was called the *Theatrum Orbis Terrarum* (Theatre of the World). It proved such a success that forty editions would eventually be published. It is interesting to see how the rediscovery of classical Greek and Roman works had a profound impact on the European mind of that time. Ortelius took pains to include a map that tried to reconcile the new findings about India with the *Periplus* and with Arrian's account of Alexander's expedition. The map identifies the location of cities like Pataliputra and Muzaris with surprising accuracy given the passage of time. In a sense, it was the first attempt to recreate the history of India's geography and is consequently a direct ancestor of this book.

THE CITY OF VICTORY

One of the most prominent features of early European maps of India is the kingdom of 'Narsinga' that covers much of the southern peninsula. Most modern Indians will have difficulty identifying this name because it refers to what is now remembered as the Vijayanagar empire, named after its capital city. It was ruled by Narasingha Raya when the Portuguese first arrived in India. He was not an especially important monarch in the history of Vijayanagar, but his name stuck and Europeans continued to mark it on their maps long after he and his empire were gone.

The city of Vijayanagar was established just after the devastating raids of Alauddin Khilji's general Malik Kafur had broken down the old power structures of southern India. Around 1336, two brothers, Hukka and Bukka, appear to have rallied various defeated groups under their banner and built a fortified new city called Vijayanagar or City of Victory. At its height in the early sixteenth century it was probably the largest city in the world.

The city was built across the river from Kishkindha, site of the monkey-kingdom described in the Ramayana. It is a dramatic landscape of rock outcrops and gigantic boulders. The choice of location, therefore, was no coincidence as the rocky terrain partly neutralized the military advantages of Turkic cavalry. An additional advantage was that the place had easy access to iron-ore from the nearby mines of Bellary, still in active use today.

A number of visitors have left us lucid accounts of Vijayanagar, including Abdul Razzaq, envoy from the Persian court, and several Europeans such as Domingo Paes and Fernão Nunes. They tell us that the city was encircled by a series of concentric walls, perhaps as many as seven of them, that enclosed a massive area. The large gap between the first and second wall was used mostly for gardens and farming. The inner walls enclosed bazaars, homes, mansions and temples. At the core of the city was a magnificent palace-complex surrounded by strong fortifications. Despite thinking of itself consciously as a bastion of classical Hinduism, the city was very cosmopolitan with sizeable populations of Muslims, Christians and even Jews. Paes tells us that 'the people of this city are countless in number, so much so that I do not wish to put it down for fear that it should be thought fabulous'. He goes on to say 'This is the best provided city in the world . . . the streets and markets are full of laden oxen so much so that you cannot get along for them'.[12]

The remains of the city can be visited at Hampi in Karnataka, and can only be described as spectacular. In my many travels across the world, I have found only the ruins of Angkor in Cambodia to be comparable to those of Hampi in terms of sheer scale. It is too large to be explored solely on foot and the visitor will need both a car and a good guide. As described by the medieval travellers, there is still a fair amount of farming that continues within the UNESCO World Heritage site, in many cases using the old canals. We even have remnants of a system of stone aqueducts that brought water into the city.

The remains of temples, palaces and bazaars make it clear that the reports about the city's size were not exaggerations. Indeed, after decades of excavations, much of the site has still not been uncovered. One of the more remarkable remains is that of Ugra Narasingha—a gigantic sculpture of Lord Vishnu as half-lion and half-man (unlike the Egyptian sphinx, it has the head of a lion and the body of a man). Given that the Vijayanagar empire was known as Narsinga by the early Europeans, this sculpture is particularly appropriate.

As already mentioned, the ruins of Vijayanagar are located right across the Tungabhadra from Kishkindha and it is worthwhile crossing the river to visit it. Although a modern bridge was almost complete at the time of writing,[13] when I visited the site in 2007 and 2008, one still has to cross the Tungabhadra in a round coracle boat piled with people, goats, motor-cycles and sacks of rice. Almost five hundred years earlier, Domingo Paes made the same crossing and wrote, 'People cross to this place in boats which are round like baskets; inside, they are made of cane and outside, are covered with leather; they are able to carry fifteen or twenty people and even horses and oxen can use them if necessary but for the most part these animals swim across. Men row them with a sort of paddle, and the boats are always turning around.'[14] I know exactly what he meant.

In 1565, Vijayanagar was attacked by a grand alliance of all the Muslim kings of the Deccan. After being defeated in the Battle of Talikota on 26 January, the Vijayanagar army withdrew instead of defending the capital. It is said that the great city was plundered for six months. It never recovered. Vijayanagar can be considered the last flash of the 'classical' phase of Hindu civilization. The second cycle of India's urbanization had begun on the banks of the Ganga but ended on the banks of the Tungabhadra.

THE CITY OF THE KING OF THE WORLD

By the late 1500s, the Portuguese and the Spanish had competition from rival European nations. In the autumn of 1580, Francis Drake returned to London after his circumnavigation of the globe. By 1588, the English had decisively defeated the Spanish Armada. However, it was the Dutch who first took on the Portuguese in the Indian Ocean. The Dutch, only recently free from Iberian rule, set up the United East India Company in 1602. It was the world's first company to issue common stock and would grow into a truly enormous multinational company. By 1603, the Dutch had a trading post in Banten, West Java and by 1611 in Jayakarta (later Batavia and now Jakarta). Soon they were challenging the Portuguese along the Indian coast and in Sri Lanka.

The Dutch were not just helped by the efficiencies of private sector enterprise, but also by the better quality of their maps. Thanks to Mercator and Ortilius, they were at the cutting edge of cartography. A map of the Bay of Bengal by Janssan and Hondius printed in the 1630s shows the improvements in the level of knowledge since Waldseemüller a century earlier. The map shows Sri Lanka, the eastern coastline of India, Bengal, the Burmese coast, the Andaman and Nicobar Islands and the northern tip of Sumatra. There is a lot of detail along the coast with both major and minor habitations marked out including *Musalipatam* and *Pallecatta*. The temple-town of Puri in Orissa is marked as *Pagod Jagernaten* after the temple to Lord Jagannath. Since it is a navigation chart, depth measurements are marked out in a number places such as the Gangetic delta. For the first time, we see some detailed knowledge of the interior of the country. For instance, the riverport of Ougely (Hooghly) is clearly marked out on the westernmost channel of the Ganga. Hooghly was then the most important trading centre in eastern India and, despite its subsequent decline, the river channel continues to bear the name of the old port even today.

Meanwhile, the English had also formed their own East India Company. By 1612, they had set up their first factory at Surat, Gujarat. Its position was strengthened a few years later by the embassy of Sir Thomas Roe to the court of Emperor Jehangir. Interestingly, Roe presented an atlas of the latest European maps to the Mughal court but it was politely returned after four days.[15] It is possible that the courtiers were unused to cartographic representations and could not understand the atlas. However, in my view, it may also have been because it showed how small the Mughal Empire was in relation to the world known to the Europeans. Maps have always had a geo-political aspect to them, and the recent friction between India and China about the depiction of Arunachal Pradesh shows that it remains the case to this day.

Shah Jehan succeeded Jehangir in 1628. The name Shah Jehan means 'King of the World' in Persian, and his reign was the golden age of Mughal architecture. Many edifices small and great, including the Taj Mahal, were built under him. He also decided to move the capital back to Delhi and build a new city in 1639. The city would be called Shahjehanabad after himself, although we now know it as Old Delhi. Completed in 1648, it had twenty-seven towers, eleven gates and a population of around 400,000. Shah Jehan had chosen a site that was farther north of the existing city, the northernmost Delhi yet. It contained a walled palace-complex surrounded by walls of red Dholpur sandstone—what we call the Red Fort. For lesser buildings, material was scavenged from the older Delhis, especially Dinpanah and Feroze Shah Kotla. The Red Fort was built along the river and, during the monsoon, water would have flowed along the palace walls. However, most of the time there was a 'beach' between the river's edge and the fort where elephant-fights and other events were organized for the entertainment of the court.

It is not easy to see the original layout of Shahjehanabad by merely visiting Old Delhi because the city has gone through many changes over the centuries. Nonetheless, one can still discern many of the key features. There was a straight and wide avenue that began at the Red Fort's western gate and ran through the main bazaar to one of the city's main gates. It remains as Chandni Chowk, named after the way the full moon once reflected on a canal that ran along the middle of the road.

The French traveller Bernier visited the city a few decades after it was completed and has left us a detailed eyewitness account.[16] One of the first things that struck Bernier was that the fortifications of both the city and the Red Fort were old-fashioned and not designed to withstand artillery. He states, 'Considerable as these works may appear, their real strength is by no means great and in my opinion a battery of moderate force would soon level them to the ground'. It is unclear why

Shah Jehan opted for designs that were already considered outdated in the mid-seventeenth century. Perhaps the empire felt so secure that he did not feel it necessary to build for a military siege. Perhaps, it is just another example of the increasing technological gap between India and the West. It would prove a major error as Shahjehanabad's walls repeatedly failed to hold off attackers over the next two centuries.

Bernier describes the opulent palaces of the nobility with their courtyards and walled gardens. He tells us that the rich had raised pavilions set in the middle of flower-gardens and open on all sides to allow the breeze to flow from any direction. The insides of the private apartments had cotton mattresses covered in cloth in summer and carpets in winter. Cushions of brocade, velvet and satin were scattered around the rooms for the use of those sitting down. This matches what we can see in Mughal paintings and buildings that have survived from that time across northern India.

However, one should not get the impression that Delhi was a city merely of grand palaces and imperial mosques. The majority of the people of Delhi were common folk— shopkeepers, artisans, servants, soldiers and so on. These people lived in huts made of mud and straw that were built between and around the great palaces of the nobility. In other words, Shahjehanabad suffered severely from slums, that perennial problem of modern Indian cities. Bernier tells us that these slums gave the city the impression of a collection of many villages. Fires were common and sixty thousand roofs had been gutted in just one year (the number is probably an exaggeration, but point taken). The problem with fires had been described 1800 years earlier by the Greek ambassador

Megasthenes when he visited Mauryan Pataliputra, but had yet to be solved in Mughal India. In other words, Mughal Delhi was a city of extremes. As Bernier puts it, 'A man must either be of the highest rank or live miserably.'

The Frenchman describes the bazaars as bustling, chaotic and dirty, not dissimilar to what Old Delhi looks like today. He tells us that there were many confectioners (i.e. halwais) all over the city but disapproved of the dust and the flies. There were also shops selling a variety of kebabs and meat preparations. Old Delhi remains home to some excellent kebab shops. The visitor can get off at the Chawri Bazar Metro stop and then take a five-minute rickshaw ride to the Jama Masjid area. Go late at night when the lane with the kebab- and sweet-shops throngs with people. With smoke rising from the open ovens and the old imperial mosque looming in the background, one could be back in medieval Delhi. Bernier, however, was quite suspicious of the kebab shops for he wrote, 'There is no trusting their dishes, composed for aught I know, of the flesh of camels, horses or perhaps oxen who have died of disease'. Perhaps he had suffered a bad case of Delhi Belly during his stay.

MONSIEUR TAVERNIER, I PRESUME

At the time that Bernier was travelling through the Mughal Empire, there were many other Europeans—merchants, officials, mercenaries, adventurers—who were also in the country and have left us colourful accounts of their experiences. One of these was Jean-Baptiste Tavernier, also a Frenchman. In the winter of 1665–66, he travelled from Agra to Bengal and wrote about the experiences. We know from his writings that the imperial highways were full of bullock-cart caravans carrying rice, salt, corn, and so on. Although most caravans consisted of one or two hundred carts, some were huge, with 10,000 to 12,000 oxen. When two large caravans going in opposite directions encountered each other on a narrow section of the road, it could take two to three days to pass each other. One can imagine the dust, the noise and the tempers.

The bullock-cart caravans were driven by nomadic castes called Manaris who travelled the trade routes with their families and belongings. At every stop a temporary village of tents would be set up. Each group had a chieftain who could be identified by a string of pearls. Often there would be quarrels between the leaders of rival caravans and matters could be escalated all the way up to the Emperor.[17] In other words, the ill-tempered truck drivers that one encounters in modern Indian highways have a long lineage.

Tavernier tells us that travellers had a choice between two kinds of transport—light carriages pulled by bullocks and palanquins carried by men. The former cost about a rupee a day and came with luxuries like cushions and curtains. The palanquins needed about six people to lift and a long journey required a company of twelve men at least so that they could relieve each other. Each man cost four rupees a month. Of course, if one wanted to make a statement, one could hire twenty to thirty armed guards who came with muskets and bows. These cost as much as the palanquin-bearers but were higher in status. In addition, Tavernier says, the English and Dutch officials also insisted on a flag-bearer who walked in front of the party in honour of their respective companies. I suppose this is the origin of the little flags that modern-day ambassadors and dignitaries have fluttering in front of their luxury cars.

On 6 December 1665, Bernier and Tavernier met each other on the banks of the Ganga near Allahabad. They drank a toast of wine mixed with water on the banks of the river—but this seems to have upset Tavernier's stomach. A couple of days later they crossed the river at Allahabad but had to wait half the day for the governor to send them entry/exit permits. Revenue officials stood on both banks, checked papers and charged octroi. Wagons were charged four rupees each and carriages one rupee. The boatman had to be paid separately.

In addition to the Sadak-e-Azam highway through the Gangetic plains, there were many other internal trade routes that continued to thrive. As per a tradition that went back to ancient times, trees were planted all along the way to provide shade. This custom survived into the twentieth century but is unfortunately no longer adhered to. In the south, the road through the Palghat Gap continued to be used to connect the ports of the Kerala coast with the interior. However, the old Dakshina Path route appears to have gone into decline during this period. Instead, there were a number of important trade routes that linked the imperial capitals of Agra and Delhi with the ports of Gujarat. For instance, a route used by Peter Mundy of the English East India Company originated in Agra and made its way south-west through Fatehpur, Bayana, Ajmer, Jalore, Mehsana, Ahmedabad and finally to Surat. An alternative route was to head more directly south from Delhi–Agra to Dholpur, Gwalior, Narwar, Ujjain and finally to Mandu.

From Mandu the route turned west to Surat. Bernier tells us that goods from Surat made it to Delhi in four to six weeks.

Some of these places were towns of importance but there were many caravan-serais along the way although their quality varied a great deal. The larger caravan-serais had spacious walled enclosures where merchants could spend the night in safety. Travellers would have been able to draw water from the wells and buy provisions. In addition, many of the busy roads would have had water-stops or 'piyaus'. The provision of drinking water to a thirsty traveller was said to gain religious merit (*punya*) and people built piyaus in memory of loved ones. Many of these have survived to modern times (indeed, new ones are still being built). The road from Delhi to Gurgaon (MG Road) used to have several old piyaus till recently. The last one was demolished in 2009 to make way for the new Metro line.

Of course, the quality of the road and accommodation could sometimes be appalling, especially on the less-frequented routes. The Portuguese Catholic priest Friar Sebastian Manrique has left us a most amusing anecdote of his travels through Orissa and Bengal during the monsoon of 1640.[18] After leaving the town of Jalesar, the priest and his companions found themselves in a small village which did not have a proper caravanserai. They were, therefore, obliged to spend the night in a large cowshed. The bovine occupants of the shed were the least of their problems for they were attacked by a swarm of mosquitoes. When they thought that matters could get no worse, it began to rain and they discovered that the roof leaked.

It was almost dawn when Sebastian Manrique was finally

able to doze off but the peace did not last. The cowshed was suddenly full of birds including two large peacocks. The friar's companions decided to kill and eat the peacocks. They were aware that the locals regarded the birds as sacred and tried to hide their activities. Unfortunately, the truth was discovered by their hosts and very soon an armed mob gathered outside. The friar's party hurriedly fled, firing muskets to cover their retreat. Such was the experience of life on the road in seventeenth-century India.

HISTORY RHYMES

By the time Bernier and Tavernier were criss-crossing India, Shah Jehan was no longer the emperor. The throne had been usurped in 1658 by his son Aurangzeb, who imprisoned his father in Agra fort and ruthlessly eliminated his siblings, including the liberal and scholarly Dara Shikoh. The new emperor next attempted the last great expansion of the Mughal empire. The governor of Bengal, Mir Jumla, pushed into the Brahmaputra valley in 1662 till he reached Garhgaon, between modern Jorhat and Dibrugarh, the capital of the Ahom kings of Assam. However, he was unable to completely eliminate the Ahoms due to torrential rains, the difficult terrain and constant guerrilla attacks.

Despite Aurangzeb's efforts in the north and in the east, his big push was into the southern peninsula. He shifted to the Deccan in 1682 and would never see Delhi again. Instead, he lived in a state of constant campaigning for the next twenty-six years. Although Aurangzeb extended the empire to its maximum geographical coverage, he also effectively destroyed it. His constant wars devastated the landscape and drained the exchequer. This is why Bernier comments that, although the Mughal emperor had revenues that exceeded the combined receipts of the Shah of Persia and the Ottoman Sultan, he could not be considered wealthy because it was all consumed by expenditure. Thus, Bernier tells us that Aurangzeb was 'perplexed how to pay and supply his armies'.

Equally important, Aurangzeb was a religious bigot who needlessly destroyed Hindu temples and re-imposed the hated jiziya tax on non-Muslims. It is said that when this tax was first announced, the Hindus of Delhi gathered in large numbers in front of the Red Fort to protest against it. The emperor set his elephants against them and many were trampled to death. Tegh Bahadur, the ninth Sikh guru, was executed in Delhi in 1675 for standing up for the Hindu Pandits of Kashmir. The Gurudwara Sis Gunj in Old Delhi's Chandni Chowk stands at the spot where he was beheaded.

Not surprisingly, the pact between the Hindu majority and the Mughals began to come unstuck. There were revolts in many places across the empire. One of the most successful revolts was led by the Maratha rebel Shivaji. The exploits of Shivaji and his band of Maratha guerrillas are so audacious that one would not believe them but for contemporary accounts of them. Using the volcanic outcrops of the Deccan Traps, the Marathas repeatedly outwitted the larger Mughal armies and remained a constant thorn in Aurangzeb's side. One of my favourite tales is about how the Marathas captured Sinhagadh by using a trained monitor lizard named Yeshwanti to scale the walls. The guerrillas tied a rope around the lizard, which climbed up a rock-face that was so steep that it had been left unguarded. A boy then climbed up the rope and secured it for the rest. The fort of Sinhagad is just outside Pune and can be easily visited. You will see cadets from the nearby military training school climbing up the hill with their heavy packs.

Another group that broke out in open revolt were the Bundelas. Their leader Raja Chhatrasaal used the low hills of the Vindhya range to wage a campaign against the Mughals. There is a colourful tale that links the Bundelas and the Marathas. Raja Chhatrasaal had a very beautiful dancer named Mastani in his court (some claim she may have been his daughter by a concubine). When the Marathas rescued the Bundela chief from a tight spot, Chhatrasaal thanked the Maratha commander Baji Rao by gifting him Mastani. Baji Rao would rise to become the Peshwa (Prime Minister) of the Marathas and Mastani would become his favourite. Although Mastani is usually left out of history books, she was a significant figure in her times and is said to have ridden with Baji Rao on his many campaigns. On the highway between Orchha and Khajuraho, there is a small but picturesque palace built on a lake by Chhatrasaal for Mastani during her younger days. Not many people know about it and visitors are likely to have it all to themselves. The surrounding hills are heavily fortified, a reminder of the turbulent times in which Mastani lived.

Nonetheless, it was not at the hands of the Marathas or the Bundelas that the Mughals suffered their first decisive defeat. This happened in the middle of the Brahmaputra in faraway Assam at the hands of the Ahom general Lachit Borphukan. The Ahoms came to India as refugees in the early thirteenth century. They were distantly related to the Thais from what is now the Burma–China border and were probably no more than a few thousand in number. Soon, they converted to Hindusim and established a kingdom that would last from 1228 till 1826. Mir Jumla's raid of 1662 had hurt them, but they had survived and were steadily clawing back territory. The conflict reached a climax in 1671 in the Battle of Saraighat, not far from modern Guwahati. The Assamese forces were far smaller but their commander cleverly avoided a battle on open ground. Instead, he coaxed the Mughals into a naval battle on the Brahmaputra river, where the smaller and more manoeuvrable Assamese boats won a decisive victory. Although seriously ill, Lachit Borphukan personally led the assault. It was the Indian equivalent of the Battle of Salamis where the ancient Greeks defeated the Persian fleet against overwhelming odds. The myth of Mughal invincibility had been shattered.

The Mughal empire may yet have survived religious bigotry, leaky public finances, Maratha guerrillas, Bundela chieftains and the Assamese navy. The foundations built up by Akbar and his immediate successors were still quite strong, but Aurangzeb committed the ultimate sin—he stayed on the throne too long. He ruled till he died at the age of ninety in 1707. As happened in the case of Ashoka and Feroze Shah Tughlaq, he was followed by a succession of weak rulers culminating in a foreign invasion. In 1739, the Persian army of Nadir Shah occupied Shah Jehan's Delhi and massacred twenty thousand of its citizens. They left with much treasure, including the famous Peacock Throne. With the prestige of the Mughals fast waning, the Marathas occupied large swathes of central India even as the governors of far-flung provinces like Bengal and Hyderabad became virtually independent. Eighteenth-century India dissolved into a chaotic scramble.

A number of foreign players saw the opportunity to extend their influence in the subcontinent. In the North West were the Afghans under Ahmad Shah Durrani, even as the Burmese eyed the North East. In peninsular India, the rivalry between the Dutch and the Portuguese had been replaced by that between the French and the English. Mercenary armies wandered the countryside, feared by rulers and common people alike. For a short while it appeared that the Marathas would replace the Mughals and establish order, but their internal rivalries let them down. Defeat at the hands of the Afghans in January 1761, in Panipat, Haryana, came as a big blow to their reputation. They would never quite regain their momentum. The scene was set for a war of maps.

THE WAR OF MAPS

As we have already seen, maps were a very important military weapon (and remain so today). One can almost trace the ascendancy of a particular European power by the relative quality of its maps. The Marathas were the only Indian power who developed some cartographic ability. Although their maps are not as rigorous as their European counterparts, they were complemented by an intuitive knowledge of the terrain. Meanwhile, the French and British cartographers replaced the Dutch at the cutting-edge of mapping. At first, it was the French who held the advantage, both on the ground as well as in the quality of their maps. By the early eighteenth century, they had a well-established network of enclaves on the Indian coast. The most important were Pondicherry, just south of Madras (Chennai) and the ancient submerged port of Mahabalipuram. There were smaller outposts like Mahé on the Kerala coast, Yanam on the Andhra coast and Chandannagar on the Hooghly channel of the Ganga, just north of the English settlement at Calcutta. The French also controlled the strategically important island of Mauritius in the middle of the Indian Ocean.

Mirroring the strategic advantage of the French, their maps of India are also superior to those of their rivals. Arguably the best of the French cartographers was D'Anville. He never visited India but appears to have collected the best available information from his Paris home. Cartographic historian Susan Gole has called him the first scientific map-maker. Unlike his predecessors, he strictly focused on geographical accuracy and refrained from eye-catching embellishments. The influence of John Mandeville was finally wearing off. Thus, when D'Anville wanted to correctly locate Satara, the Maratha capital, he asked the Portuguese ambassador to the French court for more information. The Portuguese were fighting the Marathas at that time. D'Anville was told that Satara was in the Ghats and that it was eight days' journey from both Goa and from Bombay, at the apex of a triangle formed by these two lines and the coast. For most cartographers of that time, this would have been more than enough information but D'Anville left Satara out of his map on the grounds that this was not exact enough.[19]

The British, meanwhile, were only marginally behind. The first half of the eighteenth century saw a series of British map-makers—Herman Moll, John Thornton and Thomas Jefferys.

Their records show that they keenly kept abreast of the latest French maps. There are also detailed local maps of specific ports and military installations. One of the most interesting is an English map of Maratha admiral Kanoji Angre's sea fort. From its fortified base at Vijaydurg, the Maratha navy harassed European shipping up and down the Konkan coast for several decades. Angre also defeated the Abyssinian pirates, the Sidis, but was unable to evict them from their base at Murud-Janjira.

The forts of Vijaydurg and Janjira lie south of Mumbai and are worth a visit. The fort at Janjira is built on a small island but local fishermen are happy to take visitors out on a row-boat for a small consideration. Vijaydurg is built on a peninsula but also offers spectacular views of the Arabian Sea. The eighteenth-century English map of Angre's fort shows a worryingly detailed knowledge of its defences. It also gives an amusing insight into the European attitude towards the Maratha admiral. Prominently marked is a building labelled as 'Godowns where he keeps his Plunder'. To them, he was no more than a pirate!

One of the characteristic features of European cartography till the mid-1700s is the obvious nautical orientation. By now, we have maps of India that show detailed depth measurements along the coast and even greater detail for the entrances of major ports. Yet, they remain curiously ignorant of the Himalayas, one of the most prominent geographical features on the planet. Most maps do show some awareness of mountains to the north, but the range is not systematically marked anywhere. There was a widespread belief going back to the time of Alexander that the northern mountains were a continuation of the Caucasus.

Nonetheless, the redoubtable François Bernier did visit Kashmir, and left a detailed eye-witness account of the province that was used by the Mughal Emperors as a summer retreat.[20] He tells us that there were two wooden bridges over the Jhelum at Srinagar and beautiful gardens along the river banks. Most of the houses were made of wood, although some larger buildings, including the ruins of ancient Hindu temples, were made of stone. He tells us that the rich owned pleasure boats on Dal Lake and that they threw lovely parties in the summer.

Bernier also tells us that the Mughals used their base in Kashmir to extend their influence into Little Tibet (i.e. Ladakh) and, intriguingly, Greater Tibet (i.e. Tibet itself). The cold, bleak but stunningly beautiful landscape does not seem to have impressed a contemporary chronicler who wrote, 'No other useless place can be compared with it.'[21] I could not disagree more. For me, Ladakh is the most spiritual place in the world. To experience it, spend a full-moon night—alone—on one of the lonely mountain passes. It is impossible to describe the way stars look at these altitudes and the way the moonlight reflects on the bare rocky mountainsides. The moon can be so bright that one could almost read a book by it. I have spent nights in the open in the African savannah and have watched the sun rise over the Mayan pyramids of Tikal—but nothing comes close to a full-moon night in Ladakh.

It appears that the Mughals also made some inroads into Tibet itself. The Tibetans promised to pay an annual tribute, allow the building of a mosque in their capital and to issue coins in the name of Aurangzeb. We know that the Ladakhis did allow a mosque to be built in Leh; it can still be visited at the head of the main bazaar (and just below the old palace).

However, given the difficult terrain, the Mughals had no way to ensure compliance from Tibet, and Bernier tells us that no one really believed that the Tibetans would honour the promises.

Bernier was very intrigued by the stories he heard about Tibet, including those about the institution of the Dalai Lama. He tried to question Tibetan merchants about their country but received little useful information. As we shall see, the British would have to make great efforts to get reliable information about this land in the nineteenth century. For now, the Europeans needed to find out about more about the geography of the subcontinent itself. Indeed, knowledge of India's interiors remained quite basic except for major trade routes. This would change with the Battle of Plassey in 1757 where the troops of the English East India Company, led by Robert Clive, decisively defeated Siraj-ud-Daulah, the Nawab of Bengal. With this victory, for the first time, a European power came to control a major province. Soon, the British would be acquiring large territories and sustaining campaigns in the deep interiors of the country. Accurate maps were more important than ever. Enter Colonel James Rennel.

7

Trigonometry and Steam

The Portuguese first arrived in Bengal in 1530. They set up trading posts at Chittagong in the east and Satgaon in the west. Over time, the river near Satgaon silted up and the river port of Hooghly became the main trading hub. The port was on the Bhagirathi distributary of the Ganga—although we now usually call it the Hooghly after the old port town. By the seventeenth century, other Europeans had also set up trading posts along the river—the French at Chandannagar, the Danes at Srirampur and the Dutch at Chinsurah. The English East India Company initially had its local headquarters at Hooghly. However, it seems to have had problems with the local Mughal officials and was forced to sail downriver after a skirmish in 1686. When matters were finally settled two years later, the English sent a squadron on ships from Madras (now renamed Chennai) to re-establish their presence in Bengal. The initiative was headed by the company's chief agent Job Charnock.

THE BUILDING OF CALCUTTA

On 24 August 1690, Charnock landed at a village called Sutanuti on the east bank of the river. He had already visited the spot during the retreat two years earlier and had obviously liked it. So he decided to build the new English trading post here. It would grow into the city of Calcutta, now renamed Kolkata. This was not, however, an uninhabited landscape. There were three villages in the area—Sutanuti, Gobindapore and Kalikata The city's name is derived from that of the last village. The merchant families of the Setts and Basaks already ran sizeable business establishments here. There was a fourth village nearby, called Chitpur, from where the road ran all the way to the ancient temple of Kalighat. Just off this road, in the middle of tiger-infested jungle, was a Shiva temple erected by a hermit called Chowranghi.[1] The temple no longer exists, and the place is now occupied by the Asiatic Society on Park Street. The hermit's name, however, was retained as Chowringhee Road, which would become one of the city's principal arteries. In an act of misplaced nationalism, the road was renamed after Jawaharlal Nehru in the 1980s, which is especially inappropriate since the hermit was one of the original inhabitants of the place. Fortunately most citizens of Kolkata persist with the old name.

Job Charnock probably chose this site from a standpoint of defensibility. The river ran along the west of the site while there were marshy salt lakes to the east. To the south there were dense, tiger-infested jungles, while to the north there was a creek that ran from the river to the salt lakes and was navigable by large boats. Many of these features are still discernible. The creek has long since silted up but is remembered in place-names like Creek Row and Creek Lane. The eastward suburban extensions of the 1970s, officially called Bidhannagar, are commonly called Salt Lake, recalling the marshlands. A few of the lakes still exist as the East Kolkata Wetlands that provide the city with a unique natural sewage recycling system that is now protected under the Ramsar Convention.

Most of the early British settlement was build around a pre-existing water tank called Lal Dighi that had been excavated by the Bengali merchant Lal Mohan Sett. The name Lal Dighi literally means Red Pond; there is a story that it gets its name from the colours used by the locals during the festival of Dol (or Holi). The waterbody still exists and stands in the middle of the business district. Soon, the British had built a number of substantial buildings around Lal Dighi, including a fort that they named Fort William. It stood on the site now occupied by the General Post Office and should not be confused with the later Fort William that we see today.

Commerce may have prospered but it came at a huge human cost. Surrounded by mosquito-infested swamps, the early European residents of Calcutta suffered horrible casualty rates. Alexander Hamilton, Charnock's contemporary, tells us that there were 1200 English of various ranks when he visited the city. Within six months, 460 of them died. While this may have been an especially bad year, it gives a sense of the mortality rates that the East India Company employees had to contend with. Less than three years after establishing the trading post at Calcutta, Job Charnock too died. His body was interred in a mausoleum that can be visited on the grounds of St.John's Church, just off Lal Dighi. His eldest daughter Mary died a few years later and is buried in the same tomb.

Meanwhile, Calcutta continued to grow. A map from 1757 shows that the British had built a fortified trench called the Maratha Ditch all around Calcutta to defend it from attacks by Indian rulers. The name of the ditch tells us how the threat perception had shifted from the Mughals to the Marathas since the death of Aurangzeb. Most of the area within the fortifications was still largely rural, but there is a small but significant urban cluster around Lal Dighi and along the river. Nevertheless, contemporary maps of Madras suggest that it was a much more important settlement than Calcutta at this stage.

In 1756, the Nawab of Bengal Siraj-ud-Daulah briefly occupied Kolkata and renamed it Alinagar. However, just a year later, Robert Clive defeated the Nawab of Bengal at Plassey and established British control over this large province. Calcutta now became the headquarters of a rapidly expanding empire. Over the next century, Calcutta would become the largest city in the subcontinent and one of the most important urban hubs in the world. One can see the transformation by comparing the 1757 map of Calcutta with one published by Chapman and Hall in 1842. A few of the old features are still visible. Lal Dighi still exists but is surrounded by large buildings including the Writers' Building. This is not the magnificently red Writers' Building built in 1882 that functions today as the secretariat of the state of West Bengal. The original Writers' Building was also a substantial building and was used as rent-free accommodation for clerks and other junior employees of the East India Company. The Maratha Ditch has been filled up but its outline is discerned in the 1842 map as the Upper Circular and Lower Circular roads—and they continue to be the city's arterial roads to this day, albeit with new names.

For anyone familiar with Kolkata, the 1842 map is very interesting because many of the basic contours of the modern city are clearly visible. The old Fort William has been replaced by the large star-shaped fort that is still used by the Indian Army as its eastern headquarters. The British town planners left large open spaces around the new fort in order to allow a clear line of fire for the fort's cannons. These are now the parks of the Maidan. The Victoria Memorial, of course, does not exist at this stage and its site is occupied by a complex marked as the Grand Jail. However, the site of the Turf Club already has a race course. Well-known roads such as Park Street and Camac Street have taken shape and are clearly marked. But for the fact that many of the street-names have been changed since the 1970s, one could probably find one's way around most of central Kolkata by using the 1842 map— especially since the old names remain in common use in many cases. The map also shows how, by the mid-nineteenth century, the rapidly growing city was spilling out of the confines of the old city limits marked by the former Maratha Ditch. We can see how the new suburbs of Sealdah, Ballygunge and Bhowanipur are just beginning to appear. Their conversion into fully urban settlements would happen very gradually. I remember that even in the early 1980s, some parts of Ballygunge retained a semi-rural feel with large bungalows, fish-ponds and weekly village markets. These open spaces are now occupied by multistorey residential towers, but some reminders of the past remain: the idiosyncratic lanes, the odd hut amidst modern buildings, the old village shrine stranded in the middle of the road.

By the mid-nineteenth century, Calcutta was not just a commercial and administrative hub, but also the centre of intellectual and cultural activity. Indians from across the subcontinent came here to seek their fortune. There were even sizeable communities of Jews, Armenians, Greeks and even Chinese in the city. Although these communities have dwindled in recent decades, they have left behind buildings and place-names that recall them. This multicultural milieu set the stage for the next phase of evolution of India's civilization. Over the next century, Calcutta would attract social reformers like Ram Mohun Roy, who pushed through important changes that have shaped modern India. Interestingly, these early reformers also argued in favour of providing education to Indians in the English language. This would be a profoundly important choice.

It is popularly assumed that English education was used by the colonial rulers to create a class of Indians who would be loyal to them. This view is based a note written by Thomas Macaulay in 1835 where he argued, 'We must at present do our best to form a class who may be interpreters between us and the millions whom we govern; a class of persons, Indian in blood and colour, but English in taste, in opinions, in morals, and in intellect'. In fact, the matter was hotly debated by the British officials and there were many who disagreed with Macaulay. The factor that tipped the balance was that many reformist Indians favoured English. This preference for a foreign language is not as strange as it may appear at first sight. The early reformers were very conscious that Indian civilization had been in decline for a long time and correctly blamed it on lack of technological and intellectual innovation. The knowledge of English was seen as a window to the world of ideas emanating from Europe. Far from creating a class of loyal Indians, the English-educated middle-class would be at the forefront of India's struggle for independence.

One of the important venues for the Anglo-Indian intellectual interaction of this era was a unique college founded in 1800 by Governor General Wellesley. The College of Fort William was set up for the training of British civil servants who spent their first three years studying and training there. The curriculum for the three-year course was surprisingly eclectic and tells of a generalist ethos that remains embedded in the Indian Administrative Service of today:[2]

1. Choice of Languages: Arabic, Persian, Sanskrit, Marhatta (Marathi), Tamalua (Tamil), Bengali, Telenga (Telugu).
2. Mahomedan Law
3. Hindoo Law
4. Ethics, Civil Jurisprudence, and the Law of Nations
5. English Law
6. The Regulations and Laws enacted by the Governor General in Council at Fort St. George (Madras) and Bombay for civil government in the British territories in India
7. Political Economy and particularly the commercial institutions and interests of the East India Company.
8. Geography and Mathematics
9. Modern Languages of Europe
10. Greek, Latin and English Classics
11. The History and Antiquities of Hindoostan and Deccan
12. Natural History
13. Botany, Chemistry and Astronomy

The college was meant for training civil servants, but it brought together a mix of remarkable Indian and British scholars. This interaction generated both new scholarship as well as new thinking. One of these scholars was Ishwarchandra Vidyasagar, who taught there in the 1840s. An extraordinary polymath, his contributions include giving the Bengali language its modern form, the emancipation and education of women and the teaching of Sanskrit texts to low-caste Hindus. Indian civilization would benefit enormously from this new way of thinking.

Meanwhile, the students of the college were not always immersed in their studies. A student named Mr Chisholme was sued in 1802 and brought before the court by one Jagonnaut Singh, a lawyer. A cat had been sitting in a shop near the deponent's house. The student set his dog on the cat but it fled into the lawyer's house and into the women's quarters. Mr Chisholme and his dog followed in hot pursuit. When Jagonnaut Singh objected to this intrusion, the student punched him in the forehead. In the end, Mr Chisholme admitted his guilt and was reported for proper action.

Not all the young officials of the East India Company were quite so loutish. One of the most talented was Thomas Stamford Raffles, who was sent by Governor General Minto to Penang (now in Malaysia) to keep an eye on the Dutch in South East Asia. The British and the Dutch had long been bitter rivals in South East Asia, and the English East India Company wanted to ensure that the shipping routes between India and the Far East were secure. When Napoleon annexed Holland, the British occupied the Dutch possessions in the East Indies. Raffles played a leading role in these events, and we get a wonderful insight into the man and the times from the letters he sent back to Calcutta for Lord Minto and other senior officials. It is amazing that, in the middle of organizing military operations and administrative systems in far-flung islands, people like Raffles found the time to study the flora and fauna, record local customs and investigate ancient ruins.

After Napoleon was defeated, the Dutch wanted their colonies back. There were heated negotiations between Calcutta and Batavia (the Dutch headquarters, now Jakarta). The Dutch would eventually get back most of their possessions as per the Anglo–Dutch Treaty of 1824, but not before Stamford Raffles had ensured that the British would retain effective control of the Straits of Malacca. The key to his strategy was the establishment of a new British outpost in Singapore. The island had been under the nominal control of the Sultan of Johore but Raffles was able to secure it in exchange for the payment of an annual rent and British support against the Sultan's local rival. Singapore was formally founded on 6 February 1819 with a great deal of pomp and the firing of cannons. Raffles wrote, 'I shall say nothing of the importance of the position I have taken in Singapore; it is a child of my own . . . Our object is not territory but trade; a great commercial emporium, and a fulcrum, whence we may extend our influence politically as circumstances may hereafter require'.[3]

Raffles is remembered mostly as the founder of Singapore, but his writings show an extraordinary curiosity about the natural and cultural history of South East Asia. He avidly collected samples of plants and animals and even sent back a Sumatran tapir for the Governor General's garden in

Barrackpore. He wrote extensively about the Indianized culture of Java and Bali, and is said to have 'rediscovered' the great stupa of Borobodur during the British occupation of Java. I wonder if he ever saw the panel carved with the windblown ship—a memory of an earlier age of mercantile trade. Just before he returned to England, Raffles set up an institute in Singapore inspired by Calcutta's Fort William College. It survives as the Raffles Institution, an elite school, although its original location on Bras Basah Road is today occupied by the Raffles City Shopping Mall, just across from the famous Raffles Hotel. As anyone visiting Singapore will have noticed, the liberal use of the founder's name can be quite confusing.

THE GREAT INDIAN ARC OF THE MERIDIAN

As the British became more entrenched in India, they quickly discovered the need for good maps of the country's interior to help with administration, revenue collection and military movements. Till the mid-seventeenth century, European mapping had been concentrated on the coastline but now the interiors had to be systematically charted too. The key survey tool was the perambulator—essentially a large wheel set up to allow the measurement of distance. East India Company troops would often take a perambulator along on marches and an estimate of distance would be worked out by adjusting for the twists and turns of the road. While this was hardly accurate, it provided readings that were a vast improvement on earlier estimates. For instance, a map of Sri Lanka and the Coromandel coast from this era carries the note, 'The route from Tritchinapoly to Trinevelly ascertained by a march of English troops in 1755'. This was quite typical.

With the conquest of Bengal, the British decided to carry out a more scientific survey of their new possessions. In 1765, Robert Clive assigned James Rennell, a young naval officer, the task of making a general survey of Bengal. Rennell took a detachment of sepoys and criss-crossed the countryside for seven years fixing latitudes, plotting productive lands and marking rivers and villages. It was hard and dangerous work. While surveying the Gangetic delta (the Sunderbans), Rennell wrote in his notebook 'We have no other Obstacles to carry on our Business properly than the extensive thickets with which the country abounds, and the constant dread of Tygers, whose vicinity to us their Tracks, which we are constantly trampling over, do fully demonstrate'.[4]

A tiger did carry off a soldier on at least one occasion. On another, a leopard jumped out of a tree and mauled five sepoys. In an act of extraordinary bravery, Rennell grabbed a bayonet and thrust it into the beast's mouth. On yet another occasion, Rennell sustained deep sabre wounds while fighting off bandits. At thirty-five, Rennell returned to England and produced the famous *Bengal Atlas*. He was hailed as 'the Father of Indian Geography'.

Although it was the best that has been done thus far, Rennell's work had covered only a small part of the subcontinent. As British conquests expanded, the need for further surveys was felt. The task fell to acerbic genius William Lambton, who had had a long but unremarkable career in India till he was made the Superintendent of the Great Trigonometrical Survey of India. He got the job quite by chance. In 1798, he happened to be sailing from Calcutta to Madras on the same ship as a young colonel called Arthur Wellesley. He would go on to become famous as the Duke of Wellington and the victor at Waterloo, but in 1798 he was better known as the younger brother of the Governor General and was on his way to fight against Tipu Sultan of Mysore. He seems to have been impressed with Lambton and took him along for the expedition. Tipu Sultan was defeated and killed at the siege of Srirangapatnam. Lambton played his part with distinction. By consulting the stars he was able to avert a major disaster during a manoeuvre when British troops were unknowingly marching north into enemy lines rather than south to a defensible position.[5]

It was during the campaign that Lambton came up with the idea of doing a survey of India using triangulation. Basically, this requires three mutually visible points as corners of a triangle. If one knows the length of any of the sides and can measure the angles, the length of the other sides can be established by trigonometry. The newly determined sides can then each be used to establish a new triangle and so on. It is tedious work but provides very accurate measurements. Lambton had another motive beyond just creating an accurate map of India. Using this methodology, he wanted to also use the measurements to establish the exact shape and curvature of the earth. This was not just scientific curiosity; it was of vital importance to a naval and commercial power like Britain. Lambton told Arthur Wellesley his plan, who in turn spoke to his brother the Governor General. Lambton got the job.

The first thing that Lambton did was to order a state-of-the-art theodolite to help with the survey. A theodolite is basically a telescope that has been specially adapted to allow the very accurate measurement of angles needed for triangulation. The equipment Lambton ordered weighed half a ton and had to be shipped from England. On the way it was captured by the French and taken to Mauritius. However, when the French realized that it was a scientific instrument, they gallantly repacked and sent it to Madras. At last, Lambton could start on his work.

Lambton began by establishing a baseline at sea-level in 1802. He did this just south of Chennai's famous Marina beach. From a flagpole on the beach, he ascertained the horizontal distance to the grandstand of Madras racecourse. Once he had established this base-line, Lambton set in motion a sequence of triangulation that would crisscross India for the next sixty years, consuming not just his life but that of his successor George Everest. In 1802, the East India Company had expected the work to have finished in five years! It is a testimony to the prestige and usefulness of this project that it was not stopped for six decades, despite the time and resources it would ultimately consume.

Trudging through jungles, mountains, farmlands and villages with a heavy theodolite in tow must have been very difficult work. Often there were bandits, hostile local populations, and suspicious kingdoms that were still not reconciled to British rule. Many a time there were long delays because dust and haze obscured visibility. At each location, the theodolite had to be dragged up to a height in order to provide a reading. Tall buildings were used where there were no hills. In 1808, Lambton decided to use the massive eleventh-century Brihadishwara temple in Thanjavur. The temple dedicated to Lord Shiva had been built by the Cholas at the height of their power and is a huge structure even by modern standards. Unfortunately, the ropes slipped and the theodolite was smashed. For all its size, it was a delicate and minutely calibrated instrument. A lesser man would have given up. However, Lambton ordered a new one from England at his own expense but then spent the next six weeks painstakingly repairing the damaged equipment.

Lambton worked on the survey till he died of tuberculosis, in the field, in 1823. His crumbling grave was recently rediscovered by the writer John Keay in the village of Hinganghat, fifty miles south of Nagpur. His theodolite is in better condition and is now housed in the Survey of India headquarters in Dehradun. Less than half of the project had been completed when Lambton died. Fortunately, he was succeeded by the equally dedicated George Everest. By the time Everest retired and returned to England in 1843, the Great Arc had been extended well into the Himalayas. He built a bungalow for himself at Hathipaon, near the hill-station of Mussourie. Its ruins still stand on a ridge commanding magnificent views of snow-capped peaks on one side and the valley of Dehradun on the other. It is merely a fifteen-minute drive from Mussourie town, followed by a ten minute walk up the hill. Just the shell of the house remains, although the roof was largely intact when I visited it in February 2011 and the fireplaces were clearly visible in the larger rooms. Everything else had been stripped bare. Yet, as one looked out of the broken window frames at the Indian land mass extending south into the far distance, one could feel the soul of the eccentric but determined Welshman hanging in the air.

Everest returned home to recognition and a knighthood, but it is unclear whether he had ever seen Peak XV. In 1849, surveyors in the eastern Himalayas took theodolite measurements of Peak XV from six different angles. By averaging the measurements, the Bengali computer Radhanath Sikdar calculated that the peak was 29,000 feet high. He rushed into the office of Everest's successor, Andrew Waugh, and is said to have blurted out, 'Sir, I have discovered the highest mountain in the world'. The problem was that the learned scholars of that time would have dismissed the idea of a mountain that was over 25,000 feet. They would be especially suspicious of a rounded-out figure like 29,000. Therefore, the surveyors arbitrarily added two feet to the calculation and for decades geography textbooks would carry the number 29,002 feet![6] Later measurements show the exact height at 29,029 feet or 8848 metres above sea level.

Now came the issue of naming Peak XV. The Tibetans already called it Chomolungma (Mother Goddess of the World). Unusually for the colonial period, the Survey of India tended to retain the local names where possible but in this case the temptation proved too great. It was named after George Everest. Like many people today, I used to wonder why the British would name the highest mountain in the world after the Surveyor General of India rather than after royalty or even a Viceroy. However, having read about the sheer scale of the Great Trigonometrical Survey of India, I can see that it was not so odd after all.

THE REVOLT OF 1857

By the time Mount Everest was being named, the British were very much in control of the whole subcontinent. What was not directly ruled by the British was managed through one-sided treaties with the remaining local princes. Not since the Mauryas had such a large part of the subcontinent been controlled by a single power. How did the British succeed where earlier European powers had failed? Technological advantage was important, but cannot have been the deciding factor. Unlike in the Americas, Africa or Australia, the technological gap between the Europeans and the locals was not so large as to be able to neutralize a very large numerical superiority. In many instances, there were European mercenaries and allies fighting on the Indian side. Yet, the British were repeatedly able to beat off much larger armies and then maintain control with a tiny number of officials. Why?

What is most striking about the British conquest of India is that so few British were involved. The armies of the East India Company were largely made up of Indian sepoys. Moreover, in many cases, the British received encouragement and support from the locals. For instance, at the Battle of Plassey, Robert Clive was funded and encouraged by the merchants of Bengal. Some historians tend to see this as proof that Indians did not have any sense of nationhood till the nineteenth century. However, as we have seen, Indians have had a very strong sense of being a civilization for millennia. Why did the Indians not oppose British rule more aggressively?

In my view, the real reason for this was that the collapse of the Mughal Empire in the eighteenth century had left the country in chaos. The Marathas, after showing some initial promise, had dissolved into their internal bickerings. The countryside was plagued with mercenaries and bandits of every description. Some of these privateer warlords, like Begum Samroo, became so powerful and rich that they lived openly and in style in Delhi and were considered respectable members of society. The East India Company was far from benign but, in comparison, did offer some semblance of order. There is an important additional factor. Unlike the Portuguese, the early British rulers conspicuously kept away from interfering with local culture and social norms. Even in the few instances where they did intervene, as in the abolition of the despicable custom of sati, it was done with the strong support of reformist Indians. This is why they would not have appeared as a civilizational threat to the contemporary Indian. It is not usually remembered that after his great victory at Plassey, Robert Clive did not offer thanksgiving at a church but at a Durga Puja organized by Nabakrishna Deb in Kolkata. One cannot picture Pedro Alvarez Cabral doing this.

Unfortunately, by the mid-nineteenth century, this open attitude had changed and we see growing cultural and racial arrogance. There is a distinct emphasis on 'civilizing', often meaning Christianizing, the natives. This was no secret but openly discussed. James Mill, author of *The History of British India* (1820), described Hinduism as 'the most enormous and tormenting superstition that ever harassed and degraded any portion of mankind'.[7] Evangelical missionaries began using British political control to aggressively seek converts. Not surprisingly, Indians—both Hindu and Muslim—looked on all this with suspicion.

The resultant resentment eventually erupted into a full-fledged revolt in 1857, exactly a hundred years after the Battle of Plassey. British readers will know this as the Sepoy Mutiny.

Within a few weeks, the bulk of the East India Company's Bengal Army was in open revolt and, in many cases, the British officers had all been killed. The phenomenon spread like wildfire across large parts of North and Central India. Note that the revolt did not have a centralized leadership but occurred in a number of different centres and had a number of different leaders, usually dispossessed members of the old Indian aristocracy. Delhi was one of the important centres of the uprising.

By 1857, the glory days of Shahjahanabad were a fading memory. The eighty-two-year-old Bahadur Shah Zafar was an emperor in name alone and his writ barely ran in Delhi. The royal family lived off a pension provided by the British and many of the junior branches of the family had been reduced to extreme poverty. William Sleeman, an official who visited the Red Fort a few years before the revolt, tells us of how 1200 members of the family lived in the palace off the meagre pension but were too proud to work.[8] Instead, there are amusing stories of how some of these princes would try to use their family name to swindle money. Even the palace inside the Red Fort was in a state of severe disrepair. In 1824, Bishop Herber described the palace gardens as 'dirty, lonely and wretched; the bath and fountain dry; the inlaid pavement hid with lumber and gardener's sweepings, and the walls stained with the dung of birds and bats.'[9] Things would have been worse by the 1850s.

There has been a tendency in recent years by writers like William Dalrymple to present the court of Bahadur Shah Zafar as a 'court of great brilliance' that was in the 'middle of remarkable cultural flowering' and the 'greatest literary renaissance in modern Indian history'.[10] This is inaccurate. While it is true that the court did include some excellent poets like Ghalib and Zauq, by the 1850s Delhi would have felt distinctly provincial and archaic compared to Calcutta. A 'renaissance' is about new ideas, innovation and vigour. Ghalib's poetry may be very good from a literary perspective but it is mostly a lament for a world that was collapsing around him. It contains no vision of the future.

In May 1857, several hundred mutinous sepoys and cavalrymen rode into Delhi from Meerut and instigated the local troops. Together they massacred every British resident that they could find. Indian converts to Christianity were not spared either. As more and more rebels arrived, the soldiers turned to the ageing emperor for leadership. Bahadur Shah was personally ambivalent about the offer. On one hand, he was scared that the British would return and exact retribution. On the other hand, he was faced with a large and growing number of rebels who would probably break into a riot if he refused. He opted to play along with the rebels, but would remain indecisive throughout the episode.

Meanwhile, a small British force had arrived and set up a defensible position on the ancient Aravalli ridge overlooking the walled city. From here they proceeded to pound Shahjahanabad with artillery. Their numbers were small but the disorganized rebels were unable to make a concerted attempt to capture the position. A contingent of Gurkha soldiers held off waves of rebel attacks near Burra Hindu Rao's house on top of the ridge; it's now a hospital. One of the princes, Mirza Mughal, did try to organize the mutineers, but was constantly undermined by the indecisive emperor and by the internal jealousies of his own family. It is amazing how the British had a constant flow of information from collaborators within the walled city throughout the siege.[11]

From mid-August, the British were being reinforced by fresh troops and supplies from Punjab. The artillery pounding was ramped up. A month later, Shahjehanabad had been captured and sacked. The game was over. Bahadur Shah and members of his family, proud descendants of Taimur the Lame and Ghengis Khan, fled down the Yamuna to take shelter in Humayun's grand tomb. It is not clear why they bothered since it is barely a few miles south of the city. The British soon caught up with them. Many Mughal princes were executed. Three of them, including Mirza Mughal, were stripped naked and shot dead with a Colt revolver near the archway still called Khuni Darwaza (Gate of Blood). The emperor himself was exiled to Rangoon.

The city of Delhi, shorn of its last link to Mughal grandeur, became even more of a backwater. Within the Red Fort, many of the Mughal structures were torn down to make way for the barracks that one sees today. A few years later, a large part of the old city would be cleared to make way for the railways. Only a handful of structures remain to remind one of Shah Jehan's dream. This completes the third cycle of India's urbanization. It had begun with the sacking of Prithviraj Chauhan's Delhi and ended six and a half centuries later with the sacking of Mughal Delhi. The next cycle, however, was well under way in Calcutta, Madras and Bombay.

After the fall of Delhi, the British proceeded to systematically put down the other centres of rebellion. Tens of thousands were executed as punishment. This is not the place to analyse the many reasons for the failure of the revolt. Despite the extraordinary courage shown by individuals such as Rani Laxmibai of Jhansi, the rebellion was probably too uncoordinated to succeed. The British were able to pick off each group one by one. For all its fame, the fort at Jhansi is a modest affair. It still contains two of Rani Laxmibai's cannons, of a design that would have been considered antiquated by the mid-nineteenth century and stood no chance against modern British cannonry. Standing on the ramparts of Jhansi fort, I could still feel the spirit of the twenty-two-year-old queen—her isolation, her audacity in defying the most powerful empire of that time, and the complete hopelessness of her cause.

It may hurt our nationalist pride to admit this today but many Indians either remained indifferent or were loyal to the British. Perhaps they feared a return to the chaos of the eighteenth century. Perhaps, they simply did not think that their future lay in going back to the old feudal order. The year 1857 saw another revolution that would have a much more lasting impact. Three federal examining universities on the pattern of London University were established in the cities of Calcutta, Bombay and Madras. By the time India became independent in 1947, twenty-five such institutions would have been set up. The universities would create an educated middle class that would be at the forefront of the next round of resistance to British rule.

The rebellion of 1857 also spelled the end of the East India Company. Its territories in India were put directly under government control. The Governor-General was replaced with a Viceroy, a representative of the Crown. The ratio of

Europeans to Indians in the army was pushed up to 1:3 from 1:9. The British also gave up their policy of annexing Indian kingdoms, and the existing network of kingdoms and principalities was given a permanent standing under the Imperial umbrella. This framework would broadly survive till 1947. Most importantly, the Queen's Proclamation of 1858 stated that the British would no longer 'impose Our convictions on any of Our subjects.'

The Queen's Proclamation was read out by Lord Canning on 1 November 1858. The choice of place is interesting since it was not read out in Calcutta, Bombay, Madras or even Delhi. Instead, it was done in Allahabad. It is here that the Yamuna meets the Ganga and is said to be joined by the invisible Saraswati flowing underground. The place is called Triveni Sangam, literally meaning the confluence of three rivers. It is here that Ram is said to have crossed the river and visited the sage Bharadhwaj before proceeding on his exile to the forests of central India. The association with the Ramayana is remembered in a famous Hanuman temple close to Triveni Sangam and an '*eternal* tree' under which Ram is said to have rested. It is also here that Xuan Zang (or Hieun Tsang) witnessed the great gathering of the Kumbha Mela in the seventh century AD. Overlooking the temple and the merging rivers is the fort built by Emperor Akbar which houses the Mauryan column that bears the inscriptions of three emperors—Ashoka, Samudragupta and Jehangir. In short, this is no ordinary place, but the heart of Indian civilization. The British had finally understood the nature of Indian nationhood.

In order to understand the essence of this, visit the Saraswati Ghat[12] in Allahabad at dawn in January during the annual

Magh Mela (or, if you are lucky, the Kumbha Mela). As the sun rises through the mist, one can see tens of thousands of people irrespective of age, gender, class, sect or caste take a dip at the confluence of the rivers. They chant Vedic hymns composed thousands of years ago on the banks of the ancient Saraswati, still alive in the collective memory of millions. Boatloads of villagers row across from villages far and near, their women softly singing traditional songs passed down through generations. It is a moment of eternity. The sun reflects off the ramparts built by a Muslim emperor who grew to understand this. A short walk away is the spot, marked by a column, where a global power was forced to acknowledge this ancient civilization in order to legitimize its rule.

The column commemorating the Queen's Proclamation is a short walk from Saraswati Ghat and stands neglected in an overgrown park. None of the locals seemed to know the significance of the place. This is unfortunate because the modern Indian State is the direct outcome of this Proclamation. After independence, the government capped the column with a replica of the national emblem, the Mauryan lions and the wheel. Usually I disapprove of meddling with the artifacts of history, but somehow it seemed appropriate that the dreams of Sudasa and the Mauryas are remembered at that place.

Although colonial expansion became less overt after 1858, a large gap remained between the Indians and their British rulers. The separation is visible even in urban planning. British towns were clearly segregated into the spacious 'white-towns' and crowded 'black-towns'. It is not unusual for rulers to live separately from the ruled. We see this in both the citadel of Dholavira as well as the Red Fort of Shahjehanabad. However, the elites still lived within the same cultural context as the wider population. In contrast, there was a large cultural gap between the spacious bungalows of the Civil Lines and the bazaars of the indigenous population.

Nowhere was this more visible than in the Civil Lines of Allahabad itself. The fifty years following the Revolt would be the heyday of Empire. The British considered themselves superior to the rest of humanity and were grudgingly acknowledged as such. It would be many decades before a trickle of Indians, armed with a Western education, would be reluctantly allowed into this world. Till as recently as 2005, vestiges of this era were clearly visible in the large, crumbling bungalows of Allahabad's Civil Lines. However, when I revisited it in April 2012, I found that the neighborhood had turned into a jumble of malls, shops and apartment blocks. The few remaining bungalows now hide fearfully amidst the new buildings.

THE STEAM MONSTERS

By 1820, India's population stood at 111 million, but its share in world GDP had fallen to 16 per cent compared to China's 33 per cent.[13] Together they still accounted for half of the global economy, but China was doing most of the heavy lifting. Driven by the Industrial Revolution, Britain already enjoyed a per capita income that was three times higher than that of the Asian giants. As the nineteenth century wore on, the gap between the Europeans and the Asians grew wider. By the time India became independent in 1947, its share would fall to a mere 4 per cent of world GDP.

Despite this relative decline, the second half of the nineteenth century witnessed a radical transformation of the country's economic and geographic landscape. The introduction of the railways was arguably the single most important factor that drove this change. Both commercial and military considerations lay behind the idea of building a railway network. Through the 1830s and 1840s, there were a number of discussions and proposals. The government did not have internal resources to build it but it was initially thought that private operators would easily raise the capital. However, it was soon clear that the money could not be raised in India. Investors in England also appeared lukewarm.

The discussions drifted for several years till the arrival of F.W. Simms, a railway engineer of 'tried and proved ability'. A number of routes were surveyed under his supervision. He argued that a Delhi–Calcutta line would allow the military establishment alone to make a saving of at least 50,000 pounds a year, a very large sum in those days.[14] Given these encouraging studies, the government decided to give generous guarantees to persuade investors to pump capital into the railways. These included a guaranteed return of 4.5 per cent as well as an exchange rate guarantee. These would later prove expensive and attract a lot of criticism, but at that moment they got the projects going. The very first railway line in the subcontinent ran 21 miles (34 km) from Bombay to Thane. The formal inauguration was performed at Bori Bandar on 16 April 1854 when 14 carriages with 400 guests left the station 'amidst the loud applause of a vast multitude and the salute of 21 guns'. A year later, a train left Howrah (a town across the river from Calcutta) and steamed up to Hooghly thereby establishing the first line in the east. Two years later, the first line in the south was established by the Madras Railway Company. By 1859, there was even a line between Allahabad and Kanpur.

An Indian railways map of March 1868 shows that by this time Howrah (i.e. Calcutta) had been connected to Delhi and the line was being extended to Lahore. The Lahore–Multan line had also been built, some of it with the use of four-thousand-year-old Harappan bricks. From Multan one could use the Indus Steam Flotilla to sail down to Karachi. In the west, Bombay had been connected to Ahmedabad and Nagpur but the link to the Delhi–Calcutta line was still not complete. Similarly, the link between Madras and Bombay was still

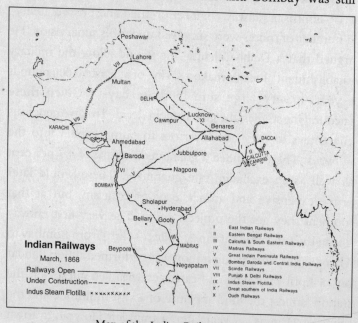

Map of the Indian Railways in 1868
(source: *Development of Indian Railways* by Nalinaksha Sanyal)

being built near Sholapur. There were a number of side lines already in operation or being built.

Given the available technology and the difficult terrain of central India, this was an impressive achievement. Yet, the pace of expansion accelerated in the 1870s with an average 468 miles (749 km) being added per year compared to 250 miles (400 km) in the previous period.[15] In 1878, 900 miles (1440 km) were added in a single year. This is incredible by any standard. By 1882, the country had a network that connected almost all major cities, and the Victorian engineers were feeling confident enough to build into the steep Himalayan hillsides in order to connect hill stations like Darjeeling and Simla.

Nonetheless, do not think of this as a seamless and integrated network. It was built in a hurry by different companies, agencies and princely states, using different standards and gauges, and with different objectives. This caused all kinds of operational inefficiencies that have not been entirely ironed out even in the twenty-first century. Still, the railway network dramatically re-ordered the economic geography of the country. Agricultural commodities could now be exported out from the hinterland while manufactured imports could be brought in cheaply. In many places, the traditional artisan economy suffered a major shock even as the old caravan routes became redundant. The Marwari merchants of Rajasthan, for instance, were forced to leave their homes and look for opportunities in the new world. Many would make their way to Calcutta where their descendants would become very successful businessmen. Their semi-abandoned but beautifully frescoed ancestral homes can still be seen in towns like Mandawa and Jhunjhunu in the Shekhawati region of Rajasthan.

Meanwhile, new towns sprouted along the railway routes even as some communities took advantage of their rapid expansion. One such group was the racially mixed Anglo-Indian (i.e. Eurasian) community that joined the railways in large numbers. They created a colourful sub-culture that has faded away in recent decades. I remember how, when I was growing up in the early 1980s, there was still a strong Anglo-Indian community in Kolkata, with its distinctive cuisine, its love of music and sport, and somewhat idiosyncratic use of the English language. Today, a few pockets remain but the Anglo-Indians are increasingly indistinguishable from the wider Indian Christian population. There is a sizeable diaspora in Australia and Canada, where too it has increasingly integrated with the wider society. Nevertheless, the memory of the old Anglo-Indian community remains alive in novels and films such as John Masters's *Bhowani Junction*. Writer Carl Muller's trilogy about the Burghers of Sri Lanka is a humorous account of the lives and attitudes of this disappearing world.[16]

As a linkage technology, the railway system was the Internet or mobile network of its time. As it carried people and goods across the country, it allowed a new form of interaction between different parts of the subcontinent. The social reformer and religious leader Swami Vivekananda used trains to criss-cross the country in the last decade of the nineteenth century. Mahatma Gandhi would do the same as he tried to re-acquaint himself with India after his return from South Africa. By 1924, 576 million passenger trips were being made per year. Of course, this does not mean that train journeys were always enjoyable, especially for the second- and third-class passengers. A report listed out the following complaints of third-class passengers in 1903:

- Overcrowding of carriages and insufficiency of trains
- Use of cattle trucks and goods wagons for pilgrims
- Absence of latrines in the coaches and their extremely unsuitable character
- Absence of arrangements for meals and insufficient drinking water
- Absence of waiting halls and their extremely uncomfortable nature when available
- Inadequate booking facilities
- Harassment at checking and examination of tickets
- Bribery and exactions at stations, platforms and in the train
- Want of courtesy and sympathetic treatment of passengers by railway staff

A century later, many of these complaints still ring true. Thankfully, cattle trucks are no longer used for passengers but the resentment still remains. An innocuous comment about 'cattle class' by Shashi Tharoor (then a minister) in 2009 would lead to an uproar.

HIGH NOON OF EMPIRE

The period between the Revolt of 1857 and the First World War was the high noon of the British Empire. Nowhere was this more evident than in Calcutta (now Kolkata), the empire's eastern capital. Extravagant buildings embodying Victorian confidence were constructed by the government, banks, companies and wealthy individuals. A surprisingly large number of them have survived into the twenty-first century, hidden behind billboards and other debris of later times. One of the positive consequences of its economic decline in the second half of the twentieth century is that Kolkata is home to the finest collection of nineteenth-century buildings that have survived anywhere in the world. The best way to see it is to wander around the financial district around Lal Dighi on a Sunday morning when the chaotic traffic and the crowds will not distract from the beauty of the old streetscape.

The area used to be called Dalhousie Square but has since been renamed after three Indian revolutionaries Binoy, Badal and Dinesh. Be sure to see the High Court, the Writers' Building, the Chartered Bank Building, the General Post Office and Guillander House. The area is also home to the exceptionally ugly Telephone Bhavan built in the twentieth century. Lal Dighi itself is half-hidden by car parks and a tram depot, sad and neglected, waiting for someone to rescue it. You may also peek from the gate at the Raj Bhavan, once the palace of the Governor General, now home to the Governor of West Bengal. However, be careful about taking photographs too close to public buildings. As I discovered, in these terrorist-plagued times, one runs the risk of being asked a lot of questions by the police!

Even as Calcutta was basking in the high noon of Empire, a rival was emerging in the western coast—Bombay (now Mumbai). It was not a new settlement. The area had been home to a major port in ancient times; the seventh-century cave temples of Elephanta Island are a testimony to those times. Nonetheless, the origins of the modern city go back to the Portuguese occupation of the area in the sixteenth century.

At this stage, Bombay was an archipelago of several marshy islands. The names of some of the islands have survived as the names of neighbourhoods—Colaba, Mahim, Parel, Worli, Mazagaon. The islands passed into British hands in 1662 as part of the dowry received by King Charles II on his marriage to Catherine of Braganza. In turn, it was then leased to the East India Company for ten pounds a year.

Initially, the settlement was not a big success because the aggressive Marathas prevented the British from expanding into the mainland. However, by the late eighteenth century, the British position was secure enough to allow the growth of a significant port and trading hub. This encouraged the British governor to initiate a series of civil engineering works, loosely dubbed the Hornby Vellard project, to connect the various islands by landfills and causeways. By 1838, the seven southern islands had been combined into one Bombay Island. By 1845, the Mahim causeway had connected Mahim to Bandra on the island of Salsette. Although all the main islands have been consolidated, the process of building linkages continues to this day. The latest is the Bandra–Worli Sealink opened in 2009 to link South Mumbai to the 'suburbs'.

One of the first to take advantage of the emerging city were the Parsis, descendants of Zoroastrian refugees from Iran who had settled along the Gujarat coast. They first moved to Bombay to work for the British as shipbuilders but, by the 1830s, became very wealthy by engaging in the opium trade with China. Nonetheless, in the mid-nineteenth century, the city was still much smaller than Calcutta or Madras. Two factors dramatically changed its fortunes in the 1860s—the American Civil War and the opening of the Suez Canal. When the blockade by the American North of the ports of the American South suddenly deprived the mills of Lancashire of raw cotton, they switched to the cotton fields of western India. The newly built railway network transported cotton directly from the fields to Bombay port. New cotton mills began to be built in Bombay itself. The opium trade with China also boomed at the same time, with 37,000 chests being shipped out every year.

With all this new money, both the government and the wealthy merchants of the city embarked on an orgy of new construction—the more extravagant the better. There was a speculative boom in cotton, land and in ambitious ventures like the Back Bay Reclamation Company. Trading was furious at the informal stock-market that had appeared under a tree in front of the Town Hall (according to legend, it was a banyan tree in what is now Horniman Circle). Migrants moved in by the tens of thousands and congested slums proliferated. A contemporary would comment, 'To ride home to Malabar Hill along the sands of Back Bay was to encounter sights and odours too horrible to describe . . . To travel by rail from Bori Bunder to Byculla, or to go to Mody Bay, was to see in the foreshore the latrine of the whole population of Native Town.'[17] The locations of the slums have changed over the last one-and-a-half centuries, but anyone who has travelled in Mumbai's suburban trains will know what the above comment means.

In 1865, the American Civil War ended and the prices of shares and cotton crashed in Bombay. By 1866, several of the city's banks and real estate companies had failed, and many previously wealthy individuals were left bankrupt. The city was strewn with half-built projects that were no longer viable. Nonetheless, the boom years had given Bombay a new status and a speculative spirit that remains very much alive to this day. Strike up a conversation with the street vendors of Nariman Point or the Fort, and you are likely to be given stock-market tips aplenty (although I would be somewhat wary of investing on the basis of this advice).

MAPPING TIBET

By the 1860s, the British surveyors had an accurate map of the subcontinent and were beginning to wonder what lay beyond the Himalayas. This was no idle curiosity; it was driven by Russian inroads into Central Asia. The 'Great Game' had begun. The problem was that the Tibetan authorities were not keen to let in Europeans inside their borders—a few who had tried had been tortured and killed. The Survey of India decided to use Indian spies disguised as traders and pilgrims. The first and most famous of these was a young schoolteacher from the Kumaon hills, Nain Singh. In 1865, he crossed from Nepal into Tibet along with a party of traders. A few days after the crossing, the traders slipped away one night with most of Nain Singh's money and left him stranded in a strange land.

Fortunately, they had left behind his most valuable possessions, concealed in a box with a false bottom—a sextant, a thermometer, a chronometer, a compass and a container of mercury. He also had a Buddhist rosary, except it had 100 beads instead of the usual 108. Nain Singh planned to measure distance by slipping one bead for every 100 paces walked. He also had a prayer wheel that concealed slips of paper on which he recorded compass bearings and distances.[18]

Nain Singh somehow begged his way across the cold and desolate landscape. In January 1865, he finally entered the forbidden city of Lhasa. He took care to behave in a manner appropriate for a pilgrim, including making a brief visit to the Dalai Lama of that time. Meanwhile, he supported himself by teaching local merchants the Indian system of keeping accounts. His position, however, was very precarious. This was brought home when he witnessed the beheading of a Chinese man who had arrived in Lhasa without permission. After this incident, Nain Singh seldom appeared in public. At night, he would climb out quietly from the window onto the roof of the small inn where he stayed. Then, he would use his sextant to determine latitude by measuring the angular altitude of the stars. He also used his thermometer to record the boiling point of water as the higher the altitude, the lower the boiling point. Using this method, he estimated that Lhasa was at an altitude of 3420 metres above sea level. This is very close to the modern measurement of 3540 metres.

Nain Singh left Lhasa in April along with a Ladakhi caravan and headed west for 800 km along the River Tsangpo. All along he kept taking readings in secret. After two months with the caravan he slipped away on his own and made his way back to India via the sacred Mansarovar Lake. He arrived back at the Survey of India headquarters on 27 October 1866. During his twenty-one-month adventure, he had surveyed thousands of kilometres, taken thirty-one latitude fixes, and determined elevation in thirty-three places and the first accurate position of the Tibetan capital. Nain Singh would return to Tibet in 1873–75 to explore a more northerly route from Leh in Ladakh to Lhasa. Some of his family members would join the dangerous profession and work for the Survey of India.

Nain Singh's reports raised an interesting geographical question. Where did the Tsangpo flow? Did it cross the Himalayas as Singh suggested, and become the river known to Indians as the Brahmaputra? In order to solve the mystery, the Survey decided to slip someone back into Tibet and float something identifiable down the Tsangpo. If it turned up in the Brahmaputra in Assam, they would know the answer.

The two man team for the job consisted of a Chinese lama living in Darjeeling and a Sikkimese surveyor called Kinthup. The Survey had badly misjudged the lama, who was more intent on enjoying himself than on getting the work done, and often got drunk. The team was stuck in one village for four months because the lama fell in love with their host's wife. When the affair became known, the lama had to pay Rs 25 in compensation and leave. Things did not improve when at last they had crossed into Tibet. The lama sold Kinthup as a slave to the headman of a Tibetan village and disappeared. From May 1881 to March 1882, Kinthup worked as a slave before taking refuge in a monastery as a novice monk. After several months of living as a monk, he received permission to go on a pilgrimage. He went to a place near the Tsangpo and spent many days cutting up 500 logs into a regular size. These he hid in a cave before returning to the monastery.

A few months later, he got permission to go to Lhasa on a pilgrimage. There he got a fellow Sikkimese to write the following message for his bosses at the Survey:

'Sir, The Lama who was sent with me sold me to a Djongpen (headman) as a slave and himself fled away with the Government things that were in his charge. On account of which the journey proved a bad one; however, I, Kinthup, have prepared the 500 logs according to the order of Captain Harman, and am prepared to throw them 50 logs a day into the Tsangpo from Bipung in Pemake, from the fifth to the fifteenth day of the tenth Tibetan month of the year called Chuhuluk, of the Tibetan calendar'.[19]

Kinthup did as he promised before returning to India. Unfortunately, the watch on the Brahmaputra had been abandoned by now and the letter arrived too late. Since we now know that the Tsangpo is indeed the Brahmaputra, the logs must have floated unnoticed down to Assam and then into Bengal. Kinthup, thus, did not receive the acclaim he deserved and he lived out his remaining life as a tailor in Darjeeling. Such was the world that inspired Rudyard Kipling to write tales of adventure like *The Man who would be King* and *Kim*.

THE LAST OF THE LIONS

Life in British India was not just about cartographic surveys and Victorian engineering. The British also enjoyed life in India. One of the popular pastimes of the rich and powerful was the hunt, particularly of tigers. According to Valmik Thapar, as many as 20,000 tigers were shot for sport between 1860 and 1960 by Indian princes and British hunting parties. Mahesh Rangarajan separately estimates that an overall 80,000 tigers may have been destroyed between 1875 and 1925, as they were considered dangerous and official bounties were paid for them.[20] Despite this devastation, it is thought that the tiger population in 1900 was between 25,000 and 40,000. So, where were the lions?

As we have seen, the British encountered the lion quite early when Sir Thomas Roe dealt with one during Emperor Jehangir's time. Accounts of lion hunts in Aurangzeb's time suggest that the animal was still fairly common in the beginning of the eighteenth century. However, their numbers seem to have dramatically fallen by the early nineteenth century. My guess is that it was a combination of two important factors. First, the rapid improvement in gun technology made it very easy to kill an animal that prefers to live in the open. Second, the collapse of Mughal power also removed imperial protection. Any rebel, mercenary or local despot with a gun could go out and shoot the animal.

Still, there was a sizeable population of lions in North India in the early 1800s. We know that William Frazer shot eighty-four lions in the 1820s and took great pride in having been personally responsible for the extinction of the species in Haryana.[21] In the 1830s, Maharaja Ranjit Singh's lancers were spearing these cats near Lahore. There are reports of large lion populations in Central India in the 1850s and of ten lions being shot in Kotah, Rajasthan, in 1866. Then, suddenly, the lions virtually disappear except for a small population in Gujarat. What happened?

In my view, habitat loss was far more devastating than hunting. According to Angus Maddison's estimates, between 1820 and 1913, the country's population jumped from 209 million to 303 million (not counting the rest of the subcontinent). This meant that agriculture had to be scaled up in order to feed this growing population. At the same time, the railways made it possible to export agricultural commodities like opium and raw cotton. In short, the open ranges needed by the lion (and the cheetah) were just gobbled up by farming within a few generations. The tiger too suffered habitat loss, but did better than the lion because it can survive in hilly and swampy terrain that is less conducive to agriculture.

By the late nineteenth century, there were reports that perhaps only a dozen Asiatic lions were left in the wild in the Gir forests of Junagarh, a princely state in Gujarat. The actual number was almost certainly larger, but at last alarm bells began to ring. Lord Curzon, the Viceroy, heard of this and refused to go on a lion hunt in Gir during his state visit to Junagarh in November 1900. The Nawabs of Junagarh, with the support of the colonial government, now became the guardians of the endangered species for the next half-century. The Gir forest was protected and hunting strictly regulated. Only the most senior British officials and Indian princes were allowed the privilege. In fact, there is a lot of correspondence to show that the Nawabs had to refuse permission to many princes and British officials who wanted to hunt in Gir. It must have been diplomatically difficult but, to their credit, the Nawabs stood their ground. Gir is still the only place where the Asiatic lion survives in the wild with a count of 411 in 2010. The Indian cheetah was not so lucky. The last documented sighting of the Indian cheetah was in Madhya Pradesh in 1947, the same year that India became independent.[22]

A New New Delhi

After the sack of 1858, Delhi dwindled to being a mere district headquarters in Punjab province. The census of 1881 showed that its urban population had dwindled to 173,393.[23] The Mughal-era city of Shahjehanabad was still the main urban hub, with European troops based inside the Red Fort and Indian troops stationed in Daryagunj. The railways had connected the city to Lahore in the west and to Calcutta in the east. To the north of the walled city, the British had built a Civil Lines with large bungalows and gardens. With its numerous historical buildings, late-nineteenth-century Delhi would have been picturesque but, compared to Bombay, Calcutta or Madras, it was a backwater. And so it remained till 1911.

Meanwhile, tiny cracks were appearing in the foundations of the British Raj. Yet again, the vagaries of nature were partly responsible for this. From 1874, India suffered a series of severe droughts. At first Bengal and Bihar were affected, but the Viceroy Lord Northbrook and famine commissioner Sir Richard Temple dealt with it reasonably competently by importing rice from Burma. Instead of congratulating them, however, British Prime Minister Disraeli's government severely criticized them for wasting money. Northbrook resigned over his growing differences with Disraeli's hawkish approach. The replacement, Lord Lytton, proved a disaster.

In 1876, the rains failed for a third year and the famine situation became acute in southern India. Lord Lytton, however, remained focused on fiscal control and even rebuked the Governor of Madras for being too generous. Sir Richard Temple, in the meantime, had learnt his lesson and had become a champion of the Malthusian approach. By 1877, the famine had spread across the Deccan and Rajasthan to the north-west, and yet, grain from surplus provinces was still being exported out to the rest of the world. The Great Famine would directly or indirectly kill 5.5 million people, more than two-thirds of them in British-controlled parts of the subcontinent. The experience was made worse by the fact that, amidst this crisis, Lord Lytton spent extravagantly on the Delhi Durbar of 1877, where Queen Victoria was proclaimed Empress of India in front of all the princes of the subcontinent. It was a shock that fundamentally undermined the moral standing of British rule in the eyes of many Indians, especially the educated. This resentment would lead to the formation of the Indian National Congress in 1885 and would ultimately build into the wider Independence Movement of the early twentieth century.

As the demands for independence gathered momentum, the colonial government began to look for ways to shore up legitimacy. One idea that gained favour was to follow the Mughals and build a new capital in Delhi as it was believed that the 'idea of Delhi clings to the Mohammedan mind'. The idea was not without its critics, but Viceroy Hardinge probably felt that this was his best chance to be remembered as the founder of a great city. Ultimately the factor that clinched the issue was the need for a grand sound-bite for the Durbar held in 1911 to commemorate the coronation of George V as Emperor of India. The proclamation was read out at Coronation Park, to the far north of the city. This is the same spot where Queen Victoria had been declared the Empress of India. A great stone column was raised to mark the event.

Almost no tourist visits the place these days and one is likely to find oneself alone with the column and the stern statutes of colonial-era worthies. King George V glares down from a pedestal removed from the canopy opposite India Gate in the 1960s. There are several pedestals without statues, as if their occupants were upset by years of neglect and have walked off.

The architects Edwin Lutyens and Herbert Baker were given the job of designing the new city. The original idea was to build the city to the north of Shahjehanabad, roughly around where Delhi University now stands. However, after a number of ground surveys, it was decided to build the new city to the south of the existing urban cluster. This had the symbolic advantage of being close to the ruins of many older Delhis—Dinpanah, Indraprastha, Feroze Shah Kotla. Note that the new city was not built as a practical hub of commerce and industry. It was meant as a display of imperial power—a city of magnificent processions and imposing symbolic structures.

The centrepiece was the palace of the Viceroy built on Raisina Hill, what we now know as Rashtrapati Bhavan. There were many opinions about what this building should look like, ranging from classical European to Indo–Sarcenic and Mughal. Lutyens's own opinion of India aesthetics was closer to those of Mughal Emperor Babur, but Baker was somewhat more sympathetic to the native style. Ultimately, the compromise was a design that combines classical European columns with Mughal and Rajput detailing. In front of the palace was a grand avenue called Kingsway (now Rajpath) inspired by the Mall in Washington DC. The intention was to impress and, more than a century later, it still impresses.

The rest of New Delhi consisted of government offices and spacious bungalows built in the mould of a garden city. It was a Civil Lines on a gigantic scale with a strict hierarchy. In the delightful politically incorrect style of the time, the residential areas were clearly demarcated on the basis of race and seniority as 'fat white', 'thin white' and 'thin black'. Since no senior Indian official was envisaged, there was no space for 'fat black'.[24] The whole thing was designed for a population of less than 60,000 including servants and other support staff. The only space for commerce was Connaught Place and its surroundings. Dubbed as 'Lutyens's Delhi', this imperial construct serves today as the capital of the Republic of India. It is *amusing* that, after independence, over-fed politicians feigning poverty in their white kurta-pyjamas would come to occupy the spacious bungalows meant for the 'fat white'.

A lot has been written about the grand buildings and bungalows of Lutyens's Delhi. However, if one looks at early photographs of the cityscape in the 1920s and 1930s, it looks very different from what we see today. It is not just that much of the city is a construction zone, but even the completed bits look somehow naked. On second glance one realizes that the difference is that the trees that we now associate with the city have not yet grown. Indeed, the systematic and careful planting of trees was a very important part of the overall design and remains a signature feature of the national capital.

The systematic planning of trees was not new in Delhi. At its height, Shahjehanabad (Old Delhi) had several private Mughal gardens belonging to the royal family and senior nobility. This included the Begum Jehanara's gardens north of Chandni Chowk and the two famous gardens within the Red

Fort—Hayat Baksh (Life-Giver) and Mahtab Bagh (Moonlit Garden). The British, however, took this to a totally different level as they tried to create a garden city. There are archival records of heated debates between foresters, horticulturists and civil servants about the ideal species to be planted. Finally the Town Planning Committee submitted a report in 1913 with a list of thirteen trees including neem, jamun and imli that were considered suitable for planting along the avenues of New Delhi.[25] Other species would be introduced in later times, but trees from the original shortlist still dominate many of the roads of Lutyens's Delhi.

The colonial town-planners also invested heavily in reforesting the Aravalli ridges around New Delhi, particularly the Central Ridge just behind Rashtrapati Bhavan. The principal tree that was used for this was the Central American mesquite or 'vilayati keekar' that would become a very common tree in Delhi. People tend to confuse it with the local keekar or babool but, in fact, it is an invasive species that has edged out many of the trees native to the area.[26] As a result of all this tree planting, Central Delhi looks extraordinarily green when seen from a height (say from the Taj Hotel on Mansingh Road). Whatever one may think of the elitism of Lutyens's Delhi, it is certainly unique.

As the construction of the new city neared completion, the British raised their own pillar in front of the Viceregal palace—the Jaipur column headed by a six-point crystal star. It is easily visible through the main gate on Raisina Hill. At its base, it is inscribed: 'In thought faith/ In word wisdom/ In deed courage/ In life service/ So may India be great.' One could take these words as being patronizing or one could think of them as a premonition that colonial rule would soon end. Perhaps recognizing their own transience, the colonial rulers merely wanted later generations to think well of them. By the time New Delhi was completed in the mid-thirties, it was abundantly clear the British rule would not last too much longer.

TO CROSS THE BLACK WATERS

As we have seen, India had withdrawn into itself from the twelfth century. I have not been able to find a good explanation for why they imposed on themselves caste rules that prohibited the crossing of the seas. It is particularly puzzling since Indian merchants and princes became very wealthy from maritime trade. Brahmin scholars also benefited greatly from the demand for their services in South East Asia. It must also be added, nonetheless, that caste rules were never watertight. Indian Muslims, and even Hindus, continued to travel to foreign lands. There are remains of a large Indian trading post in far away Azerbaijan. Built in the seventeenth and eighteenth century, the Ateshgah of Baku includes the remains of a Hindu temple and inscriptions invoking the gods Ganesh and Shiva. There are also records of Indian merchants in Samarkand and Bukhara. Still, it must be admitted that these overseas outposts were a shadow of the thriving Indian networks that had once extended from China to the Middle East.

It was in the nineteenth century, under British rule, that Indians began again to travel abroad in large numbers. An important driver of migration was the demand for indentured labour in British colonies after the abolition of slavery in 1834.

The initial demand came from sugar cane plantations, but soon Indians were being used to build railway lines and work mines. In the early years, the workers expected to come home at the end of the indenture period, but the British decided that it was cheaper to encourage Indians to settle in the colonies. Thus, Indian women were encouraged to join their menfolk. The indentured workers faced a hard life, but the migration process was given a boost by the Great Famine of 1877. In this way, large Indian communities came to settle in faraway British colonies like Fiji, Trinidad, Guyana, Malaya, South Africa and Mauritius. The French colony of Reunion and the Dutch colony of Surinam also received substantial numbers. The place where half a million Indian workers landed in Mauritius is preserved as 'Aapravasi Ghat' (Immigration Depot) and now is a UNESCO World Heritage Site.[27]

A surviving example of a contract for an indentured worker of that period reads as follows:[28]

I, Peroo, engage to proceed to Mauritius to serve E. Antard, pere, or such other persons as I may be transferred to (such transfer being made by mutual consent, to be declared before a public officer), as a khidmutgar, for the space of five years from the date of this agreement, on consideration of receiving a remuneration of Company's rupees ten (10) per month, and food and clothing as follows; viz

Daily:
14 chittanks rice, 2 chittanks dholl, ½ chittanks ghee, ¼ chittanks salt.

Yearly:
1 blanket, 2 dhooties, 1 chintz mirjace, 1 lascar's cap, 1 wooden bowl

. . . also one lotah or brass cup between four persons, and medicine and medical attendance when required; also to be sent back to Calcutta at the expiration of my period of service, free of all expense to myself, should such be my wish, subject to the terms of my general agreement. Executed this day _____ of November 1837.

The contract is followed by a short note signed by F.W. Birch, Superintendent of Calcutta Police that describes Peroo as 'Height, 5 feet, 3 inches; age 28 years; colour, light; particular marks, none; caste Mussalman.' Hundreds of thousands of Indians would have left their homes with contracts like these. It is estimated that less than a third returned. Many perished during the sea journeys and the years of hard labour. Yet, enough of them survived to form the Indian communities scattered across these faraway lands.

Soon, Indian traders and clerks also began to follow the British to the colonies. Gujarati merchants and shopkeepers established a network in eastern and southern Africa. The Tamil Chettiar community was especially active in South East Asia and established a network in Burma, Malaya, Singapore and even French-controlled Vietnam. As they settled in these areas, they would have found tiny remnants of Indian merchant communities that had survived from ancient times. The 'Chitty' community, for instance, had survived for centuries in Malaya with little contact with the original homeland. They had intermarried with local women and adopted local dress, but somehow had retained their Hindu religion and customs. The community is now rapidly merging with the broader Tamil community in modern Malaysia.

Although this network of Indian communities was created

and maintained by British power, the diaspora played an important role in India's struggle for independence from colonial rule. Mahatma Gandhi, for instance, was part of the Indian community in South Africa between 1893 and 1914, and he developed his political and spiritual philosophy of non-violence while fighting for the rights of Indians there. The incident in June 1893 that changed the course of his life was his eviction, on racial grounds, from the first-class compartment of a train, despite the fact that he had a valid ticket. This took place at Pietermaritzburg station—visitors will see a plaque on the platform marking the spot where he was thrown out. Gandhi would return to India only in 1915, at the age of 46, but would soon become the country's leading political figure.

Singapore, by contrast, was the hub of a very different effort to rid India of its colonial masters. When the Japanese captured the island-city during the Second World War, Netaji Subhash Bose used the opportunity to form the Azad Hind Fauj or Indian National Army, by recruiting Indian civilians and soldiers held as prisoners-of-war. The first review of the troops took place in July 1943 on the Padang, a large open field that still exists at the heart of the city. There is a small memorial near the Singapore Cricket Club that marks the event. The original had been demolished by the British after the war, so the current memorial dates only from 1995. You are likely to encounter a few Indian tourists getting themselves photographed in front of it.

A twenty-minute walk will take you to Dhoby Ghat where Bose declared the formation of the Provisional Government of Free India. The proclamation was read out at the Cathay

Cinema Hall. The building has been demolished, but a part of its façade has been preserved as part of a new shopping mall. Bose's army would fail in military terms alongside the defeat of its Japanese sponsors, but it fundamentally undermined the confidence of the British colonial government in the loyalties of its Indian troops. Although seven decades have passed, there are still a few Singaporean and Malaysian Indians alive who personally witnessed and participated in these events. I found it remarkable that these people, many of whom had been born in these parts and had never seen India, had been willing to die for the idea of a civilization.

8

The Contours of
Modern India

After centuries of foreign domination, India finally became independent on 15 August 1947. Unfortunately it was not a time of unmitigated celebration. The subcontinent was partitioned at birth into Muslim-dominated Pakistan and Hindu-majority India, which predictably was a very bloody affair. The matter did not end there. Over a third of the country was ruled by local princes who were less than enthusiastic about losing their kingdoms. There were even enclaves still ruled by the French and the Portuguese, leftovers from the age of colonial conquest. Add to this the fact that the long border with China (initially Tibet) was disputed. Thus, the borders of modern India were not established in August 1947, but evolved to their current shape only in the mid-1970s, when Sikkim was incorporated into the Union. The continued disputes with China and Pakistan mean that the

contours are still not set in stone. We now turn to the story of
how modern India came to have its present borders.

THE PARTITION

Much has been written about the political events that led to
the partition of India. Given the geographical focus of this
book, I do not wish to recount these events except to say that,
at its core, it was the result of a fundamental disagreement
about the nature of India's civilizational nationhood. Indeed,
Mohammad Ali Jinnah explicitly stated his demand for Pakistan
in civilizational terms on several occasions. It is not a
divergence in world view that appeared suddenly with Jinnah
in the 1930s. It can be traced back centuries to the differences
between the Emperors Akbar and Aurangzeb. In fact, the
intellectual origins of Pakistan are derived from a sixteenth-
century Islamic scholar from Punjab, Ahmad al-Sirhindi. A
prominent member of the Naqshbandi Sufi order, Sirhindi
loudly denounced Akbar's eclectic beliefs and his liberal
attitude. In order to understand the subsequent history of
Pakistan, therefore, it may be more instructive to read Sirhindi
rather than Jinnah.

As the country hurtled towards independence in the mid-
1940s, the demands of the Muslim League became increasingly
strident. Amid growing tensions and frequent riots, the decision
was taken to divide India along religious lines. The meeting
that finalized Partition was held on 2 June 1947 in Viceroy
Mountbatten's study, under a large oil painting of Robert
Clive.[1] The Indian National Congress was represented by
Jawaharlal Nehru, Sardar Patel and Acharya Kripalani. The

Muslim League was represented by Jinnah, Liaquat Ali Khan and Rab Nishtar. In addition, there was Baldev Singh representing the Sikhs. Lord Ismay and Sir Eric Miéville, two of the Viceroy's key advisers, sat along the wall. The decision was announced at 7 p.m. on 3 June on All India Radio. The Viceroy spoke first, followed by Nehru and then by Jinnah. Pakistan was a reality.

No date had been announced for the handover. However, when Viceroy Mountbatten was later asked about it at a press conference, he replied that the final transfer of power to Indian hands would happen on 15 August—just seventy-two days later! It appears that this was a unilateral decision Mountbatten made—he had not consulted the Indian National Congress, the Muslim League or even Downing Street about it. It was a shock to everyone. It is unclear why Mountbatten opted for this date; it may have been no more than a sentimental attachment to the day on which the Japanese had surrendered to the Allies in 1945. It is instructive how the twists and turns of history can often be based on the most arbitrary of factors.

The partition of India was a major project. Writers Lapierre and Collins have aptly dubbed it 'the most complex divorce in history' and yet it had to be completed within a few weeks. Everything from the apparatus of the State, including the army, to government assets and debts had to be divided fairly between two sovereign countries. Even chairs, tables, petty cash, books and postage stamps had to be divided. There were many arguments, and often over very petty things. Sets of Encyclopaedia Britannica in government libraries were divided up. There is a story of how the instruments of the police band in Lahore were divided up—a drum for India, a trumpet for Pakistan and so on. In the end, the last trombone was left and the two sides almost came to blows over it. As often happens, the madness of the situation is best captured in fiction; Manto's 'Toba Tek Singh' is a short story about how the inmates of Lahore's mental asylum had to be divided up along communal grounds.

The frictions over dividing government property were minor compared to the real business of dividing territory, particularly the two large provinces of Punjab and Bengal. This job fell to a London barrister, Sir Cyril Radcliffe. He was considered one of the most brilliant lawyers of his time but had had nothing to do with India. His unfamiliarity with India was considered a major advantage as it was felt that this was the only way to ensure impartiality. On 27 June he was called to the office of the Lord Chancellor and given the job. Radcliffe must have been stunned when he heard this. He was being asked to decide the fate of millions of people with no previous knowledge of the territories that he was expected to divide. He must have known that, no matter what he did, his decisions would lead to unhappiness and bloodshed. It was the worst job in the world.

Radcliffe set to work in the sweltering July heat from a lonely bungalow in the Viceregal estate in Delhi. Given the paucity of time, he had no opportunity to visit the lands that he had to divide. Instead, he had to trace out a boundary line on a Royal Engineers map with merely population statistics and maps for company. If he had not already known it, he would soon have realized the near-impossibility of what he was expected to do. The Hindu and Muslim enclaves were haphazardly mixed up. The city of Lahore, for example, was split exactly between the Muslim and the Hindu–Sikh populations (600,000 each). Similarly, Amritsar was a holy city for the Sikhs, but was surrounded by Muslim-majority areas. There were other factors to be considered as well. In Bengal, Calcutta was the main industrial cluster and had a Hindu majority. However, the raw jute for its jute mills came from the Muslim-majority east. In Punjab, critical irrigation systems had to be severed. The barrister would have pondered these issues in the solitude of his bungalow.

Even as Radcliffe was drawing his line, communal violence continued to escalate across the countryside. Refugees were already on the move even before the border had been demarcated. The maps that would decide the fate of millions was delivered to the Viceroy on 13 August, but they were not made public for seventy-two hours. Thus, when India became independent on 15 August, many Indians along the borderlands did not know in which country their homes would fall. The maps were made public a day later and the bloodbath began. People were on the move—on trains, on bullock-carts and on foot—holding on to whatever they could salvage of their former lives. It is estimated that about 7 million Muslims moved from India to Pakistan and a similar Hindu–Sikh population shifted from Pakistan to India. Meanwhile, a disenchanted Radcliffe returned to his London chambers. He returned the 2000 pounds that he had received for his services.

The Hindus and Sikhs who fled West Pakistan were directed to hundreds of refugee camps. One of the largest camps was in Kurukshetra, the battlefield where the Pandavas and Kauravas are said to have fought each other in the

Mahabharata. The camp was planned for 100,000, but three times the number came to inhabit it by December 1947.[2] Half a million refugees, mostly from West Punjab, came to Delhi. These desperate people squatted wherever they could, including the pavements of Connaught Circus. In time, they would build homes in 'colonies' allotted to them in the south and west of Lutyens's garden city. We know them today as Lajpat Nagar, Rajendra Nagar, Punjabi Bagh and so on. A smaller group of refugees from East Pakistan also made their way to Delhi and were settled in East Pakistan Displaced Persons Colony. Now renamed Chittaranjan Park, it retains a distinct Bengali identity. Thus, within a few decades, Delhi had gone from being city of Mughal memories to a grand Imperial dream and then to a city of refugees.

If the migration happened in one big rush in Punjab, it was spread over many years in Bengal. A series of anti-Hindu riots in East Pakistan in 1949–50 forced a second spike in refugee movements, with 1.7 million coming to West Bengal in 1950 alone.[3] A steady trickle continued for over a decade. Indeed, many members of my mother's family made the shift only in the early sixties. The luckier refugees stayed with relatives and friends but, as in Delhi, many squatted wherever they could—in railways stations, unoccupied homes, vacant land and even barracks. There have been accusations, arguably true, that the national government in Delhi did far less to rehabilitate the Bengali refugees than their Punjabi counterparts. Still, unlike in West Pakistan, a sizeable Hindu population continued to live in East Pakistan. They would face a second crisis two decades later.

Despite all their troubles, the Punjabis and Bengalis at least had provinces, namely West Bengal and East Punjab, that they could call their own. The sorriest communities, therefore, were those that could no longer lay claim to any territory. For instance, the Sindhi Hindus found that their entire province was part of Pakistan. Many of them headed for Bombay, where they were accommodated in five refugee camps. A concentration of Sindhis remains in Ulhasnagar, an industrial suburb of Mumbai. Over the years, however, they have migrated all over the world and today run a network of international businesses. Hong Kong, for instance, has a significant number of successful Sindhi business families. I have attended Sindhi community gatherings in the former British colony. It is touching to see how old customs have been lovingly kept alive by a generation that has had no contact with the original homeland.

ABSORBING THE PRINCELY STATES

The partition of British India was not the only territorial problem faced by the country at independence. Over a third of the country was ruled by princes, over 500 of them. Some of them ruled kingdoms that were as big as major European countries, while others ruled only a few villages. Some of them had survived from before the Islamic conquests. It says a lot about the spirit of the times and the persuasive powers of the negotiators that, after a lot of grumbling, the occasional theatrics and some last-minute bargaining, almost all of them signed over their kingdoms to the new democracy by the 15 August deadline (of course, some also opted for Pakistan). There were three important exceptions to this—Junagarh in the west, Hyderabad in the south, and Jammu and Kashmir in the extreme north. The first two had Muslim rulers but a Hindu-majority population, while the reverse was true of Jammu and Kashmir.

Junagarh was not just wedged within Indian territory but was also of great symbolic value. Within its borders were the ancient temple of Somnath and the sacred hill of Girnar with its numerous Hindu–Jain temples. At the base of the hill, and a short walk from the Junagarh fort, are the rock inscriptions of Ashoka, Rudradaman and Skandagupta. In addition, it is home to the last Asiatic lions left in the wild. In 1947, it was ruled by Nawab Mohabat Khan, best remembered for his love of dogs. It is said that he owned 2000 pedigree dogs and that when two of his favourites mated, the 'wedding' was celebrated as a State event.

In the summer of 1947, Mohabat Khan was on holiday in Europe but had left the country in hands of his Dewan, Sir Shah Nawaz Bhutto, a Sindhi politician and the father of future Pakistan Prime Minister Zulfikar Ali Bhutto. When the Nawab returned, Bhutto convinced him to opt out of India. On 14 August 1947, just hours before the handover, Junagarh declared itself for Pakistan! A few weeks later, Pakistan accepted the accession. The local population, 82 per cent Hindu, and India's leaders were enraged. Deputy Prime Minister Patel, himself a Gujarati, responded by getting two of Junagarh's vassal states to declare for India. A small military force was sent in to support them. Meanwhile, a popular agitation began to gather momentum. The Nawab panicked and fled to Karachi, taking with him a dozen of his favourite dogs! With his back to the wall, Sir Shah Nawaz agreed to a plebiscite that overwhelmingly voted in favour of India.

The period of political uncertainty in Junagarh meant that the lions of Gir suffered. With the Nawab's protection crumbling, several lions were hunted down in the later months of 1947. It is said that some of the hunters were princes of neighbouring principalities who simply took advantage of the confusion to add to their private collections. Thankfully, order was restored by early 1948. This was not merely an act of wildlife conservation. The lion, as depicted on the Mauryan pillar in Sarnath, was now the national emblem. There had been some who argued in favour of the elephant but a committee headed by future president Rajendra Prasad had ruled in favour of the lion in July 1947. The same committee also decided that the flag of the Indian National Congress would be adopted as the national flag after replacing the symbol of the 'charkha' (spinning wheel) with that of the spoked wheel from the same Mauryan column—the ancient symbol of the Chakravartin or Universal Monarch. After thousands of years, Sudas's dream was still alive.

Even as the Junagarh crisis was being resolved, a fresh crisis was brewing in Hyderabad, a leftover from Aurangzeb's invasion of southern India. It was the largest of the princely states and its ruler Nizam Osman Ali Khan was famous as one of the richest and most miserly men in the world. Although the state had an overwhelming Hindu majority, the Muslims dominated the police, civil service and the landowning nobility. It even had a sizeable army that included armoured units as well as Arab and Afghan mercenaries. Faced with the withdrawal of the British, the Nizam first attempted to negotiate some form of independence and then hinted that he would opt for Pakistan.

The threat was never really tenable since Hyderabad was a landlocked state surrounded by Indian territory. Still, the Nizam was persuaded by Kasim Razvi, an Islamic fanatic, to allow the creation of an irregular paramilitary group called the Razakdars, which had 200,000 members at its height. As the political situation deteriorated, the Razakdars unleashed a reign of terror in the countryside. India responded by tightening an economic blockade. Finally in September 1948, more than a year after independence, Deputy Prime Minister Patel decided to move. The military action was named Operation Polo, supposedly because of the large number of polo grounds in Hyderabad.

The Indian army columns entered Hyderabad state on 13 September and were met with some resistance from the Razakdars as well as from regular troops. However, the result was never in doubt and, by the morning of 17 September, it was all over. The surrender was surprisingly meek. *Time* magazine (issue of 27 September 1948) tells the story of how the surrender took place a few miles outside the city. The commander-in-chief of Hyderabad's army, a black-mustached Arab called Major General Syed Ahmed El Erdoos drove up in a shiny Buick. He then walked up to Major General Chaudhuri, the Indian field commander. 'They shook hands, lit cigarettes and talked quietly while the spellbound villagers looked on'.[4]

The story of Jammu and Kashmir, however, is very different. Here a Hindu prince ruled over a Muslim-majority kingdom. However, the overall Muslim majority obscured a more complicated situation on the ground. The north-east of the state was Ladakh, a large but sparsely populated area dominated by Buddhists. To the north-west were the equally sparsely populated areas of Gilgit and Baltistan. The population here was Muslim but from the Shia and Ismaili sects rather than the Sunni branch. In the middle was Kashmir itself, including the Valley, relatively densely populated and largely Sunni, albeit with significant Sikh, Hindu and Shia minorities. Finally, to the south was Jammu, home to the Dogra Rajputs who had conquered this kingdom, with a Hindu population boosted by recent refugees from West Punjab. Unlike Junagarh and Hyderabad, moreover, this state shared borders with both India and Pakistan. This meant that it was feasible for it to choose sides. Yet, Maharaja Hari Singh had visions of remaining independent as some sort of Asian Switzerland. The situation could not have been more complex.

One will never know how things may have eventually resolved themselves because the flow of history was hijacked by an unexpected turn of events. On 22 October 1947, thousands of armed Pakhtun tribesmen from Pakistan's North West poured into Kashmir. No one knows for sure exactly who organized or instigated them, although they certainly had the support of newly formed Pakistan. Their initial progress was quick and largely unopposed. The remote mountain valleys were cut off from the rest of the world and even Hari Singh had no idea what was happening. The ruler only realized the seriousness of the situation when the invaders blew up Mahura power station, plunging the state into darkness. The tribesmen were just 75 km away from Srinagar, the capital. At this stage, they could just have driven down the short undefended and well-paved road and taken over. However, greed overpowered strategy and religious fervour. The tribesmen indulged in an orgy of rape and plunder where they spared neither Hindu nor Muslim. They also stopped to rape the European nuns of a Franciscan mission in Baramullah, barely 50 km from the capital. All this delayed their progress by a critical forty-eight hours.

The Indian authorities in Delhi first heard of the invasion from a very curious source. Remember that this was barely two months after independence, and the Commanders-in-Chief of both the Indian and Pakistani armies were British. The Commander-in-Chief of the Pakistan army was Major General Douglas Gracey who received secret intelligence reports of what was going on in Kashmir.[5] The first thing he did was to pick up his phone in Rawalpindi and call his Sandhurst classmate Lt. General Rob Lockhart, the Commander-in-Chief of the Indian army! It did not take long for Mountbatten and Nehru to find out what was happening.

Given the desperate situation, it was not difficult to convince a panicky Hari Singh to sign an Instrument of Accession in favour of India. By the morning of 27 October, Indian troops had secured Srinagar airport and were landing men and supplies. The tribesmen had lost the initiative and had been stopped at the gates of the city. Jinnah was furious. Bit by bit, the Indians began to push the invaders out even as the bitterly cold winter set in. It bears mention here that one of the heroes of the Indian side was Brigadier Mohammad Usman, a Muslim officer who had opted to stay with India. He would later be killed in battle in July 1948.

The first Indo–Pak war in Kashmir dragged on through 1948. Although Srinagar had been secured, western Kashmir, Gilgit and Baltistan remained in Pakistani hands. For a while, Pakistan even took over the strategically important towns of

Kargil and Dras and threatened Ladakh. However, by November 1948, Indian troops had cleared the two towns and secured supply lines to Ladakh. (Half a century later, Pakistan would try to recapture the towns in what is now known as the Kargil war of 1999.) Given the momentum, some Indian commanders wanted to push ahead. However, they were refused permission. The matter now shifted to the United Nations. The cease-fire positions of December 1948 have come to be the effective boundary between the two countries. This border was designated the 'Line of Control' as per the Simla Accord of 1972.

On 26 January 1950, the country threw off the last vestige of British rule by declaring itself a Republic. By now, India's borders were recognizably like those that we know today. The country had a population of 359 million or 14.2 per cent of the world's population (by comparison, China had 546 million people and the United States 152 million). However, its share of world economy stood at a mere 4.2 per cent in 1950 compared to 16 per cent in 1820, and a far cry from the 30–33 per cent that it had enjoyed in ancient times. Note that in 1950, the United States was by far the largest economy in the world with a 27 per cent share. Ravaged by war, the Chinese economy was just a tad larger than India's. After adjusting for relative population sizes, even dirt-poor India had a per capita income level that was 40 per cent higher than the Chinese level.[6]

THE LAST COLONIAL

With the British withdrawal complete and the princely states absorbed, the Indian government now turned to the tiny enclaves along the coast held by other European powers. These were remnants of an era of European exploration and conquest before Robert Clive changed the rules of the game. The French had five such enclaves. The largest was Pondicherry, south of Chennai and close to the ancient port of Mahabalipuram. The others included Chandannagar (just north of Calcutta), Yanam (on the Andhra coast), Mahe (on the Kerala coast) and Karaikal (on the Tamil coast).

As pressure from the Indian government and the local population grew, the French attempted to delay re-integration. However, they showed remarkable restraint compared to how they reacted in Algeria and Vietnam. Perhaps they recognized the inevitable. In June 1949, Chandannagar opted to merge with India, and a year later it was integrated with the state of West Bengal. The French hung on to their enclaves in southern India for a few more years, but the situation was growing increasingly tense on the ground. Finally, in 1954, the French handed over the rest of the territories.[7]

Pondicherry, renamed Puducherry, is today a Union Territory (i.e. a province directly ruled by the central government) but most Indians do not realize that it also includes the three other enclaves of Yanam, Mahé and Karaikal. French influence lives on in many ways. The main town of Puducherry retains many colonial-era buildings as well as the rigid street-grid designed by the French. Many locals even hold French citizenship, descendants of those who chose to remain French at the time of the handover. Perhaps the most thriving of French legacies, however, is also the most unexpected: a community set up by a Bengali revolutionary, Aurobindo Ghosh, who fled British India in 1910 to avoid arrest and was granted asylum by the authorities in Pondicherry. Here he shifted his focus from politics to spirituality and attracted a huge following. Although the movement has branches all over India and abroad, Pondicherry remains home to many institutions as well as a commune inspired by the spiritual leader.

Having tackled the French, New Delhi now turned its attention to the Portuguese. The Portuguese held several small enclaves along the western coast. Goa was the single largest territory, but there were also Diu, Daman, Dadra, and Nagar-Haveli. In the sixteenth century, the Portuguese had used a network of such enclaves to enforce their control over the Indian Ocean. Although much diminished in power by the twentieth century, they had survived Vijayanagar, the Mughals and the British. They saw no reason why they should leave just because India had been declared a Republic. The Portuguese dictator Antonio Salazar condescendingly declared that Goa represented the 'light of the West in the Orient'.

For all their bravado, the Portuguese should have recognized their situation when, in the summer of 1954, a small group of local activists simply took over the government in Dadra and in Nagar-Haveli. It was not immediately absorbed into India and for a while it remained an independent country in the eyes of international law! The Portuguese responded by bolstering their defences in the remaining territories with African troops from Portuguese East Africa (now Mozambique). Protests and strikes were severely put down and thousands were arrested. Prime Minister Nehru had hoped that the matter would be eventually resolved through negotiation but, by late 1961, patience had run out.

Operation Vijay began with the Indian Air Force bombing Dabolim airport at dawn on 18 December 1961. This is the same airport that tourists use today when they fly to Goa. Within hours, Indian ground troops were pouring into Goa from the north, south and east. The Indian Navy pressed in from the west. Similar operations were carried out simultaneously against the other enclaves of Daman and Diu. Lisbon had instructed the defenders to fight to the end, but they simply had no chance against such overwhelming force. The only show of defiance came from *NRP Alfonso de Albuquerque*, the sole Portuguese warship in Goa. Built in the 1930s, it was a medium-sized frigate that was outmoded and hopelessly outgunned by the large, modern fleet it faced on the morning of 18 December. By noon, it was engaged by two Indian frigates at the entrance of Marmagao port. The two sides exchanged fire but, within half an hour, *Alfonso de Albuquerque* was no longer a functioning ship. The crew then ran it aground near Dona Paula beach and used it as a fixed battery. They defiantly kept firing the guns for another hour and a half till they stopped due to mounting casualties and a lack of ammunition. The Portuguese had come to India with cannons firing from their ships, and they left in the same way. Yet another of the circularities of Indian history.

Barely thirty-six hours after the invasion began, the Portuguese Governor General Vassalo e Silva saw the futility of his position and signed the document of unconditional surrender. It was Christmas season, but Lisbon was in mourning. 'Cinemas and theatres shut down as thousands marched in a silent parade from Lisbon's city hall to the cathedral, escorting the relics of St. Francis Xavier'.[8] Vassalo e

Silva returned home to a hostile reception. Salazar had him court-martialed and then exiled. I must admit that I feel somewhat sorry for the last colonial.

Reading press reports about the liberation of Goa half a century after the event, I was struck by the extreme hostility with which Western diplomats and media of that time reacted to Indian actions. The United States and Britain pushed for a UN resolution against India, but it was vetoed by the USSR. Press reports railed against Indian aggression and shed many a tear for Goa's Christians, ignoring the fact that leading pro-liberation activists like Tristão de Braganza Cunha were themselves Christian.[9] A *Time* magazine article 'India: End of an Image' dated 29 December 1961, openly called Nehru a hypocrite who preached peace abroad but used force at home. The magazine appears not to have noticed that after waiting for fourteen years for the Portuguese to come to the table, the Prime Minister was looking increasingly ridiculous.

DUELS WITH THE DRAGON

Taking Goa from a spent power like Portugal was one thing, but it was quite another to deal with Mao's China. The Sino–Indian border can be divided into two sectors. In the east, it is defined by the McMahon Line which had been agreed upon between the Tibetans and the British as per the Simla Agreement of 1914. It was named after Sir Arthur Henry McMahon who was the chief negotiator for the British side. It generally followed the crest of the Himalayan range eastwards from Tawang near the Bhutan tri-border and defined the northern boundary of the North East Frontier Agency[10] (what we now know as the state of Arunachal Pradesh). An early version of the Line had also been endorsed by a Chinese representative, but the final detailed version was signed only by Tibet and British India.

In the middle Himalayas, India and China were separated by three kingdoms—Nepal, Bhutan and Sikkim (the last was then an Indian protectorate). The border resumed in the western Himalayas and ran along what are now the states of Uttarakhand and Himachal Pradesh and finally ran into Ladakh. Here, India had inherited the territorial claims of the former kingdom of Jammu and Kashmir. However, there was uncertainty about a large but uninhabited territory that is now Chinese-controlled Aksai Chin. Nineteenth-century British surveyors had demarcated the border on two separate occasions, using two different natural contours.[11] The first demarcation is called the Johnson Line, drawn in 1865 between Kashmir and Turkestan (this was during the Dungun revolt, when the Chinese were not in control of the area). This line used the Kunlun mountains as the natural boundary which left Aksai Chin within Kashmir.

The famous explorer Francis Younghusband visited Aksai Chin in the 1880s and reported that the area largely uninhabited except for a few bands of nomadic herdsmen, and a small fort in the cold and barren landscape, intermittently manned by the Maharaja of Kashmir. In 1899, however, the British drew a new border called the Macartney–Macdonald Line. This time, they used the Karakoram range as the natural boundary and left out Aksai Chin, possibly to create a defensible buffer against Russian expansion in the region. The British then went on to use both the lines in their maps till 1947. It must be added here that no Chinese map showed Aksai Chin as part of China before the 1920s, and a map of Xinjiang from the 1930s also shows the Kunlun rather than the Karakoram as the customary boundary.[12] In short, Aksai Chin's status was unclear and it was up for grabs, although the Indian claim was probably a bit stronger.

After independence, India's focus remained on Kashmir's western border, leaving the eastern boundary essentially unmarked and unpatrolled. Sino–India relations in the early 1950s were marked by great shows of friendship by Premiers Nehru and Chou En-Lai. It was the age of 'Hindi-Chini Bhai-Bhai' (meaning Indians and Chinese are brothers). It appears that Nehru was led to believe that the Chinese accepted the McMahon Line in the east and that any disagreements over the western border could be ironed out by friendly negotiations. Thus, it came as a shock when it was found in 1957 that, over the previous year, the Chinese had quietly built a highway between Tibet and Xinjiang that went right through Aksai Chin. The Indian government did not even know about such a major project being constructed on territory that it claimed!

Matters really heated up from there. An official Chinese magazine published a map in 1958 that showed large parts of Ladakh and the North East Frontier Agency (NEFA) as part of Chinese territory. If any reader was not convinced about the importance of cartography in history, I hope they have changed their mind by now. Nehru wrote angry letters to Chou En-Lai. The Chinese responded that Aksai Chin had always been Chinese territory and that the McMahon Line was not valid as it had been concluded between British imperialists and the

Tibet Region of China (implying that a mere province had no business negotiating the national boundary). In the middle of all the letter-writing, in March 1959, the Dalai Lama fled to India via Tawang and was granted asylum.

The Chinese had long claimed suzerainty over Tibet and had occasionally exercised it. However, as the Mughals had discovered in the seventeenth century, the hostile terrain made it very difficult to enforce control. Thus, Tibet had been effectively independent for a long time when the communists invaded and annexed it in October 1950. Nehru had, at that time, preferred to look away despite Sardar Patel's warning, just a few weeks before he died, that 'In the guise of ideological expansion lies concealed racial, national or historical claims'.[13]

By the time the Dalai Lama arrived in India, there were regular skirmishes between Indian and Chinese border patrols. Alarm bells were going off everywhere. General Thimayya, the army chief, repeatedly requested an equipment upgrade and the redeployment of troops to the China border. Some units of the army were still armed with .303 Enfield pea-shooters from the First World War. Yet, Prime Minister Nehru and Defence Minister Krishna Menon disregarded the warnings. When asked to introduce Belgian FN4 automatic rifles, Menon retorted that he did not want 'NATO arms' in the country. Dogma came first.

One of the reasons for Thimayya's growing unease was that he had received a first-hand account of Chinese activities in Tibet from a very unlikely source: the adventurer Sydney Wignall. Thimayya had recruited the Welshman who wanted to climb Himalayan peaks on the Nepal–Tibet border (although he had almost no mountaineering experience). He was arrested by the Chinese and interrogated. Wignall was unfazed and told them outrageous stories that Coleridge's *Kubla Khan* was a coded message and that his password, straight out of Welsh rugby, was 'Keep passing to left, boyo'. The Chinese eventually decided that he was mad and let him go—but Wignall reported back to Thimayya that the Chinese were building significant military infrastructure along the border.[14]

With calls for his resignation mounting, Menon decided to promote Brij Mohan Kaul, an officer known to be close to Nehru, to the rank of lieutenant general. Thimayya was furious and threatened to resign. Kaul had not only superseded twelve senior officers but had no field experience. His main experience so far had been in developing real estate on army land. Worse, on 3 October 1962, he was put in charge of defending NEFA!

On 18 October, barely a fortnight after arriving, Kaul complained of chest pains and was evacuated to Delhi. Thus, when the Chinese launched a full-fledged attack on the night of 19 October, the Indian troops were outgunned, outnumbered and leaderless. The Chinese had attacked Ladakh too, but there the Indian army had fallen back to defensible positions and held their ground. In NEFA, however, they were overrun and the Chinese took control of Tawang on 25 October. Here, they halted their advance to construct supply roads. The Indians should have used the time to build up a more defensible position at Bomdila where it would have been easier to resupply from Assam. However, Kaul insisted that the Indians should defend a position farther up at Sela Pass. When the Chinese restarted their advance on 14 November, they simply went around Sela and cut off the Indian troops from behind. There was a massacre and Bomdila fell soon after. When this news arrived in Assam, there was panic. The town of Tezpur was abandoned and even the inmates of the local mental asylum were let loose. In a broadcast, Nehru stated 'My heart goes out to the people of Assam'.[15] It was interpreted to mean that the North East would be abandoned and is still strongly resented by the Assamese.

Then, as suddenly as they had come, the Chinese declared a unilateral ceasefire and withdrew roughly to their pre-war position. We still do not know for sure why they came in and why they left. The most likely reason is that winter was fast approaching and supply lines through the Himalayas would have been difficult to sustain. In the end, nature proved a better defender of the Indian Republic than its politicians. Today, the road from Tezpur to Bomdila is a beautiful drive through dense forests and high mountains. In the lower reaches, wild elephants often hold up traffic. From Bomdila, one can carry on through Sela Pass (4200 metres above sea level) to the monastery at Tawang. Still, the memory of the Chinese invasion lingers. Convoys of army trucks make their way up the mountains to supply military bases that dot the region. The Chinese, too, have not forgotten the past. They still mark the province as 'Southern Tibet' in their maps and made an awful fuss when the Dalai Lama visited Tawang in 2009.

The war had left thousands of Indian soldiers dead or wounded. Nehru's personal reputation lay shattered. The removal of Defence Minister Menon, Lt. General Kaul and army chief General Pran Nath Thapar could not hide Nehru's own strategic miscalculations. As 1963 dragged on, everyone became aware of the obvious—Prime Minister Nehru was an old man who had been in power for sixteen years. History appeared to be repeating itself: an ageing leader who had been on the throne for a long time, unclear succession and war. Indeed, the sixties was a time of great uncertainty. Nehru died in 1964, Pakistan and India fought a war in 1965, Nehru's successor Shastri died in January 1966, the Congress Party split and the economy stagnated.

Out of all this, Nehru's daughter Indira Gandhi emerged as prime minister. In the early seventies, she would play an important role in a major shift in the political geography of the subcontinent.

BANGLADESH

Different perceptions of nationhood had led to the partition of India in 1947, but Pakistan faced the same problem in the 1960s. The basis of its nationhood was the idea of Islamic civilization. However, while they shared a religion, there were major cultural differences between East and West Pakistan. In the east, there was a strong sense of being Bengali. This was strengthened by resentment that political power lay in the hands of politicians and generals based in West Pakistan, who were blatantly insensitive to the needs of the east. It seemed that East Pakistan had just exchanged one form of colonialism with another. As Bengali demands gathered momentum, the response became more repressive. The openly expressed view by the West Pakistani military rulers was that the Bengalis were too influenced by Hindu culture. Particularly suspect was the significant Hindu Bengali population that had continued to live in East Pakistan. Frequent riots, supported tacitly by the State, broke out against the minorities in the mid-60s. Nonetheless, demands for autonomy and fairness continued to grow.

Once again, an act of nature triggered the sequence of events. In November 1970, a major tropical cyclone 'Bhola' struck East Pakistan and killed between 300,000 and 500,000 people. It is considered one of the worst natural disasters on record but, what really incensed the Bengali population was the lukewarm relief efforts of the military dictatorship. So when Pakistan's military leaders finally allowed elections in late December, East Pakistan voted overwhelmingly for the Bengali-nationalist Awami League, which won 167 of 169 seats in the province. Since East Pakistan was more populous than West Pakistan, it raised the prospect that the Bengalis would now rule the country as a whole. This was certainly not palatable to the military brass or to Zulfikar Ali Bhutto, leader of the largest party in West Pakistan. The elections were 'cancelled' and East Pakistan broke into open revolt.

The military government of Yahya Khan responded by sending in the troops. The result was a genocide in which as many as three million people, particularly minorities and intellectuals, were killed. The residential halls of Dhaka University were particularly targeted. Up to 700 students were killed in a single attack on Jagannath Hall. Several well-known professors, both Hindu and Muslim, were murdered. Hundreds of thousands of women were systematically raped in the countryside. By September 1971, ten million refugees had poured into eastern India. Although this was one of the worst genocides in human history, it is barely remembered by the rest of the world. *Time* magazine of August 1971 quoted a US official saying 'This is the most incredible, calculated thing since the days of the Nazis in Poland'.[16] The article goes on to describe the streams of refugees who were pouring into India, carrying with them their few remaining possessions, their children and the infirm:

> They are silent, except for a child whimpering now and then, but their faces tell the story. Many are sick and covered with sores. Others have cholera, and when they die by the roadside there is no one to bury them. The Hindus, when they can, put a hot coal in the mouths of their dead or singe the body in lieu of cremation. The dogs, the vultures and the crows do the rest. As the refugees pass the rotting corpses, some put pieces of cloth over their noses.

The response of the international community to the massacres was shameful. The Chinese premier Chou En-lai sent a letter of support to the Pakistan government and even hinted at military support should the 'Indian expansionists dare to launch aggression against Pakistan'. Meanwhile, the Western world was aware of what was happening. We now have copies of desperate cables sent by diplomat Archer Blood and his colleagues at the US consulate in Dacca (now Dhaka) pleading with the US government to stop supporting a military regime that was carrying out genocide.[17] Instead, President Nixon concentrated on threatening Indira Gandhi to stay out. He would even send the US Seventh Fleet to cow her down.

Fortunately, Prime Minister Indira Gandhi held her ground and began to prepare for war. Strengthened by promises of support from the US and China, Pakistan's military commanders ordered pre-emptive air strikes against India on 3 December 1971. The next morning, the *Statesman* newspaper carried the headline 'It's War'. The Indian response was swift and sharp. With support from the civilian population as well as the Mukti Bahini, an irregular army of Bengali rebels, the Indian army swept into East Pakistan. It was winter and the snow-covered Himalayas prevented any immediate Chinese intervention. Nixon was too bogged down in Vietnam to do more than issue threats. On 16 December, the Pakistanis signed the instrument of surrender in Dacca. Thus, Bangladesh was born. However, given its implied acquiescence, the international community has conveniently forgotten about the genocide and no Pakistani official has ever been indicted for it.

In 1975, India absorbed the protectorate of Sikkim into the Union. The principality had been ruled by the Chogyal, a ruler of Bhutiya extract, who was unpopular with the ethnic Nepali majority. This led to constant friction and demands for popular representation. The Indians were also concerned that the Chinese would press claims that Sikkim was part of Tibet and move in. When elections were finally held, the anti-monarchist Sikkim National Congress won all the seats but one. The Chogyal was forced to abdicate and a referendum in April 1975 overwhelmingly voted to join India. My father was one of the first Indian officials sent in to manage the handover and administer the new state. Thus, my earliest memories are of the beautiful snow-clad peaks of the Kangchenjunga. As one can see, it took almost three decades after British withdrawal for the national borders of the subcontinent to look like what we know them today. They are still not set in stone. India has serious border disputes with China and Pakistan. Even with Bangladesh, there are issues left over from Partition involving tiny enclaves that lie trapped within each other's territory.

MODERNIST BRUTALITY

Almost a century ago, Mahatma Gandhi is said to have commented that 'India lives in its villages'. This was not a comment on population statistics but one about the soul of India. It is a deeply ingrained view that India is somehow a fundamentally rural country, unchanging and eternal. Yet, for all the extraordinary continuities of Indian civilization, the country has gone through many dramatic changes and cycles of urbanization over the millennia. By all indications, it is now embarking on a phase of rapid urbanization that will make India an urban-majority country within a generation. At one level, this will transform the economic, social and physical landscape of the country. At another level, Indian civilization has seen many such changes before and will take the shift in its stride.

When India became a republic in 1950, the share of urban population stood at 17 per cent, while China at 12 per cent was even more rural. The largest cities in India at that stage were Kolkata with a population of 2.6 million, followed by Mumbai at 1.5 million, Chennai at 0.8 million and Delhi at 0.7 million.[18] The Chinese cities of Shanghai and Peking (now Beijing) were much larger, at 3.8 million and 1.6 million respectively. Despite the damage done by war, Tokyo was the largest Asian city, with a population of 6.3 million. Tiny Singapore had less than one million, and not all of this population was urban.

Kolkata, or Calcutta as it was known then, was the country's pre-eminent city in the first two decades after independence. The political capital had shifted to New Delhi but Calcutta was the most important industrial, commercial and cultural hub of the country. It was the headquarters of many of the country's largest companies as well as of leading multinationals. Although it had lost part of its hinterland to East Pakistan, Calcutta's industrial cluster included British-era factories as well as new public sector establishments like Chittaranjan Locomotive Works. The nightlife in Park Street was said to be liveliest in Asia and the city's elite clubs buzzed with the rich and famous.

Unfortunately, it was too good to last. The rise of communism and militant trade unionism from the late sixties sapped the city's entrepreneurial spirit. Through the seventies and eighties, the city was repeatedly brought to a halt by strikes against 'capitalists', 'American imperialism', the central government and even against computers. One by one, the companies left and with them left the patronage for the arts and culture. Educational institutions also suffered from politicization. By the 1980s, the middle class, including me, began to leave in search of education and jobs. Mumbai clearly replaced Kolkata as the country's commercial capital; the latter has never made a serious bid to regain its position.

By the 50s Delhi had reverted to becoming a patchwork of cities rather like what Ibn Batuta had witnessed six centuries earlier. There was Old Delhi, including Shahjehanabad and Civil Lines. Then there was Lutyens's Delhi, which was dominated by the national government. As already discussed, there were also the numerous refugee resettlement colonies.[19] Soon, the city had to deal with yet another influx—that of civil servants and public sector employees needed to run the centrally-planned, socialist economy. The Public Works Department (PWD) went into overdrive and created whole new government colonies. This led to the construction of Bapanagar, Kakanagar, Satya Marg, Moti Bagh and many others. In the seventies, a large new township called Rama Krishna Puram was built to the south-west.

These government areas were built to standardized plans and according to a strict hierarchy denoted as AB, C-1, C-2, D-1, D-2 and so on. The civil servant was expected to slowly make his/her way up this hierarchy over the course of his/her career. Note that a similar housing ladder existed for the military, the public sector, university professors and even for the private sector. Smaller versions of it were created in the state capitals and in industrial townships.

As the son of a civil servant, I too spent my childhood moving up this housing ladder. Life in the government colonies had its pros and cons. Design and maintenance was poor. Painted in lime-wash, the walls flaked off to the touch. The doors and windows expanded and contracted with the seasons—one had to master special techniques to open and close each of them. At the same time, housing for the more senior officials, at least, was spacious, centrally located and had access to parks and other amenities. One interesting aspect of this hierarchical system was the fact that everyone moved up the system at about the same rate. This meant that one grew up with roughly the same group despite changing homes every few years.

By the late eighties, the children who had grown up in this system began to marry each other irrespective of their origins. Till then the Indian middle class had been made up of the Tamil middle class, the Bengali middle class, the Punjabi middle class and so on. I am not suggesting that they were not proudly Indian; after all, these groups had been at the forefront of the freedom movement. However, their roots were firmly tied to their home provinces. This changed as the children of the middle class intermarried. Suddenly, there was a rapidly expanding group whose world view was essentially pan-Indian, their identity forged by the common experience of the housing colonies, the high-pressure education system, Bollywood films and cricket. We will return to this group later.

One of the unfortunate aspects of urban growth between the mid-fifties and the mid-eighties was the influence of 'brutalist' modernism. To socialists and fascists alike, the industrial starkness of reinforced concrete had a great attraction that is difficult to understand. Yet, the architects were somehow able to design buildings that are simultaneously unfriendly to the user, difficult to maintain and astonishingly ugly. Thus it came to be that India, land of the sublime symmetry of the Taj Mahal and the organic orchestra of Palitana, is also home to some of the ugliest buildings in the world. Every major city has them—Nehru Place and Inter-State Bus Terminal in Delhi, the Indian Express Building in Mumbai and the Haryana State Secretariat in Chandigarh.

Fascists and socialists have another thing in common—the urge to impose rigid master-plans on cities. In 1950, Prime Minister Nehru invited Le Corbusier, a French fascist, to design the new city of Chandigarh. Although the new city was to be built at the heart of ancient Sapta-Sindhu and very close to the Saraswati-Ghaggar, Corbusier was specifically asked by Nehru to create a city that was 'unfettered' by India's ancient civilization. Enormous resources in land, material and money were poured into building the new city. At the same time, rigid master plans were imposed on existing cities. Delhi was master-planned in 1962 into strict zones according to use. However, the static master plan is to the city what socialist planning is to the economy. Both cities and economies are organic and rapidly evolving eco-systems. Just as the Mahalonobis model of central planning damaged the Indian economy, the country's urban thinking was severely damaged by Le Corbusier's philosophy that buildings were machines for living.

This mechanical world view is echoed in the Delhi Master Plan of 1962 which proclaimed that 'there is undesirable mixing of land-uses almost everywhere in the city'. Just as the government had the right to control the economy through licences, it also had the right to tell people where to live and where to work. The problem is that such an approach cannot create a living ecosystem. New industrial cities like Durgapur never took off, and today's successful cities are still those with British-era roots. Even Chandigarh, the expensive poster-child of master-planning, has generated little of economic or cultural value after half a century of existence. Much of its apparent 'cleanliness' comes from simply having left no space for the poor within city limits. It remains a sterile and heavily subsidized city of tax-consuming bureaucrats that encourages neither entrepreneurship nor tax-generating jobs despite being the capital of two prosperous states. To the extent that the city has shown any energy at all, it comes from the evolving suburb of Mohali rather than from Corbusier's Chandigarh. Nehru had wanted Chandigarh to be the symbol of India's future. Instead, the face of twenty-first-century India is a city that is chaotic, unplanned, infuriating but undeniably dynamic: Gurgaon.

Laissez-faire City

Gurgaon lies to the south of Delhi and, according to legend, is said to have belonged to Dronacharya who taught martial arts to the Pandav and Kaurav cousins in the Mahabharat. Indeed, the name Gurgaon literally means the 'village of the teacher'. Despite its proximity to Delhi, however, the settlement of Gurgaon was never particularly large. Its population was estimated at a mere 3990 in 1881 and nearby towns like Rewari and Farrukhnagar had much larger populations. The *Gazetteer* of 1883–84 tells us that the British used Gurgaon as a district headquarters and that the town consisted of a small market (Sadar Bazaar), public offices, dwellings of European residents and a settlement called Jacombpura named after a former Deputy Commissioner.[20] An old road connected Gurgaon to Delhi via Mehrauli. The road is now the arterial MG Road, but the contours of the British-era settlement can just about be discerned if one goes to Mahavir Chowk, the busy marketplace in Old Gurgaon. If one looks closely enough, one can still see the remains of an old serai that would have been used by caravans heading to and from Delhi.

For the first few decades after independence, Gurgaon remained a relatively small town in a largely rural district. The first major change came when Sanjay Gandhi, son of then-Prime Minister Indira Gandhi, acquired a large plot of land to start an automobile company in the early 1970s. This is now the Maruti-Suzuki factory, but the project was not initially successful. From the early eighties, however, a number of real estate developers, particularly DLF, began to acquire farmland along the Delhi border. The idea at this stage was to build a mostly low-rise suburbia for Delhi's retiring civil servants. Although the Maruti car factory did get going by 1983, no one really envisaged Gurgaon as an independent growth engine.

The whole dynamics changed after India liberalized its economy in 1991, which coincided with the communications and information technology revolutions. As India globalized, a number of multinational companies discovered that call centres and back-office operations could be outsourced to India. Delhi was a good location for this because of available human capital and a well-connected international airport. However, the necessary real estate could not be created because of Delhi's rigid master plan. The old planners had never envisioned white-collar factories. The outsourcing companies, therefore, jumped across the border to Gurgaon and began to build huge facilities for this new industry.

This attracted young workers to Gurgaon. Many of those seeking their fortune in the newly liberalized economy were the children of civil servants, public sector employees, military officers and schoolteachers. The influx of so many young people, in turn, encouraged the construction of malls and restaurants. As this generation intermarried and set up home, the single-house format was abandoned in favour of condominiums more suited to the lifestyles of corporate executives. Schools and other educational institutions too began to multiply. The pace of expansion can be gauged from a lone milestone that survives on MG Road under the elevated Metro line (in front of Bristol Hotel). This is now the effective city-centre but the milestone confidently proclaims that Gurgaon is 6 km away!

The construction of Gurgaon was not planned, although a 'plan' did exist in theory. It was made possible by a combination of a lack of rules and the blatant disregard of rules. There was always a whiff of the robber baron. Yet, what was a sleepy small town till the mid-1990s has become a throbbing city of gleaming office towers, metro-stations, malls, luxury hotels and millions of jobs. I am not suggesting that Gurgaon does not have serious civic problems ranging from clogged roads and erratic power supply to the doings of unscrupulous property developers. I have more than enough personal experience of all these issues. It is also true that, with a little imagination, Gurgaon could have been done a lot better. Nonetheless, it is hard to deny the bursting energy of the city. It is a good metaphor for modern India with its private-sector dynamism, the robber-baron element and a government that is struggling to keep up.

THE URBAN FRONTIER[21]

One of the important things that I learnt over years of travelling through the interiors of India is that the children of farmers no longer want to farm. This is true across the country. Well-known sociologist Dipankar Gupta has also documented this phenomenon.[22] There are many reasons for this change. For one, literacy and television are changing attitudes and aspirations. Nevertheless, in my view the biggest reason is economic. The farm economy now generates a shrinking 13 per cent of GDP and the rural population can see where the money is.

City folk tend to have a view that rural migrants get squeezed out of rural areas by the atrocities of feudal landlords who pitilessly exploit the poor villagers. This is an image that derives from old Hindi films and is completely inaccurate on the ground. In fact, there are few large landholdings left in rural India. The real issue is that property rights are unclear because of a shoddy legal system, incomplete records, disregard for common rights and arbitrary land acquisition (often by the State using eminent domain powers). The combination of small landholdings and weak property rights has discouraged long-term investment by farmers in their land. As a result, Indian farming is hopelessly inefficient and uneconomical. The children of farmers want to opt out. Who are we to stop them? Rural India needs reforms and investment, not subsidies.

Meanwhile, urban India needs to prepare for large-scale migration: large cities will grow larger, small towns will grow big and brand new cities will be built. In some ways, India is merely witnessing what all developed countries have experienced at some stage of their evolution. Development is ultimately about shifting people from subsistence farming to other activities; urbanization is merely the spatial manifestation of this process. For instance, England's urbanization level jumped from 20 per cent in 1800 to 62 per cent in 1890.[23] More recently we have seen how China's urban population has jumped from 12 per cent in 1950 to over 50 per cent by 2012. My guesstimate is that urban India will have to absorb some 300–350 million people over the next three decades. This will be one of biggest human events of the twenty-first century.

The explosive growth of cities like Gurgaon shows that India's rapidly expanding economy may well be able to generate enough jobs. The real problem is to match hundreds of millions of migrants to jobs, housing, and amenities while maintaining overall social cohesion. Slotting so many individuals into the urban fabric according to their respective skills and financial abilities is a colossal task. China used draconian social control systems to manage the process over the last two decades. In most other countries, slums played this role. Even in China, 'urban villages' have been an integral part of the migration process.

Most people tend to be overwhelmed by the poor living conditions that prevail in Indian slums. The usual reaction is to treat this as a housing problem. Over the decades, we have seen many well-meaning slum re-development projects that have attempted to resettle slum-dwellers into purpose-built housing blocks (often on the outskirts of the city). Yet, almost all these efforts have failed. More often than not, the former slum-dwellers sell, rent out or abandon the new housing blocks and move back into a slum. The problem is that these schemes view slums as a static housing problem whereas slums are really evolving ecosystems that include informal jobs inside the slum, information about jobs outside the slum, social networks, security and so on. Thus, slums play an important role as 'routers' in the urbanization process. They absorb poor migrants from the rural hinterland and naturalize them into the urban landscape. In doing so, they provide the urban economy with the armies of blue-collar workers— maids, drivers, factory-workers—who are essential to the functioning of any vibrant city. As we have seen, slums existed in Harappan Dholavira, Mughal Delhi and in colonial Bombay.

Slums are not unique to India. The slums of New York and London were legendary in the nineteenth and early twentieth century. We need to distinguish here between urban decay and slums. Urban decay describes the condition of blight and abandonment that one sees in Detroit, New Jersey, and northern England. In contrast, as writers like Jeb Brugmann have pointed out, Indian slums are full of enterprise and energy.[24] Indeed, Indian slums are remarkable in how safe and cohesive they are. Most readers of this book will be able to walk through the average Indian slum even at night without fear of being harmed. This cohesion comes from the fact that migrants do not view slum life as a static state of deprivation but as a foothold into the modern, urban economy. Life may be hard but, in a rapidly growing economy, there is enough socio-economic mobility to keep slum-dwellers hardworking, enterprising and law-abiding. I am not glorifying slums or arguing that they do not need help. Clearly, we need to provide the urban poor with better sanitation, public health, education and so on. The point I am making is that real slums are not the places of static hopelessness portrayed in popular movies like *Slumdog Millionaire*.

URBAN VILLAGES, SLUMS AND THE NEW MIDDLE CLASS

The expansion of cities usually happens by engulfing the surrounding countryside. In some cases the old villages are swept away. However, in most parts of India, the old villages often survive despite being engulfed by the expanding urban sprawl. Scattered across modern Indian cities, there remain enclaves where the contours of the old villages can be clearly discerned decades after the surrounding farmlands were converted into offices, roads, houses and shops.

In some ways, this is in keeping with Indian civilization—the ability to allow the past to live on in the present. Tucked away behind modern buildings, the former villages make their presence felt in many different ways—as the source of vagrant cattle, as homes to armies of informal workers, as the place to visit if one wants to buy bathroom tiles or electricals. Many of these villages have been newly absorbed into the urban fabric, but some are very old and have been embedded in the city for generations. In Mumbai, the villages of Bandra and Walkeshwar retain strong vestiges of their origins despite being located at the heart of a throbbing megapolis.

For the purposes of this book, I will limit myself to the experience of urban villages in and around Delhi. My studies suggest that, roughly speaking, these villages go through the following cycle. In the first stage, the farmers sell their farmland to the government or to a developer but the village settlement itself is usually left alone. This settlement, dubbed as 'lal dora', is exempt from the usual municipal and building codes. The former farmers now notice that there is inadequate housing for the legions of workers, contractors and suppliers who have descended on the construction site. They, therefore, use their newly acquired capital and the exemption to build a mish-mash of buildings within the lal-dora area. Often built with little regard for safety or ventilation, these become home to construction workers and suppliers. Thus, the village turns into a slum with the former villagers as slumlords.

A few years pass and construction work in that particular area begins to wind down. The construction workers drift away to other sites. New migrants move in—security guards, maids, drivers and other people who work in the newly built urban space. The shops selling construction material and hardware are steadily replaced by shops selling mobile phones, street-food, car-parts and so on. For the first time we see private and, occasionally public, investment in amenities such as common toilets. As the migrants become more permanent, they bring their families in from their ancestral villages. This leads to an interesting supply-side response—the 'English Medium' school! In my experience, language is seen by the poor as the single most important tool for social climbing. Nathupur village in Gurgaon, circa 2009–10, was an example of a village in this second stage.

After another ten to fifteen years, the village goes through a third transformation. By this time, the surrounding area is well settled and open agricultural fields are a distant memory. We now see students, salesmen, and small businessmen move into the village. Some of them may be the newly educated children of migrants but they are now a higher social class. The old villagers still continue to be the dominant owners of the land but they begin to invest in improving their individual properties in order to elicit higher rents (after all, they now have a location advantage in the middle of an established city). In many instances, the owners have become politically important enough to lobby for public investment in basic drainage and sanitation. The shops upgrade themselves and the old street-food-sellers become cheap restaurants. An 'Aggarwal Sweets' is almost obligatory in the larger settlements.

The final stage of transformation is that the old village gentrifies. This can happen in a number of ways. Since the early nineties, Hauz Khas village has become a warren of boutique shops, art galleries and trendy restaurants. Mahipalpur, near the international airport, has seen an explosion of cheap hotels in the last decade. Anyone driving to or from the airport will have seen the screaming neon signs that remind one of Hong Kong's Wan Chai district. Similarly, Shahpur Jat has become home to numerous small offices and designer workshops. In many cases, the old villagers have encashed their real estate and the ownership pattern has become much more mixed. The areas now grapple with the problems of prosperity such as inadequate parking.

Out of this messy process of migration, social-climbing and urban evolution, a new India is emerging. It will be dominated by the newly middle class children of migrants. The country's old middle class was the product of the British and socialist eras. However, it is now being swamped by those climbing into the middle class from the slums and small 'mofussil' towns. Unlike the incumbents, the newcomers are usually the first generation that can speak some English. Their parents would have been the first literate generation and their grandparents would often have been illiterate subsistence farmers. One sees them working in call-centres or as shop-assistants in the malls. Even the changing social background of India's sports heroes hints at the shift. India has never witnessed such social mobility.

Moreover, as the new middle class climbs the social ladder, its tastes and attitudes will impact the mainstream. This is already visible from Bollywood music to television news. The superhit Bollywood song *Munni Badnaam Hui* (Munni is Notorious) is an example of how 'mofussil' music is being mainstreamed. No matter what the snobs of the old middle class may say, this is generally a good thing.

Diaspora—Being Indian in the Twenty-first Century

As we have seen in the previous chapter, Indians had again begun to travel and migrate abroad during the colonial era. The fortunes of these various diasporas changed with the withdrawal of British rule. In some places like Singapore and Mauritius, the Indian community would thrive. However, in many places, they faced severe persecution. In 1962, the Indian community in Burma was expelled by the dictator Ne Win and its properties were expropriated. A similar fate befell the Gujarati community in Uganda under Idi Amin in 1972. Some of these groups returned to India but others sailed farther afield. The Ugandan Gujaratis, for instance, moved to Britain in large numbers and would become a successful business community.

After independence, the nature of Indian migrations changed. There was one wave in the '50s and the '60s, with Punjabis moving to the United Kingdom as industrial workers. Another was of Anglo-Indians who migrated to Australia and Canada. By the 1970s, the oil-rich Arab states in the Persian Gulf began to import Indians in large numbers to work in construction sites. The single largest source of this migration was Kerala and, as already discussed in Chapter 5, many of these workers were descendants of Arabs who had come to India in the Middle Ages to trade. By the 1990s, large Indian communities would come to agglomerate in hubs like Dubai.

Thus far, Indian migrations had been predominantly of blue-collar workers and of traders. From the late sixties, a new kind of emigration took shape: that of middle-class Indians in search of education and white-collar opportunities. By this time, India's socialist economic model was beginning to fray and the optimism of the early years of independence was fading. What began as a trickle became a flood by the late 1980s, and it was commonplace for middle-class Indian students to take the SAT and GMAT tests and apply to foreign universities. The United States was the biggest recipient of this flow, although smaller streams also went to Britain, Canada and so on. By the late '90s, yet another sub-category emerged—Indian professionals who were hired into the global economy. This group clustered around important cities like Singapore, London, New York and Dubai, and were concentrated in sectors such as medicine, law, finance and information technology.

Over the years, many of these groups have mixed and merged, but traces of each stream can still be discerned in the early twenty-first century. What is interesting is the extent to which 'Indianness' has been consciously retained by most of these expatriate communities even when they have been away from the subcontinent for generations. I remember two gentlemen, both Swedish citizens, whom I met on a boat trip from Dar-e-Salaam to Zanzibar in May 2010. Their ancestors were Gujarati Muslims who had settled in Zanzibar in the late nineteenth century but were forced out by race riots in the mid-1960s. They were on a trip back to rediscover their roots. I found them in the cabin chatting away in Kutchhi and, when they discovered I was Indian, they insisted that I share their supplies of Gujarati snacks. They had never visited India, but I was amazed by how strongly Indian they felt. Indeed, they were very proud of India's recent economic successes and were planning a trip to see their ancestral homeland.

This brings me to a fundamental point about what it means to be Indian in the twenty-first century. The Indian diaspora is said to be around twenty-five to thirty million strong and spans the world. Through hard work, education and entrepreneurship, its members have become very successful in fields ranging from business and politics to literature. With success has come a new confidence in its identity. Thanks to globalization and technology, these expatriate communities can now maintain business, personal and cultural links with India in ways that would have been unthinkable a generation ago. Richer and better connected, they share passions ranging from Bollywood to cricket with their cousins back in India.

Note that this is not a one-way relationship. Indians tend to be inordinately proud of the personal achievements of people of Indian origin even if they have had no direct link to the subcontinent. An Indian-origin governor of an American state, a Nobel Prize winner or a CEO of a multinational company can make headlines in Indian newspapers. In other words, both sides share a very palpable sense of shared identity. This is not unique to Indians since the Jewish and Chinese diasporas also share similar sentiments. The point is that India's civilizational nationhood includes people who are neither citizens nor live on the subcontinent. In recent years, the Indian Republic has tried to deal with this reality by creating, perhaps clumsily, different shades of citizenship in the form of Overseas Citizen of India and Person of Indian Origin. Such has been the journey of the 'global Indian': from the docks of Lothal to the boardrooms of London, New York and Singapore.

GONDWANA TO GURGAON

The journey from Gondwana to Gurgaon has been a long one. In this book, I have hopefully given the reader a sense of the twists and turns, the abrupt shifts as well as the surprising continuities. It is remarkable how the artifacts of this long history sit juxtaposed and piled up next to each other. The brand new city of Gurgaon, for instance, is being constructed right next to the Aravalli ridges, the oldest discernible geological feature on this planet. If you look north from one of Gurgaon's tall office blocks, you will see the Qutub Minar, built by a Turkish slave-general to commemorate the conquest of Delhi. Just below the medieval tower, globalized Indians enjoy Thai and Italian food at the expensive restaurants of Mehrauli, an urban village that is steadily gentrifying. Metro trains slither nearby on their elevated tracks.

Similarly, a short drive south of the imperial inscriptions of Junagarh, the Asiatic lion is making a slow comeback. A survey in 2010 suggests that there are now 411 lions in Gir. In fact, the sanctuary in Gir is proving to be too small for the expanded population and some of these animals are now wandering into the surrounding countryside. Some have even been seen on the beaches of Kodinar. Just across from this beach is the island of Diu, a Portuguese stronghold for four centuries. At some point, the Portuguese had presented a group of African slaves to the Nawab of Junagarh. Their direct descendants now live in hamlets just outside Gir National Park. Thus, the country's bubbling genetic mix has come to include a barely-remembered community of African Indians! The Sidi community of Sasan Gir is nominally Muslim but retains customs, music and dances from its African past.

The last hundred years have not been kind to India's tigers. It is estimated that barely 1706 of them remain in the wild, down from over 3600 in the 1990s. Poaching is a major problem but even more important is the destruction of their habitat through illegal encroachments, logging and mining. The imagery of the lion and the tiger, however, remains alive in the human mind. Every year, the drums of Kolkata beat for Goddess Durga, astride her lion, at war with Evil. In Singapore, tourists take snaps of the Merlion, half-lion and half-mermaid, a mythical beast that through many twists and turns recalls the influence of ancient Indian merchants who brought their culture to these distant shores. These distant cultural memories can have very important symbolic meaning for modern people. In 2009, the Sri Lankan army, flying a lion flag, decimated the separatist Tamil Tigers to end a long-running civil war.

Even as I was writing this book, the Indian government came up with a proposal to re-introduce the cheetah into the country from Africa. Furious debates rage on whether or not the African and Asian cheetahs belong to the same species. There are even more furious debates about mining. The primordial forests of Gondwana are now rich coal fields in Jharkhand. India's economic expansion is hungry for energy and covets the coal that lies below the beautiful, rolling hills of the state. No matter which side one takes in the debate, my tour of the coal mines of Hazaribagh suggested that the extraction of resources needs to be done in a way that significantly reduces the social and environmental costs of this activity. These natural resources are not renewable and we must have good reason for exploiting them today rather than leaving them for future generations.

We live in a time of massive change—mass urbanization, climate change, globalization, and a shifting global order. India has seen all this before, but the human inability to learn from the past is sometimes astounding. I write these lines in Varanasi as I watch the evening 'aarati' on the ancient ghats along the Ganga. The priests chant the glories of the great river and seek her blessings, but the river is clearly dying from the assaults of human interference and thoughtless civil engineering. Perhaps the Harappans chanted hymns extolling the glories of the Saraswati as they impotently watched the river dry up. Perhaps they desperately invoked Indra to break the dams and let the waters flow again.

As we have seen, despite all this change, Indians have retained an intuitive memory of their civilization. It continues to influence Indian attitudes in surprising ways. A lot can be discerned about a people from the way they remember their darkest hour. When New York observes an anniversary of the 9/11 attacks, there is a sombre service and speeches by leading political figures. Contrast that with how Mumbai commemorated the terrorist attacks of 26 November 2008. A day after the fourth anniversary, a flash mob of 200 young boys and girls suddenly appeared in the middle of Chhatrapati Shivaji Terminal, a busy train station that had witnessed one of the massacres on that night of horror. The flash mob then proceeded to dance for five minutes to a popular Bollywood number *Rang de Basanti* (roughly translates as 'The Colour of Sacrifice'). Then, when the music stopped, the mob disappeared into the crowd. In any other country this would have been considered sacrilege but in India it was widely seen as appropriate. The whole episode was filmed and became an instant hit on the Internet. But, why do Indians remember a horrible event by dancing?

The key to resolving the paradox is to realize that Indians view history not in political but in civilizational terms. When Americans raise their flag at the 9/11 sites, they reaffirm the resilience of their nation state. When Indians dance at the site of the 26/11 massacre, they celebrate the triumph of their civilization.

The history of India's geography and civilization reminds us of the insignificance of each generation in the vastness of time. The greatest of India's monarchs and thinkers too felt it. So they left behind their stories and thoughts in ballads, folktales, epics and inscriptions. Even if these memories are not always literally true, what matters is that they carry on the essence of India's civilization. On the island of Mauritius, descendants of Indian immigrants have transferred their memories of the river Ganga to a lake, Ganga Talao, that they now hold as sacred. A very long time ago, their distant ancestors would have similarly transferred the memory of the Saraswati to the Ganga. Geography is not just about the physical terrain, but also about the meaning that we attribute to it. Thus, the Saraswati flows, invisibly, at Allahabad.

Notes

INTRODUCTION

1. The 2011 tiger census came up with a count of 1706. This is up from 1411 from the 2007 census. It is unclear if the increase is due to better conservation or better counting.
2. The Gayatri Mantra is one of the most popular hymns in the Hindu tradition. It is contained in the Rig Veda and has been translated and interpreted by many scholars. Here is my attempt: 'As you light up the Heavens and the Earth, O Radiant Sun, So light up my Mind and Soul'.
3. *India, A History*, John Keay. HarperCollins, 2001.
4. *The Lost River: On the Trail of the Sarasvati*, Michel Danino. Penguin, 2010.

1. OF GENETICS AND TECTONICS

1. 'The Making and Unmaking of a Supercontinent: Rodinia Revisited', Joseph Meert and Trond H. Torsvik. *Tectonophysics*, vol. 375, November 2003.
2. The story of the siege of Delhi is fascinating. The interested reader should read *The Last Mughal* by William Dalrymple. Penguin Viking, 2006.
3. 'Study on Restoration of Dying Lakes: Case study on Balsamand Lake in Jodhpur', published by The Sustainable Planet Institute and AFPRO, February, 2010.

4. There was probably an intermediate but short-lived super-continent called Pannotia prior to the formation of Pangea.

5. 'The biogeographic and tectonic history of India', John Briggs. *Journal of Biogeography*, 2003.

6. 'Bones to Pick', Uday Mahurkar. *India Today*, 8 November 2010.

7. 'Fossil find in Gujarat tweaks India's breakaway story', *The Indian Express*, 27 October 2010; 'The first keroplatid species from the Lower Eocene amber of Vastan, Gujarat, India', Monica Kraemer and Neal Evenhuis. Zootaxa, 2008.

8. It appears that India was not entirely ecologically isolated during its northward drift. John Briggs has found that India still received some new mainland species during the period. The process is not yet entirely understood. 'The biogeographic and tectonic history of India', John Briggs. Journal of Biogeography, 2003.

9. http://www.monstersandcritics.com/science/nature/news/article_1069908.php/Mammoth_genes_resemble_those_of_Asian_elephant_scientists

10. 'World's most ancient race traced in DNA study', Steve Connor. *The Independent*, 1 May 2009.

11. 'Major genomic mitochondrial lineages delineate early human expansions', Nicole Maca-Meyer et al. *BMC Genetics*, 2001.

12. There may have been another related group that struck north towards the Levant. It is unclear if this group made a separate crossing from Africa via the Sinai or split from the original band soon after the first crossing.

13. We have learnt a lot in recent decades about the early migrations of modern humans from archaeology and genetic data. However, it is still an evolving area of research, and there is a confusing and, sometimes, contradictory array of research. For a good survey of the material read *The Incredible Human Journey*, Alice Roberts. Bloomsbury, 2009; *Out of Eden: Peopling of the World*, Stephen Oppenheimer. C&R, 2003.

14. *The Circulation of the Persian Gulf*, J. Kampf and M. Sadrinasab, Ocean Science Discussions, 2005. http://www.ocean-sci-discuss.net/2/129/2005/osd-2-129-2005

15. There is controversial new research that, during this period, modern humans may have even mated with Neanderthals. The Neanderthals were a closely related but parallel species and it was long considered that they left behind no descendants. However, new research by Harvard Medical School and the University of California, Santa Cruz, suggests that they have left behind tiny traces of their genes amongst us. While I am not entirely convinced by the study, it is strange to think that many of us may not be 'pure' modern humans! See: http://www.newscientist.com/article/dn18869-neanderthal-genome-reveals-interbreeding-with-humans.html?full=true

16. Comment by K.K. Abu-Amero et al. in 'New Light on Human Pre-History in the Arabo-Persian Gulf Oasis', Jeffrey Rose. *Current Anthropology*, December 2010.

17. 'Reconstructing Indian-Australian phylogenetic link', Satish Kumar et al. *BMC Evolutionary Biology*, July 2009.

18. *The Story of India*, Michael Wood, BBC Worldwide, 2008.

19. 'Shoreline Reconstructions for the Persian Gulf since the last Glacial Maximum', Kurt Lambeck. *Earth and Planetary Science Letters*, ANU, 1996.

20. 'New Light on Human Prehistory in the Arabo-Persian Gulf Oasis', Jeffrey Rose. *Current Anthropology*, December, 2010.

21. 'Recent Marine Archaeological Finds in Khambat, Gujarat', S. Kathiroli et. al. *Journal of Indian Ocean Archaeology*, 2004.

22. *Guns, Germs, and Steel*, Jared Diamond, Vintage, 2005.

23. Readers should recognize that genetics is a young science and still evolving. In addition, subsequent migrations have obscured many of the markers of the original migrations. Therefore, the schematic framewords discussed in this section is at best a broad description. The reality would have been far more messy, with groups and sub-groups going back and forth and interbreeding with yet other groups.

24. 'Polarity and Temporality of High-Resolution Y-Chromosome Distributions in India Identify Both Indigenous and Exogenous Expansions and Reveal Minor Genetic Influence of Central Asian Pastoralists', Sengupta et al, *The American Journal of Human Genetics*, February 2006.

25. 'Reconstructing Indian Population History', David Reich et al., *Nature*, September 2009.

26. Geneticist Thangarajan, one of the co-authors of the study, said in a press interview that the ASI group may date to 60,000 years ago and the ANI to 40,000. So, we are dealing with very old populations.

27. The genetic sub-groups are named by adding letters or alphabets to a lineage. So, R1a1 is a subgroup derived from R1a that in turn is derived from R1 and so on.

28. 'Separating the post-Glacial coancestry of European and Asian Y chromosomes within haplogroup R1a', Peter Underhill et al., *European Journal of Human Genetics*, 2010.

29. 'A prehistory of Indian Y Chromosomes: Evaluating demic diffusion scenarios', Sanghamitra Sahoo et al, University of Cambridge, November 2005.

30. 'A prehistory of Indian Y Chromosomes: Evaluating demic diffusion scenarios', Sanghamitra Sahoo et al. The National Academy of Sciences, USA, 2006.

31. 'Mystery of Our Origins', Dr. Lalji Singh, *NAAS News*, October–November 2009.

32. I collated material from various sources but the reader could use 'Separating the post-Glacial coancestry of European and Asian Y chromosomes with reference to R1a', Underhill et al., *European Journal of Human Genetics*, 2009: 'The Indian origin of paternal haplogroup R1a1 substantiates the autochthonous origin of Brahmins and the caste system', S. Sharma et al., *Journal of Human Genetics*, January 2009; 'The Genetic Heritage of the Earliest Settlers Persists Both in Indian Tribal and Caste Populations', Kivisild et al, *American Journal of Human Genetics*, 2003.

33. 'The Indian origin of paternal haplogroup R1a1 substantiates the autochthonous origin of Brahmins and the caste system', S. Sharma et al., *Journal of Human Genetics*, January 2009.

34. It is possible that the varna framework was no more than an intellectual effort to understand and rationalize the bubbling milieu of jatis. Scholarship based purely on texts has allowed the tail to wag the dog.

2. PEOPLE OF THE LOST RIVER

1. *The Lost River: On the Trail of the Sarasvati*, Michel Danino. Penguin, 2010.

2. *A History of Ancient and Early Medieval India*, Upinder Singh. Pearson, 2009.

3. Discussions at international seminar on 'How Deep are the Roots of Indian Civilization?', Delhi, 25–27 November 2010.

4. 'A new approach to tracking connections between the Indus Valley and Mesopotamia: Initial Results of Strontium isotope analysis from Harappa and Ur', J. Mark Kenoyer et al, *Journal of Archeological Science*, May 2013.

5. *Beyond the Three Seas: Travellers' Tales of Mughal India*, (ed.) Michael Fischer. Random House India, 2007.

6. *The Lost River: On the Trail of the Sarasvati*, Michel Danino. Penguin, 2010.

7. *India: A History*, John Keay. HarperCollins, 2000.

8. *The Lost River: On the Trail of the Sarasvati*, Michel Danino. Penguin, 2010.

9. *The Penguin History of Early India*, Romila Thapar. Penguin, 2002

10. *The Penguin History of Early India*, Romila Thapar. Penguin, 2002

11. *The Saraswati Flows On: The Continuity of Indian Culture*, B.B. Lal. ABI. New Delhi, 2002.

12. *The Lost River: On the Trail of the Sarasvati*, Michel Danino. Penguin, 2010.

13. *Indo-Aryan Origins and Other Vedic Issues*, Nicholas Kazanas. Aditya Prakashan, 2009.

14. *The Quest for the Origins of Vedic Culture*, Edwin Bryant. Oxford University Press, 2001.

15. *A History of Ancient and Early Medieval India*, Upinder Singh. Pearson, 2009.

16. It can even be argued that Dasa refers to the Daha tribes of north-eastern Iran.

17. The words 'krishna ayas', black bronze, may not mean iron. In that case, even the Atharva Veda is ignorant of iron and we can date the Vedas even earlier, in the third millennium.

18. 'Beginnings of agriculture in the Vindhya–Ganga Region', Radha Kant Verma, Chapter 3 in *History of Science Philosophy and Culture in Indian Civilization*, (ed.) D.P. Chattopadhyay, Centre for Studies in Civilizations, 2008. Also in *A History of Ancient and Early Medieval India*, Upinder Singh, Pearson, 2009.

19. 'The Horse and the Aryan Debate', Michel Danino, *Journal of Indian History and Culture*, September 2006.

20. Hymn LXI, Book VI, Rig Veda calls the Saraswati 'seven-sistered, sprung from three fold source'.

21. *The Lost River: On the Trail of the Sarasvati*, Michel Danino. Penguin, 2010.

22. http://www.edgeofexistence.org/mammals/species_info.php?id=65, http://www.iucnredlist.org/apps/redlist/details/41756/0

23. Rig Veda Hymn LXIV of Book X describes the wider Vedic landscape and includes the Saraswati, the Sarayu and the Indus. It speaks of forests, mountains, 'tribes of varied sort' and, most interestingly, of 'thrice-seven wandering rivers'. The 'thrice-seven' rivers are mentioned in several other hymns. One does not have to literally take this to mean twenty-one rivers but the Sapta-Sindhu is obviously a sub-set of the overall Vedic landscape.

24. Rig Veda, Book VII, Hymn XXXVI, Stanza 6.

25. See Mandala 7 of the Rig Veda (there are many translations but one can use *The Hymns of the Rigveda VI*, (trans.) Ralph Griffith, 1896—http://www.sanskritweb.net/rigveda/griffith.pdf).

26. The Bharatas are also referred to as the Trtsu in the Rig Veda.

27. Panini was a grammarian from around the fifth century BC. In an explanation of grammatical forms, he states that saying, 'Eastern Bharatas' is superfluous as everyone knows that the Bharatas are an eastern tribe. Of course, Panini lived many centuries after the Rig Veda but we have no reason to disbelieve him as his statement agrees with the other circumstantial evidence.

28. *A History of Ancient and Early Medieval India*, Upinder Singh. Pearson, 2009. Also see Mandala 7 of the Rig Veda (use *The Hymns of the Rig Veda VI*, (trans.) Ralph Griffith, 1896. http://www.sanskritweb.net/rigveda/griffith.pdf).

29. *The Quest for the Origins of Vedic Culture*, Edwin Bryant. Oxford University Press (OUP), 2001.

30. This is how the term 'Hindu' came to mean Indians and eventually gave its name to the country's dominant religion.

31. http://www.yeziditruth.org/yezidi_religious_tradition, 'Yezidism: Historical Roots', by Tosine Reshid, *International Journal of Kurdish Studies*, 2005.

3. THE AGE OF LIONS

1. *The Penguin History of Early India*, Romila Thapar. Penguin, 2002.

2. *Kim*, Rudyard Kipling, 1901.

3. 'Ravana worshipped on Dussehra in Madhya Pradesh', *The Times of India*, 5 October 2011.

4. *The Lost City of Dvarka*, S.R. Rao, Aditya Prakashan, 1999 and *An Ancient Harbour at Dwarka*, A.S. Gaur et al. National Institute of Oceanography, *Current Science*, May 2004.

5. *China: A History*, John Keay. HarperCollins 2008.

6. The Mahabharata also contains a sub-plot about Ulupi, a Naga princess, and her rivalry with Chitrangada over Arjuna. This is interesting given the modern-day frictions between the Nagas and the Manipuris. Since I am not sure that today's Naga tribes

relate to the Naga tribe mentioned in the Mahabharata, I have left this out of the main text. Nonetheless, there are some interesting coincidences. Arjuna and Ulupi had a son called Iravan, a minor character in the epic, who is depicted in folk art in faraway Tamil Nadu as a decapitated head. The tribes of Nagaland practised headhunting into living memory. One wonders whether there is a link.

7. *China: A History*, John Keay. HarperCollins 2008.

8. *The Story of Asia's Lions*, Divyabhanusinh Chavda. Marg Publications, 2008.

9. This continued into much later times—Singapore was named after a lion whereas the animal in question was almost certainly a tiger.

10. The April 2010 census showed that Gir has 162 mature females, 97 mature males and 152 cubs. This is up from around 180 in the 1960s.

11. *The Story of Asia's Lions*, Divyabhanusinh Chavda. Marg Publications, 2008.

12. *The Penguin History of Early India*, Romila Thapar. Penguin, 2002

13. It is difficult to date this compendium but a version of this document probably existed by the third century BC. The text clearly states that surgery was a well-established science by the time the compendium was written. So, it is reasonable to say that this body of knowledge was systematized in the late Iron Age. However, it appears to have been repeatedly edited in later centuries. The current version of the text may be as late as the fifth century AD.

14. *The Roots of Ayurveda*, Dominik Wijastyk. Penguin, 2001.

15. *The Invasion of India by Alexander the Great as described by Arrian, Q. Curtius, Diodorus, Plutarch and Justin*. J.W. McCrindle, Archibald Constable & Co., 1896. Reprinted 1984 by Eastern Book House.

16. *The Invasion of India by Alexander the Great as described by*

Arrian, Q. Curtius, Diodorus, Plutarch and Justin. J.W. McCrindle, Archibald Constable & Co., 1896. Reprinted 1984 by Eastern Book House.

17. Some scholars argue that Kautilya and Chanakya were different people but I have stuck to the traditional view here.

18. *The Invasion of India by Alexander the Great as described by Arrian, Q. Curtius, Diodorus, Plutarch and Justin*. J.W. McCrindle, Archibald Constable & Co., 1896. Reprinted 1984 by Eastern Book House.

19. There is another tradition that he remained a minister into Bindusara's reign.

20. *The Story of India*, Michael Wood. BBC Worldwide, 2008.

21. Presumably from wounds and famine.

22. Dhamma (Dharma) is an important concept in both Hinduism and Buddhism. It is difficult to translate but broadly relates to the duty to do the right thing.

23. *The Penguin History of Early India*, Romila Thapar. Penguin, 2002.

24. The empire was larger than modern-day India and its overall population would have been around 75–80 million. These are my own guesstimates.

25. *From Stone Quarry to Sculpturing Workshop: A Report on the Archaeological Investigations around Chunar, Varanasi and Sarnath*, Vidula Jayaswal, Agam Kala Prakashan, 1998.

26. *The Story of Asia's Lions*, Divyabhanusinh Chavda. Marg Publications, 2008; *The True Chronology of Ashokan Pillars*, John Irwin, *Artibus Asiae*, XLIV, IFA, NYU, 1983.

27. Note that Megasthenes's *Indika* has been lost but sections have been preserved in other Greek writings.

28. *The Penguin History of Early India*, Romila Thapar. Penguin, 2002; ASI (http://asi.nic.in/asi_exca_imp_bihar.asp)

29. *The Arthashastra*, Kautilya, (trans.) L.N. Rangarajan, Penguin, 1987.

4. THE AGE OF MERCHANTS

1. *The Penguin History of Early India*, Romila Thapar. Penguin, 2002.

2. *The Story of India*, Michael Wood. BBC Worldwide, 2007 (as translated by Dr Sivakkolundu).

3. *The Sanskrit Language*, Thomas Burrow. Faber & Faber, 1955; 'Rigvedic Loanwords', F.B.J. Kuiper, in *Studia Indologica*, 1955.

4. *The Commerce and Navigation of the Erythaean Sea* and *Ancient India as described by Ktesias the Knidian*', John W. McCrindle. Westminister Edition 1901. Reprinted by Eastern Book House 1987.

5. http://www.archbase.com/berenike/english6.html

6. *Ancient India as Described in Classical Literature*, John W. McCrindle. Westminster Edition 1901. Reprinted by Eastern Book House, 1987.

7. By the time of Christ, Hebrew was no longer the language commonly spoken. Its role was somewhat similar to that of Sanskrit—a language for formal use. As with the Prakrits in India, Aramaic dialects were the language of the common people. It is only in modern Israel that Hebrew was revived as a language for common use.

8. *A History of South-East Asia* by D.G.E. Hall, 4th edition, Macmillan, 1981.

9. Literally means: 'Memory of the Three Kingdoms'.

10. 'Maritime Heritage of Orissa', Atul Pradhan, Utkal University (taken from the official website of Orissa state government).

11. http://news.bbc.co.uk/2/hi/south_asia/4302115.stm & http://news.bbc.co.uk/2/hi/south_asia/4312024.stm

12. *The World Economy: Historical Statistics*, Angus Maddison. OECD 2003.

13. 'The Sewn Boats of Orissa', Eric Kentley, in *Maritime Heritage of India*, (ed.) K.S. Behara, ABI, 1999.

14. *Travels of Fa-Hian and Sung-Yun*, (trans.) Samuel Beal, Trubner & Co., London, 1869. Reprinted by Asian Education Services, 2003.

15. When I revisited the Iron Pillar in 2011, I saw what looked like a few rusty patches. The patches are small and superficial, but one wonders if acid rain may at last be getting the better of this extraordinary example of ancient metallurgy.

16. *Travels of Fa-Hian and Sung-Yun*, (trans.) Samuel Beal, Trubner & Co., London, 1869. Reprinted by Asian Education Services, 2003.

17. 'Pleasure and Culture', Shonaleeka Kaul, in *Ancient India: New Research*, (ed.) Upinder Singh and Nayanjot Lahiri, OUP, 2009.

18. *The Travels*, Marco Polo, (trans.) R. Latham. Penguin, 1958

19. The report could also relate to the Magh Mela—the smaller annual event at the same location. However, Xuan Zang's description suggest a grand affair that better fits with the Kumbh itself.

20. *Buddhist Records of the Western World* by Hiuen-Tsiang, (trans.) Samuel Beal, 1884. Reprinted by Oriental Books, 1969.

21. *Nagapattinam to Suvarnadwipa*, K. Kesavapany et al., ISEAS, 2009.

22. *Kalhana–the Chronicler*, K.N. Dhar, Shri Parmanand Research Institute, Srinagar (http://www.koausa.org/Glimpses/Kalhana.html). *Kalhana's Rajataringini: A Chronicle of the Kings of Kashmir*, vol. 1, Elibron Classics, Adamant Media, 2005.

23. *The Penguin History of Early India*, Romila Thapar. Penguin, 2002.

5. FROM SINDBAD TO ZHENG HE

1. 'World's Second Oldest Mosque is in India', *Bahrain Tribune Daily*, 7 July 2006.

2. *Al-Hind: The Making of the Indo–Islamic World*, vol. 1, André Wink. OUP, 1999.

3. *Al-Hind: The Making of the Indo–Islamic World*, vol. 1, André Wink. OUP, 1999.

4. *The Great Arab Conquests*, Hugh Kennedy. Da Capo Press, 2007.

5. *Al-Hind: The Making of the Indo–Islamic World*, vol. 1, André Wink. OUP, 1999.

6. Not all Mappilas are of Arab origin. It is a very diverse group that includes local converts as well as non-Arab Muslim sailors.

7. Means 'Story of Sanjan'. Sanjan was the name of a town in Khorasan from where the refugees had come (it's near Merv in modern Turkmenistan). The Parsis probably named their first settlement after their lost homeland.

8. http://articles.timesofindia.indiatimes.com/2008-01-21/patna/27750686_1_muharram-procession-hazrat-imam-hussain-month-of-islamic-calendar

9. 'A newly discovered founder population: the Roma/Gypsies', Luba Kalaydjieva et al., Bio-Essays, Wiley, 2005.

10. There is some reason to believe that originally there were 64 shakti-peeths but I have stuck here to the current convention.

11. *India: A History*, John Keay, Harper Collins 2000.

12. *Al-Hind: The Making of the Indo–Islamic World*, vol. 1, André Wink. OUP, 1999.

13. As quoted in *Ashoka*, Charles Allen. Little, Brown, 2012.

14. The English translation by John Briggs is available as *The History of the Rise of Mohammedan Power in India*. Reprinted by Sang-e-Meel Publications, New Delhi, 1981.

15. *Rambles and Recollections of an Indian Official*, W.H. Sleeman, vol. II, Asian Education Services (reprinted 1995).

16. Gazeteer of the Delhi District 1883–84, Sang-e-Meel Publications, Lahore (reprinted 2000)

17. *Delhi: A Thousand Years of Building*, Lucy Peck. Roli-INTACH, 2005.

18. *The Travels of Ibn-Batuta*, (ed.) Tim Mackintosh-Smith. Picador, 2002.

19. *India: A History*, John Keay. HarperCollins, 2000.

20. One should not take this literally as meaning a thousand pillars—it merely denotes a very large number.

21. *A History of India*, vol. 2, Percival Spear. Penguin, 1990.

22. *India: A History*, John Keay. HarperCollins, 2000.

23. *The Baburnama*, (trans.) Wheeler Thackston, The Modern Library NY, 2002.

24. *The Baburnama*, (trans.) Wheeler Thackston, The Modern Library NY, 2002.

25. Note that the process of reconciliation with the Hindus had already begun with the Suris. The commander-in-chief of the Suri army was Hemu, a Hindu.

26. *India: A History*, John Keay. HarperCollins, 2000.

27. *The Baburnama*, (trans.) Wheeler Thackston, The Modern Library NY, 2002.

28. *The Story of Asia's Lions*, Divyabhanusinh Chavda. Marg Publications, 2008.

29. *The Story of Asia's Lions*.

30. *The Story of Asia's Lions*.

31. *The Story of Asia's Lions*.

32. *The Story of Asia's Lions*.

33. *The Indian Renaissance*, Sanjeev Sanyal. Penguin, 2008,

34. *The Travels of Ibn-Batuta*, (ed.) Tim Mackintosh-Smith. Picador, 2002.

35. *A History of South-East Asia*, D.G.E. Hall, Fourth Edition. Macmillan, 1981.

36. *Admiral Zheng He and Southeast Asia*, (ed.) Leo Suryadinata. ISEAS, 2005.

37. *Cheng Ho and Islam in Southeast Asia*, Tan Ta Sen. ISEAS, 2009.

38. *Cheng Ho and Islam in Southeast Asia*, Tan Ta Sen. ISEAS, 2009.

6. THE MAPPING OF INDIA

1. *India Within the Ganges*, Susan Gole. Jayaprints, 1983.

2. The Indian peninsula does look somewhat like a roseapple. So, it is possible that the term Jambudwipa did also have a geographical meaning. However, none of the texts that I read seem to build on this in a systematic cartographic sense. It is possible that such texts did exist but have been lost.

3. *The Riddle and the Knight*, Giles Milton. Hodder & Stoughton, 2001.

4. *The Riddle and the Knight*, Giles Milton. Hodder & Stoughton, 2001.

5. *The Travels*, Marco Polo (trans.) R.E. Latham. Penguin, 1953.

6. *Empires of the Monsoon*, Richard Hall. HarperCollins, 1998.

7. *Empires of the Monsoon*, Richard Hall. HarperCollins, 1998.

8. *Empires of the Monsoon*, Richard Hall. HarperCollins, 1998.

9. *The World Economy: A Millennial Perspective*, Angus Maddison. OECD, 2001.

10. *India Within the Ganges*, Susan Gole. Jayaprints, 1983.

11. *The Mapmakers*, John Noble Wilford. Pimlico, 2002.

12. *Hampi*, John Fritz, George Michell and John Gollings. India Book House, 2003; *A Forgotten Empire: Vijayanagar*, Robert Sewell, 1900. Reprinted by Asian Education Services, 2007.

13. Its construction has been delayed for years. When work commenced in 2009, several workers were killed in an accident.

14. *Hampi*, John Fritz, George Michell and John Gollings. India Book House, 2003.

15. *India Within the Ganges*, Susan Gole. Jayaprints, 1983.

16. *Travels in the Mogul Empire: AD 1656–1668*, François Bernier. Reprinted by Asian Education Services, 2004.

17. *Beyond the Three Seas: Travellers' Tales of Mughal India*, (ed.) Michael Fisher. Random House, 2007.

18. *Beyond the Three Seas: Travellers' Tales of Mughal India*, (ed.) Michael Fisher. Random House, 2007.

19. *India Within the Ganges*, Susan Gole. Jayaprints, 1983.

20. *Travels in the Mogul Empire: AD 1656–1668*, François Bernier. Reprinted by Asian Education Services, 2004.

21. *India, A History*, John Keay. Harper Collins, 2000.

7. TRIGONOMETRY AND STEAM

1. *European Calcutta*, Dhrubajyoti Banerjea. UBSPD, 2008.

2. *European Calcutta*, Dhrubajyoti Banerjea. UBSPD, 2008.

3. As cited in *In the Footsteps of Stamford Raffles*, Nigel Barley. Penguin, 1991.

4. *The Mapmakers*, John Noble Wilford. Pimlico, 2002.

5. *The Great Arc*, John Keay. HarperCollins, 2001.

6. *The Mapmakers*, John Noble Wilford. Pimlico, 2002.

7. Cited from *India, A History*, John Keay. HarperCollins, 2000.

8. *Rambles and Recollections of an Indian Official*, W.H. Sleeman, vol. II, Asian Education Services (reprinted 1995).

9. *Trees of Delhi*, Pradip Krishen. Dorling Kindersley, 2006.

10. *The Last Mughal*, William Dalrymple. Penguin, 2006.

11. *The Last Mughal*, William Dalrymple. Penguin, 2006.

12. In yet another act of cultural vandalism, part of the Saraswati Ghat was renamed after Jawaharlal Nehru in the nineteen eighties.

13. *The World Economy: A Millennial Perspective*, Angus Maddison. OECD, 2001.

14. *Development of Indian Railways*, Nalinaksha Sanyal. University of Calcutta, 1930.

15. *Development of Indian Railways*, Nalinaksha Sanyal. University of Calcutta, 1930.

16. *Yakada Yaka, The Jam Fruit Tree* and *Once Upon a Tender Time*, Carl Muller.

17. *Maclean's Guide to Bombay*, J.M. Maclean, as quoted in *Kipling Sahib: India and the Making of Rudyard Kipling 1865–1900*, Charles Allen. Abacus, 2007.

18. *The Mapmakers*, John Noble Wilford. Pimlico, 2002.

19. As quoted in *The Mapmakers*, John Noble Wilford. Pimlico, 2002.

20. *The Story of Asia's Lions*, Divyabhanusinh Chavda. Marg Publications, 2008.

21. *The Story of Asia's Lions*, Divyabhanusinh Chavda. Marg Publications, 2008.

22. There are unconfirmed reports till 1967.

23. Gazeteer of the Delhi District, 1883–84, Sang-e-Meel Publications, Lahore (reprinted 2000).

24. *Delhi Metropolitan*, Ranjana Sengupta. Penguin, 2007.
25. *Trees of Delhi*, Pradip Krishen. Dorling Kindersley, 2006.
26. *Trees of Delhi*, Pradip Krishen. Dorling Kindersley, 2006.
27. http://www.aapravasighat.org/
28. *The Encyclopedia of the Indian Diaspora* edited by Brij Lal; Didier Millet, 2006

8. THE CONTOURS OF MODERN INDIA

1. *Freedom at Midnight*, Dominique Lapierre and Larry Collins. Vikas Publishing House (2010 edition).
2. *India after Gandhi*, Ramachandra Guha. Picador India, 2007.
3. *India after Gandhi*, Ramachandra Guha. Picador India, 2007.
4. 'The Happy War', *Time* magazine, 27 September 1948.
5. *Freedom at Midnight*, Dominique Lapierre and Larry Collins. Vikas Publishing House (2010 edition).
6. *The World Economy: A Millennial Perspective*, Angus Maddison. OECD, 2001.
7. The de jure transfer would have to wait till August 1963.
8. 'India: End of an Image', *Time* magazine, 29 December 1961.
9. The ancestral home of Tristão de Braganza Cunha in the village of Chandor is an interesting place to visit. It is a beautiful and well-preserved colonial bungalow with a wealth of Portuguese-era books, artifacts and furniture.
10. It was first called North-East Frontier Tracts, then North-East Frontier Agency from 1951 and, finally, Arunachal Pradesh from 1972. It was initially a Union Territory but became a state in 1986.
11. 'India–China Border: Learning from History', Mohan Guruswamy, *Economic and Political Weekly*, 27 September 2003.
12. *India after Gandhi*, Ramachandra Guha. Picador India, 2007.
13. *India after Gandhi*, Ramachandra Guha. Picador India, 2007.
14. 'Sidney Wignall', Obituary, *The Economist* , 5 May 2012.
15. *Encyclopaedia of Northeast India*, vol. II, H.M. Bareh. Mittal Publications, 2001.

16. 'Pakistan: The Ravaging of Golden Bengal', *Time* magazine, 2 August 1971.

17. US Consulate (Dacca) cable, 6 April 1971. It was signed by 21 American officials based in Dacca at that time and make a desperate plea to the US to stop supporting a military government that was systematically carrying out massacres.

18. *Lands and Peoples*, vol. IV, Grolier Society, 1956. The estimate for Delhi may not fully reflect the entire refugee population.

19. The use of the term 'colony' to denote a township or neighbourhood is a curious use of the term, especially for a country just coming out of colonization. I have not been able to find a satisfactory explanation for it although many theories persist.

20. *Gazetteer of the Gurgaon District 1883–84*, Sang-e-Meel Publications, Lahore (reprinted 2000).

21. Many of the issues discussed in this section were discussed in greater detail in a series of columns that I wrote for the *Business Standard* newspaper between 2009 and 2011. Also see, 'Re-imagining Urban India', Sanjeev Sanyal, in *India 2010*, BS Books, 2010.

22. *The Caged Phoenix*, Dipankar Gupta. Penguin, 2009.

23. *The World Economy: A Millennial Perspective*, Angus Maddison. OECD, 2001.

24. *Welcome to the Urban Revolution*, Jeb Brugmann. 2009.

Index

9/11, 304–05
26/11, 304–05

Aceh,
  earthquake, 119
Afghanistan,
  Turkic invasions, 144–45, 154–58
Africa,
  prehistoric hominids, 20
Ahoms, 4, 28, 31, 202, 204
Aibak, Qutubuddin, 151–52
Ain-i-Akbari, 137
Akbar, 4, 137, 156, 162–70, 205, 232, 260
Al Adrisi, 177
Al–Biruni, 171
Al–Sirhindi, Ahmad, 260
Alexander the Great, 65, 90–94
Ambhi, King, 90
American Civil War, 241–42
Amin, Idi, 299
Anthropological Survey of India, 23
Arabs, 138–39
  merchants, 140, 182, 185

Arthashastra, 50–51, 92, 101–02
Aryabhatta, 127, 176
Aryans/Persians, 66–67, 83
  Cyrus the Great, 89
Ashoka, 6, 95–97, 100, 128, 159, 164, 205, 232
  Buddhism, 100
  pillars and chakra, 98–99, 104, 125, 169
Asiatic lion, 70, 81–85, 105, 247–48, 267, 302
Assyrians, 66, 68
Aurangzeb, 9, 202–03, 205, 209, 247, 260
Awami League, 282
Ayodhya, 74, 80
Ayurveda, 88

Babur, 159–61, 166–67, 251
Back Bay Reclamation Company, 242
Baker, Herbert, 251
Banabhatta, 136
Bangladesh, 281–84
Batuta, Ibn, 127, 153–58, 171, 286

Bernier, Francois, 167, 196, 198, 200–03, 209–10

Bharatas people, 62–64, 67, 80

Bhaskara, 132

Bhimbetka, 56

Bhutto, Zulfikar Ali, 266, 282

Bindusara, 94–95

Bishnupriya people, 79

Borphukan, Lachit, 204–05

Bose, Subhash Chandra, 257–58

British Raj, 3–6, 12–13, 73, 210, 226, 246
  and economy of India, 234–35
  and railways, 236–39
  establishing control, 232
  Indians travelling abroad, 254–55
  as labourers, 256–57
  maps, 214–16, 220–23, 243
  naming Mt. Everest, 225
  Queen's Proclamation, 223–33
  Sepoy Mutiny, 227–30, 234
  training civil servants, 217–18
  Town Planning Committee, 253

Bronze Age, 24, 32, 44, 51–53, 55, 80, 126

Buddha, 86–88

Buddhism, 118, 128–29, 170
  attacked, 147–48
  spread of, 107–08, 123

Bundelas, 204–05

Cabral, Pedro Alvares, 185–86, 226

Cambay Shale, 17

Cambrian Explosion, 14

Canning, Lord, 232

Cantino, Alberto, 188

Catherine of Braganza, 241

Chanakya, 92–94, 100–02

Chandragupta I, 124

Chandragupta II (Vikramaditya), 7, 18, 125

Chandragupta Maurya, 92–94, 97, 100–01, 105

Charnock, Job, 211–13

Chauhan, Prithviraj, 147, 151

China, 89, 187, 271, 285, 293
  ancient civilization, 80
  conflict with India, 195, 275–80
  dominating the seas, 175
  opium trade, 242

Chola dynasty, 134–35

Churchill, Winston, 5

Clive, Robert, 210, 221, 226–227, 260, 272

Columbus, Christopher, 179, 181

Curzon, Lord, 248

da Gama, Vasco, 181–85, 187

Dae Jung, Kim, 118

Dakshina Path, 71–73, 75–76, 86, 87, 94, 103, 106, 109, 154, 200

Dalai Lama, 210, 244, 278, 280

Danino, Michel, 49–50

Daulah, Siraj–ud, 210, 214

Daulatabad, 154, 158

Deccan Traps, 4, 15, 203

DELHI,
  age of, 148
  and refugees, 264
  excavations, 149–50
  in Mughal times, 195–98
  population, 149
  Turkish occupation, 147

Dias, Bartholomeu, 181

Drake, Sir Francis, 194

Druhya tribe, 65

Dutch colonial expansion, 194

EARLY INDIA,
  and Bali, 117
  and cartography, 176–78,
    188–91, 195, 207–08
  and continental drift, 11–12,
    14–19
  and genetics, 31–33
  and Mongolia, 106–07
  anthropological roots, 19–24,
    64–66
  'Aryan invasion theory', 27–
    30, 37, 45, 55–56
  caste system, 34
  contact with Far East, 116–19,
    135–36
  earthquakes, 17–18, 40–41, 48,
    58
  Great Flood myth, 25, 32
  history and civilization, 3–5,
    8–10, 19, 37–42, 53

  farming, 27
  internal migrations, 28
  Jewish settlers, 114–15
  maritime trade, 107–13, 116,
    120, 143, 171, 176
  prehistoric flora and fauna, 19
  prehistoric fossils, 15, 19, 56
  Roman contact, 111–15, 120
  sculpture, 131
  shipbuilding design, 121
  Stone Age sites, 24

Egyptian civilization, 37, 193

En–Lai, Chou, 277, 283

English East India Company,
  195, 200, 210–15, 218, 227–28,
  241

Europe,
  Neanderthals, 20–22

Everest, George, 223–25

Frazer, William, 247

Funan, 116–17

Gandhi, Indira, 281, 283, 290

Gandhi, Mahatma, 94, 238, 257,
  284

Gandhi, Sanjay, 290

Gangetic plain, 70–72, 74, 78, 80,
  90, 122

Gene mutations,
  M458, 32
  R1a1, 31, 32, 34-35, 69
  R1a1a, 32, 69
  R1b, 32, 33

George V, King, 8, 250–51
Ghalib, 229
Ghosh, Aurobindo, 272–73
Grand Trunk Road, 73, 162
Great Trigonometrical Survey
    of India, 221, 225, 243–45
Gulf of Khambat, 26
Gupta empire, 103, 105, 124–32
Gurgaon, 1, 13, 77, 289–93, 297,
    302
Guru Nanak, 164

Hampi, 73–75, 192–93
Harappan civilization, 8, 27–28,
    36–45, 50–58, 102
    and horses, 55–57
    and lions, 82–83
    decline, 45–48, 68
    Dholavira, 8–9, 39–42, 48, 50,
        233
    influence on modern India,
        49–50
    Kalibangan, 48, 50
    Lothal, 43, 56
    Meluhha, 42–44
    Mohenjodaro, 38–39, 42, 85
Hardinge, Lord, 250
Harshcharita, 136
Harsha, 134, 138
Hastings, Lord Warren, 18
He, Zheng, 117, 170, 173–74,
    178, 181
Herber, Bishop, 228
Hindus, 4, 68, 128–29

perception of the British, 227
    spread to South East Asia, 172
Hittites, 67
Huangdi, Qin Shi, 80, 90,
    93–94
Hui of Qin, King, 89
Humayun, 161–62, 165–66
Hunas (Huns), 132
Hurrian people, 68

Iltutmish, Sultan, 148
Indian ancestral groups, 30
    Ancestral North Indian (ANI),
        29–31
    Ancestral South Indian (ASI),
        29–31
Indian National Army, 257–58
Indian National Congress, 250,
    260–61
Indian Navy, 274
Indian Ocean, 4
Indian wildlife,
    dolphins, 59–60
    hunting, 167–69, 246
    lions, 81, 247–48
    rhinoceros, 167
    tigers, 81, 246–48, 303
Indus Steam Flotilla, 236
Iran, 67
Iron Age, 70, 72–73, 77–80, 107
    late, 85–86, 102, 109
Islam, 140
    and India, 139, 142
    and South East Asia, 174

Jainism,
  temples, 87
Jehangir, 168–70, 195, 232, 247
Jinnah, Mohammad Ali, 260–61,
  270
Jumla, Mir, 202, 205

Kafur, Malik, 148, 191
Kalhana, 136–37, 170
Kamasutra, 129–30
Kashmir,
  Indo–Pak wars, 270
Kaul, Brij Mohan, 279–80
Kausambi, 85–86
Khan, Ghengis, 160, 230
Khan, Kublai, 180
Khan, Nawab Mohabat, 266–67
Khan, Nizam Osman Ali,
  267–68
Khan, Yahya, 282
Khilji, Alauddin, 152–53, 191
Khilji, Bakhtiyar, 147
Kinthup, 245–46
Kipling, Rudyard, 37, 73, 246
Kochi,
  ancient trading post, 113
  Christian missionaries, 114–15
Kolkata, 212–16, 219, 237,
  239–40, 285–86
  Raj-era buildings, 240
Kozhikode (Calicut), 184, 186
Kripalani, Acharya, 260
Kumaragupta, 127
Kurds, 68

Lambton, William, 221–24
Lapierre, Dominique, 261
Laxmibai, Rani of Jhansi, 231
Le Corbusier, 288
Lockhart, Rob, 270
Lutyens, Sir Edwin, 6, 251–52
Lytton, Lord, 249–50

Macedonians, 90–93, 101, 103
Madras, 241
Madras Railway Company, 236
Magadh, 81, 93
Mahabalipuram, 116, 119–120
Mahabharata, 65, 70–71, 76–80,
  84, 131
  sites, 77–79
Mahmud of Ghazni, 144–47, 171
Majapahit empire of Java, 174
Mandeville, Sir John, 178–80,
  189, 207
Manipur, 79
Manrique, Friar Sebastian,
  201–02
Manto, Saadat Hasan, 262
Manu, 25, 30, 62
Mauryan Empire, 73, 76, 92–106,
  125–26, 176, 233
McMahon, Sir Arthur Henry, 275
McMahon Line, 275, 277
MEDIEVAL INDIA,
  and Jewish settlers, 9
  Arab traders, 9, 138–41
  economy before European
    colonization, 188

European colonization, 199,
211
exporting steel swords, 140
Parsis in Mumbai, 141, 241
Portuguese colonization,
183–88, 191, 211
travelogues, 199 –200
European colonies, 206–07
redefining borders, 206–08
Vijayanagar empire, 191–93
Megasthenes, 101, 103, 198
Menon, Krishna, 278–80
Mercator, Gerardus, 189–90, 194
Mercury, Freddie, 183
Mesopotamia, 42–44, 82, 90, 107
Mieville, Sir Eric, 261
Mill, James, 227
Milton, Giles, 179
Minto, Lord, 219
Mittani people, 67–68
MODERN INDIA,
diaspora, 298–301
disputes with neighbouring
countries, 259
over J&K, 268–70
with China, 275–78, 284
droughts and famines, 249–50
economic growth, 2–3
English education, 216–17, 231
Great Famine, 250, 255
independence, 250, 259, 263
accession of Goa, 274
and princely states, 265–66,
268

national flag, 267
union territories, 272–73
liberalization, 290–91
Line of Control 271
migrants, 299–300
mixed communities, 238
Anglo–Indians, 238
nationhood, 5, 260
new middle class, 287, 295–98
pan–Indian identities, 287
Partition, 259–65
communal violence,
263–64, 269–70
drawing the lines, 263
Sikkim, 284
slums, 294–95
technological development, 1
urban development, 1, 194,
284–88, 293, 296–98
Mountbatten, Lord, 260–61, 270
Mughal empire, 4, 10, 13, 18, 73,
160–65, 195, 203
decline, 205–06, 226–231
Muhammad Ghori, 147, 151
Muller, Carl, 238
Mumbai, 240–43
Muslim League, 260–61

Nehru, Jawaharlal, 94, 260–61,
270, 273, 275, 277–80, 288–89
New Delhi, 4, 6–7, 77, 251–53,
286–89
and the Aravallis, 11–14, 253
Feroze Shah Kotla, 6, 158, 161,
196

Lodhi Gardens, 159
Qutub Minar, 7–8, 151–52
New Testament, 52
Nikator, Seleucus, 93
Nixon, Richard, 283, 284
North East Frontier Agency
(NEFA), 277–79
Northbrook, Lord, 249
Nunes, Fernão, 192

Ortilius, Abraham, 189–90, 194

Paes, Domingo, 192–93
Pakistan, 47–48, 66, 263–65,
270–71, 283
East –, 264–65, 281–83
Pallava dynasty, 119
Panini, 88
Parsus, 64, 67
Pataliputra, 3, 86, 92, 101, 103, 124,
127–28, 130, 132, 162, 190, 198
Patel, Sardar Vallabhbhai, 260,
266, 268, 278
Periplus, 111–12, 177, 190
Pliny, 114
Plutarch, 92
Polo, Marco, 131, 155, 178, 180
Portugal, 181
colonial expansion, 182–87
control over Indian Ocean,
185–87
explorers in Africa, 183
Porus, King, 65, 90
Prasad, Rajendra, 267

Pratap, Rana, 13
Prophet Muhammad, 138–39
Ptolemy, 111, 177–78, 180
Pulaksen II, 134
Puru tribe, 90

Radcliffe, Sir Cyril, 262–63
Raffles, T.S., 218–20
Raja Bhoj, 145–46
Rajasthan, 13
Rajatarangini, 136–37
Ramayana 70–75, 78, 80, 191
in Java, 118
Rana Pratap, 164
Rao, Baji, 204
Rashtrakutas, 138
religious conflict, 163
religious pacifism, 169
religious pillage, 151–52, 159
Renaissance,
Europe, 180
Rennel, Col. James, 210, 221
RIVERS,
Asi, 87
Belan, 56
Brahmaputra, 4, 245–46
Ganga, 18, 46, 48, 52–54,
58–59, 81, 86, 189, 232, 305
Ghaggar, 45–48, 53, 57, 59,
61–63
Helmand, 53, 67
Indus, 46–48, 58, 61, 90, 137,
189
Kabul, 52

Markanda, 59

Narmada, 49, 112

Sabarmati, 43

Saraswati, 4, 37, 52–53, 57, 61–62, 83, 133, 144, 232–33, 305

drying up, 56–60, 68

Sutlej, 46–48, 53, 58, 61, 62

Tapti, 49

Tons, 59

Varuna, 87

Yamuna, 46, 48, 53, 58–61, 63, 232

Roe, Sir Thomas, 169, 195, 247

Roy, Ram Mohun, 216

Salazar, Antonio, 273, 275

Samudragupta, 124–25, 169, 232

Sangam literature, 109–10, 120

Sanskrit language, 171

evolution of, 109

Sarnath, 18, 87–88

lions, 99

Schliemann, Heinrich, 78

Shah Jehan, 150, 195–97, 202

Shah, Nadir, 205

Shahjehanabad (Old Delhi), 165, 195–97, 228–30, 233, 249, 251–52, 286

Shakti worship, 110, 143

Shankaracharya, Adi, 110, 143, 177

Shastri, Lal Bahadur, 281

Shivaji, 4, 15, 203–04

Shunga dynasty, 106

Sikdar, Radhanath, 225

Sikhs,

persecution, 203

Silapaddikaram, 108

Silva, Vassalo e, 274–75

Simms, F.W., 235

Singapore, 219–20, 257

origins, 173

Singh, Maharaja Hari, 269–70

Singh, Maharaja Jai, 9

Singh, Maharaja Ranjit, 247

Singh, Nain, 243–45

Sri Lanka, 84–86, 100, 108, 122, 303

Skandgupta, 125

Slumdog Millionaire, 295

Spain, 181

Spear, Percival, 156

Srivijaya, 117, 134–35, 170, 172, 174

Sudasa, 55, 62–65, 80, 233

Sumerian civilization, 25, 37–38, 82

Suri, Sher Shah, 18, 73, 161–62

Sushruta, 88

Suvrata, 137

Taimur the Lame, 10, 159–61, 169, 230

Tamil language, 109–10

Tavernier, Jean–Baptiste, 43, 198–200, 202

Thapar, Romila, 49, 97

Tibet, 244–45, 276, 278, 280

Tipu Sultan, 88, 222
Tughlaq, Feroze Shah, 6–7, 158–59, 166, 170, 205
Tughlaq, Muhammad, 154–58
Tughlaqabad, 153–54, 158, 164

United East India Company, 194
United Nations, 275
United States of America, 271
Uttara Path, 71–73, 81, 87, 162

Valmiki, 73, 75
Varahamihira, 9, 132
Varanasi, 87–88, 98–99
Vedas, 51–53, 60–61
  Rig, 51–55, 57–58, 62–64, 80
    devas and asuras, 67
    mention of lions, 83–84
    Sapta–Sindhu, 60–63, 66, 71, 83, 107, 149
Velho, Alvaro, 183–84
Victoria, Queen, 8, 250
Vivekananda, Swami, 238

Waugh, Andrew, 225
Wegener, Alfred, 11–12
Wellesley, Lord, 217, 222
Win, Ne, 299

Xian, Fa, 121–24, 126–28, 132
Xiongnu, 107

Yezidi people, 68
Younghusband Francis, 276
Yueh–Chin tribe, 107

Zafar, Bahadur Shah, 10, 13, 228–30
Zang, Xuan, 127, 132–34, 138, 232
Zarathustra, 66
Zayd, Abu, 140
Zedong, Mao, 94
Zoroastrianism, 66–67, 141

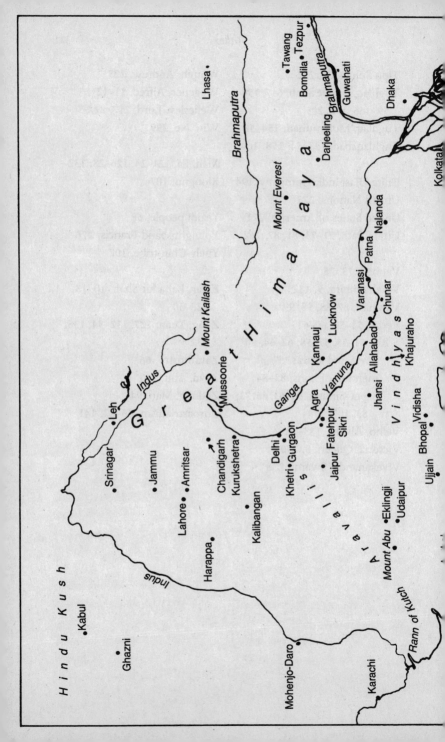

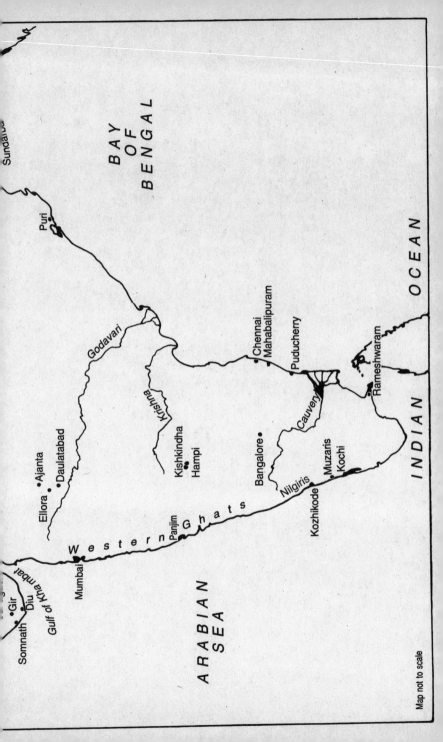

Map not to scale